Demographic Change and Intergenerational Justice

Joerg Chet Tremmel
Editor

Demographic Change and Intergenerational Justice

The Implementation of Long-Term Thinking in the Political Decision Making Process

Springer

Foundation for the Rights
of Future Generations
P.O. Box 5115
61422 Oberursel
Germany
kontakt@srzg.de
www.srzg.de

This publication was financed by a printing subsidy from the Bertelsmann Stiftung.

ISBN 978-3-540-77083-1 e-ISBN 978-3-540-77084-8

DOI 10.1007/978-3-540-77084-8

Library of Congress Control Number: 2007940373

Typesetting and production: le-tex Jelonek, Schmidt & Vöckler GbR, Leipzig, Germany
Cover design: WMX Design GmbH, Heidelberg, Germany

Printed on acid-free paper

9 8 7 6 5 4 3 2 1

springer.com

Preface

Dear reader,
Intergenerational justice[1] and demographic change are intimately linked, because it is the size of a generation that determines a great share of its fate. But, for better, or for worse?

The relationships between generational justice and demographic change are extremely complex, and not one-directional. This anthology aims at shedding some light on these. Both rapid population growth in developing countries, and projected population decline in most developed countries are considered a threat for future generations in the respective countries.

Although shrinking societies are usually growing older, and growing societies usually become younger, for analytical purposes the elements of demographic change can be separated into changes in population size (growth, shrinking), and changes in median age (aging, juvenescence). Each of the ensuing four possible combinations has different effects on policy fields, and indicators for the wellbeing and the welfare of a generation. As the negative effects of high population growth rates in developing countries have been extensively studied, the authors of this book concentrate on the less often described relationship between aging/shrinking and intergenerational justice.

In the first part of this book, the demographic changes are described in detail on a global and national level. The dynamics of population growth (decline) and aging (juvenescence) must be laid out, because they set the statistical basis for the rest of the volume. The second part examines the impact of demographic change on key sustainability indicators in certain areas of interest such as public debt, retirement systems, competitiveness, environment, the labor market, and the education system in more detail.

Regarding the quality of the environment, food safety, job opportunities, and access to educational institutions, each member of the next generation is probably better off if his generation is smaller than the previous one. However, for other sustainability indicators (e.g., stability of the social security system, or the reduction of state debt per head), it is probably better for a member of the

[1] The terms "intergenerational justice" and "generational justice" are used synonymously. Just like "gender justice" inevitably means, by its inner logic, justice between the genders (and not within one gender group), "generational justice" is bound to mean justice between generations, and not within one generation. Hence, the prefix "inter" is dispensable.

next generation that his generation be bigger than the previous one. A similar connection ties the ageing and juvenescence of a society. Some sustainability indicators are aided by an ageing population (e.g., democratic stability), whilst others benefit from a juvenescent society (e.g., ability to innovate).

Of course, these assumptions are debatable. And debating these is exactly what the authors of Part II do.

In the third part, we ask how intergenerational justice is affected if sustainability indicators change due to demographic change. In the context of population shrinking and aging, the next generation might be better off ecologically, but worse off economically. How can we then make a statement about intergenerational justice? This section of the book draws a balance. In addition to that, it examines the implications of ever increasing life expectancy on intergenerational justice.

The fourth part addresses the ethical legitimacy of population policies. If we can influence the wellbeing of our descendants (including, but not limited to, adopting certain family or population policies), should we do so? Governmental regulations on permissible number of births raise profound ethical questions. Undoubtedly, they are a form of governmental interference in individuals' and families' freedom of choice. Having a baby is an intimate, private affair, and at the same time, a process of great relevance to society as a whole. This dual character is one of the key reasons why debates on this subject are so explosive and emotionally charged.

The fifth and last part of the book addresses the issue of institutionalizing our responsibility for future generations. Democracies face a structural problem, namely, the tendency to prefer the present, and to forget future implications of present decisions. Every party tries to obtain a majority, and therefore has to concentrate on the short-term perspective, namely, the preferences of the present electorate. In this bid for votes, the future generation is neglected. Thus, politicians (of all parties) who want to look further ahead than the next election have a disadvantage in the competition with their short-term-thinking political rivals. The framework for a fair, future-orientated generational political system could be mended by an institutional establishment of generational justice. Thereby, the glorification of the present in everyday politics would decrease. Part V of the book examines ways to institutionalize intergenerational justice in order to abate this structural problem of "short-termism" in democracies.

Most of the chapters derive from a call for papers for the scientific symposium "Demographic Change, Intergenerational Justice and the Implementation of Long-term Thinking", which was held from 6–7 November 2006 in Berlin, Germany. The symposium was organized mainly by the Foundation for the Rights of Future Generations, and the Bertelsmann Foundation. The Bertelsmann Foundation strives to encourage social change, and to contribute to society's long-term viability. The Foundation for the Rights of Future Generations is a research institute on the interface of science and politics. The main purpose of the foundation is to conduct research on the themes of intergenerational justice and sustainability. This mission is realized primarily through the development of research projects, the organization of academic meetings and symposiums, as well as the release of scientific publications. But, as an advocacy think-tank, FRFG's mission is not only to describe society, but to actually improve it.

This book is far from a solo effort. I am grateful to many people for their assistance, namely Catherine Barrow and Michelle Wenderlich for their translations, and Silvia Hurlebaus, Maren Ziegler, and Gudrun Hüther for their formatting work. I am further indebted to the production editor, Katja Röser and her colleagues from the le-tex company, for their meticulous support in preparing the final manuscript for publication. I am additionally grateful to Brigitte Reschke from Springer Publishing for her careful, candid, and supportive guidance. Many articles were discussed at the scientific symposium "Demographic Change and Intergenerational Justice", held from 5–7 November 2006 in Berlin, Germany. This book owes a great deal to the discussions that were going on there. The symposium was mainly sponsored by the Bertelsmann Stiftung who also funded the printing costs of this book. I am extremely grateful for the foundation's financial support which was made possible by Dr. Johannes Meier and Dr. Ole Wintermann. No expression of gratitude on my part could possibly repay the debts that I have been fortunate enough to incur.

Responses to this collection, especially be email to kontakt@srzg.de, on ways to make future editions of this volume more useful are very welcome.

Oberursel, Germany
January 2008

Dr. Joerg Chet Tremmel
Foundation for the Rights
of Future Generations

Contents

Contributors

Daniel Blobel studied geo-ecology at Karlsruhe University, Germany until 1998. In addition to a comprehensive education in natural sciences, he took courses in economics and environmental law. In 1995 and 1996, he spent 7 months in Russia for study purposes. After completing his studies, he received additional training in the field of landscape planning at the Institute for General and Applied Ecology in Hardegsen. In his work for the EU coordination office of the German League for the Protection of Nature (DNR) in 2001, Daniel Blobel was the author of many articles on European environmental policy for the monthly "EU-Rundschreiben" (EU Bulletin). In 2000 he carried out investigative and editorial work for the journals *punkt.um* and *politische ökologie* at Ökom publishers in Munich, which specialize in sustainability and environmental policy issues. Blobel is a Fellow with the Institute for International and European Environmental Policy (Ecologic) in Berlin.

Dr. Ulrich Feeser-Lichterfeld was born in 1968, and has received a Diplom (M.A.) in Theology and Psychology and a Dr. theol. From 2000–2005, he was a Research Assistant and Assistant Lecturer at the Department of Pastoral Theology at the University of Bonn, Germany; since 2005, he is a Research Assistant at the Institute of Science and Ethics in Bonn. Dr. Feeser-Lichterfeld has several publications on gerontological topics, e.g., *How "adult" is the religiosity of adults? Normative implications of empirical theological research into religious development in the second half of life* (ed. with T. Kläden in: J.A. van der Ven/M. Scherer-Rath). His current project is "Life Prolongation and Deceleration of Human Aging: Individual Assessment, Social Consequences, Ethical Analysis and Normative Judgement" [NRW-Exzellenzinitiative "Geisteswissenschaften gestalten Zukunftsperspektiven"].

Peter Friedrich was born in 1972, and is a **Member of the German Parliament**. He is nondenominational, married, and has two children. After completing his alternative civilian service at a nursing home in 1992, he began his studies at the University of Constance. In 2001 he was scientific assistant at the *Lernagentur Bodensee Impuls* (Impulse Learning Agency of Lake Constance), in Constance.

In 2004 he was project director of *translake*, the cooperation aiming to promote the standing of the European Union. Friedrich was Chairman of AWO (Workers' Welfare Association) in Constance, and member of the union ver.di. His political life started when he joined the SPD (Social Democratic Party) in 1990. In 1992 he was Acting Chairman of Juso (youth organization of the Social Democratic Party), and then he became their president in 1997. He became Member of the German Bundestag in 2005, and is director at the Youngsters of the SPD faction.

Prof. Dr. Michael Hüther was born in 1962, and studied economics and history at the Justus-Liebig-University of Gießen (Germany). He received his doctorate in 1990 (summa cum laude), after which he held several positions as a scientific assistant. From 1995 to 1999, he was Secretary General of the expert advisory board for the survey of Germany's macroeconomic development, and he then became head economist of the DekaBank in Frankfurt/Main (1999 to 2004). Since 2001, Hüther is Honorary Professor at the European Business School, and since 2004 Director and member of the Steering Committee of the Institut der Deutschen Wirtschaft Köln (Institute of the German Economy Cologne). He currently holds several memberships of societal associations, executive boards, advisory committees, and administrative boards.

Michael Kauch was born in 1967, and is a Member of the German parliament. He studied economics and social sciences at the University of Dortmund, Germany. He has been member of the FDP (Free Democratic Party) since 1989. From 1993 to 1995, he was Deputy Federal Chairman of the Junge Liberale (Young Liberals), and in 1994 worked within the Department of Public Relations of the FDP faction in the Mecklenburg-Western Pomeranian parliament. From 1995 to 1999, he was Federal Chairman of the Junge Liberale, and from 1995 to 2001 member of the federal board of the FDP. Since 1998, he has been District Chairman of the FDP district chapter Dortmund. Kauch was managing director of the Bundesverband Junger Unternehmer (German Association of Young Entrepreneurs) from 1999 to 2003. Since 2003 he is a Member of the German Bundestag. Since 2005 he is member of the Committee on the Environment, Nature Conservation and Nuclear Safety, member of the Parliamentary Council on Sustainable Development and a substitute member of the Committee on Health. Currently he is the spokesman of the FDP Parliamentary Group for environment as well as for ethics in medicine. Additionally he is chairman of the Social Policy Commitee of the party.

Doris Knoblauch began her political science studies at the Ruprecht Karls University of Heidelberg. She has been at the Otto Suhr Institute of the Berlin Free University since 2002. Her studies focus on international development policy, North–South relationships, as well as global climate and environmental policy. Knoblauch has been a Research Assistant with the Institute for International and European Environmental Policy (Ecologic) in Berlin since January 2006.

Her work focuses on European Environmental Governance. She is currently working on projects concerning European Impact Assessment, and the integration of environmental requirements into other policy areas.

R. Andreas Kraemer worked in the petrochemical industry before studying environmental engineering and sciences at the Technische Universität Berlin, and the Université de Paris VII. From 1986 to 1991, Kraemer worked for a range of policy institutes: Science Center Berlin (WZB), the Institut für ökologische Wirtschaftsforschung (Institute for Ecological Economy Research, IÖW), and the Research Unit for Environmental Policy of the Free University of Berlin. From 1991 to 1995, he was Senior Fellow at the nonprofit Institute for European Environmental Policy (IEEP), with offices in various European capitals and a European-wide network of correspondents. R. Andreas Kraemer has been Director of Ecologic (Institute for International and European Environmental Policy) in Berlin since its foundation in 1995, and he is also a Visiting Assistant Professor of Duke University, lecturing on European integration and environmental policy in Duke's Berlin Program. With a strong background in institutional analysis, and capacity building in environmental policy and resource management, he now focuses on integrating environmental concerns into other policies, notably EU General Affairs, trade, development, and external relations. He is renowned for his expertise in international water management and policy. Kraemer is Co-chairman of the advisory board of ÖkoWorld, a group of ethical and "green" investment funds or mutual trusts that sets criteria for global investment, and of Oekom Research, a rating agency specializing in corporate and sovereign debtors' ethics and sustainability. He also serves on the boards of the Bellagio Forum for Sustainable Development, and the French-Alsatian NGO Solidarité Eau Europe, and is a coordinator of the British German Environment Forum.

Prof. Dr. Thomas Lindh was born in 1952. He did his B.Sc. in Mathematics in 1985, his Ph.Lic. (Fil. lic.) in Economics in 1987, and his Ph.D. (FD) in Economics in 1991 at Uppsala University. He was Associate Professor (Docent) in Economics at the Social Science Faculty, 1997, and by 2000, a Professor in Economics at Uppsala University. Lindh was also a Research Fellow at the Institute for Housing and Urban Research, Uppsala (1997 to 1998), and at the Department of Economics, Uppsala University (1998 to 1999). In November 2001, Lindh completed guest research at the Department of Economics at the School of Business Economics and Law, Göteborg, and in October 2002 at the Institut für Demographie, Vienna. Since 2004, he is the Research Director of the Institute for Futures Studies, Stockholm. His research focuses on structural aspects of growth and productivity, with a strong emphasis on the effects that demographic change has on the economy. In collaborative work with Bo Malmberg, he investigated correlations between the age structure of the population and not only economic growth, but also inflation, investment rates, and other macroeconomic variables. An important part of his research has been the development of methods to make use of these connections for forecasting. One of his latest publications is *Demography and housing demand – what can we learn from residential construction data?*

Anna Lührmann was born in 1983, and is the youngest member of the German Parliament. She currently is a student of policy and organization at the Distance University of Hagen, Germany. Since October 2000, she has been a member of the German division of the Youth for Understanding committee, and in 2001 she joined the JEF (*Young European Federalists*). She has been member of the Grüne Jugend (Green Youth) since 1997, and has joined the party Bündnis90/Die Grünen (The Greens) in 1998. She has been spokesperson of the Grüne Jugend, at first of Kassel, later of Hessen for several years (discontinuously), and has been a Member of the German Bundestag since 2002.

Prof. Dr. Wolfgang Lutz was born in 1956, and studied Philosophy, Mathematics and Theology at the University of Munich, Germany. He received his M.A. in Social and Economic Statistics at the University of Vienna in 1980, and an additional M.A. in Demography at the University of Pennsylvania, USA in 1982. In 1983 he received his Ph.D. (with distinction) in Demography at the University of Pennsylvania. In 1988 he received his Habilitation (second doctorate; right to teach and apply for a chair at the university) in Demography and Social Statistics at the University of Vienna. Since 1994, he has been the Leader of the World Population Program, IIASA (International Institute for Applied Systems Analysis), and since 2002 he has been the Director of the Vienna Institute of Demography (VID) of the Austrian Academy of Sciences. In one of his previous positions, Lutz was the Demographic Coordinator of the EU Observatory for the Social Situation, Demography and the Family, an official body of the European Commission (2000 to 2005). Among other activities, he has published 21 scientific books (including two single-author books, three co-authored books, and 16 edited volumes and special issues of scientific journals).

Prof. Dr. Bo Malmberg. After his doctoral defense in Education at Linköping University in 1990, Bo Malmberg has in his research and education been interested primarily in the situation of older people from a social psychological point of view. Many older people are confronted with reduced strength, and withering social networks. In recent years he has, together with colleagues at the Institute of Gerontology, Karolinska Institute, and Pennsylvania State University, USA, been the principal investigator in a study of gender differences in health in older years. Malmberg is the Research Leader for the theme "Demographically Based Future Studies", and Professor at Stockholm University. He is also the President of the School of Health Science-Research Committee. His publications include *Age structure effects on economic growth – Swedish evidence* and *Age structure effects and growth in the OECD, 1950–90*, which he wrote together with Thomas Lindh.

Dr. Johannes Meier was born in 1963, and studied information technology at the University of Applied Sciences in Aachen. He then completed his Ph.D. at the University of Hawaii, as part of an interdisciplinary program in Communications and Information Science. From 1990 to 1998, he held a number of positions in the Hamburg, Hong Kong, and Munich offices of the management consulting firm McKinsey & Co. In 1998, he joined the GE CompuNet Computer AG Executive Board as Director of the IT, Service and International Management division. From May 2000 to April 2003, he served as Chairman of the GE CompuNet Computer AG Executive Board. On 1 October 2003, Johannes Meier joined the Bertelsmann Stiftung Executive Board.

Anneke von Raggamby started her studies in political science, geography, and public law at the Rheinische Friedrich Wilhelms University in Bonn. After finishing her intermediate exam, she continued her studies in political science at the Free University Berlin, where she completed her final exam in November 2000. Anneke von Raggamby has been working for Ecologic (Institute for International and European Environmental Policy) in Berlin since 1998. From August to December 2001, she worked for the Institute for European Environmental Policy (IEEP) in London, where she was involved in projects concerning the Enlargement of the European Union, and the Cardiff process for integrating environmental concerns into other policy fields. In 2002, she completed a Certificate in European Law at the University of Constance-Landau. Anneke von Raggamby is Senior Fellow at Ecologic in the field of European Environmental Policy.

Dr. Vegard Skirbekk graduated in economics from the University of Oslo, Norway in 2000, and also studied at Adelaide University, Australia. In 2005 he completed his PhD at the University of Rostock, Germany. In 2000–2001 Dr. Skirbekk participated in the Advanced Studies Program in International Economics, held by the Institute for World Economics in Kiel, Germany. From 2001 to 2003 he worked at the Max Planck Institute for Demographic Research in Rostock, Germany. He joined the World Population Program at IIASA in October 2003 as a Research Scholar. Skirbekk's research interests include understanding and describing fertility patterns, estimating productivity variation over the life cycle and conducting regional and national population projections. He has published in leading journals including Science, Demography and Population and Development Review.

Prof. Dr. Thomas Straubhaar did his Lic. rer. pol. in 1981, and his Ph.D. in 1983 at the University of Bern, Switzerland. From 1985 to 1986, he was a Postdoctoral Fellow at the University of California Berkeley, USA. His Habilitation took place in 1987 at the University of Bern, Switzerland. Straubhaar was Professor of Economics at the University of Federal Armed Forces, Hamburg, Germany (1992 to 1999), and since 1994 he is a Ph.D. Advisor at the Friedrich-Naumann Foundation. He is also Professor of Economics at the University of Hamburg since 1999, and Director of the Hamburg Institute of International

Economics (HWWI) since April 2005. In addition, Prof. Straubhaar is a Policy Fellow at the Institute for the Study of Labor, Bonn, and received the public award "Economist of the Year" of the economic magazine "Made in Germany" (Deutsche Welle TV) in 2006.

Dr. Joerg Chet Tremmel was born in 1970, and has an M.B.A. in Business Administration from the European Business School (1997), and an M.A. in Political Sciences from the University of Frankfurt (2003). He completed a Ph.D. in Social Sciences at the University of Stuttgart in 2005. A second Ph.D. from the University of Düsseldorf, in Philosophy, will be completed in spring 2008. The title of his first dissertation is "Bevölkerungspolitik im Kontext ökologischer Generationengerechtigkeit" (Population policies in the context of ecological social justice between generations; Wiesbaden: DUV 2005), and the title of his second dissertation (forthcoming) is "A theory of intergenerational justice". Tremmel is Director of the "Foundation for the Rights of Future Generations" (FRFG), a nonprofit and nonpartisan research institute that he founded in 1997. In this function, Tremmel has been responsible for the organization of several symposia and congresses, as well as the "Award of Intergenerational Justice". Since 2006, also director of FRFG's subunit "Institute for a Better Demographic Future".

In winter semester 2007 Tremmel is Visiting Lecturer at the Johann-Wolfgang-Goethe-University Frankfurt, the Albert-Ludwigs-Universität Freiburg, the University of Düsseldorf, and the University of Stuttgart. His main publication in English (as editor) is: *Handbook of intergenerational justice*; Edward Elgar Publishing, Cheltenham, 2006.

Marco Wanderwitz is a lawyer and Member of the German Bundestag. He was born in 1975, and studied law in Potsdam and Dresden. He is Assistant Chairman of the CDU's Chemnitz chapter. He furthermore volunteers his time to serve on the city council in Hohenstein Ernstthal. In the Bundestag, he is Chairman of the "Junge Gruppe" of the CDU/CSU, Assistant Chairman of the German-Portuguese parliamentarian group, and a member of the executive board of the CDU/CSU. He is also a member of the Committee for Legal Affairs, the Committee for Cultural and Media Affairs, and the Subcommittee for New Media. Additionally, he is a substitute member of the Committee for Family Affairs, Senior Citizens, Women and Youth, and takes an active part in the Committee for Sustainable Development.

Harald Wilkoszewski, born in Munich in 1976, studied Political Science at the universities of Augsburg (Germany), Cork (Ireland), and Munich (Germany), and graduated in 2002. In the following years, he attended different courses in the fields of Demography (International Max Planck Research School for Demography, and University of Rome "La Sapienza", Italy), and quantitative methods (University of Michigan, Ann Arbor, USA). He has been doing his Ph.D. at the Max Planck Institute for Demographic Research in Rostock since 2003. He is also Ph.D. Fellow in the Social Policy Department at the London

School of Economics and Political Science. In addition, he started working as Research Scientist at the Rostock Centre for the Study of Demographic Change, in October 2004. Among other things, he is member of the German Society for Demography (DGD), and of the "Aging and Society" section of the German Society for Sociology (DGS). One of his books is *Die verdrängte Generation. Politische Parteien und die alternde Gesellschaft in Deutschland (2003).*

Dr. Ole Wintermann completed his Masters degree in Social Economics at the University of Kiel, Germany, in 1992. Beginning in 1993, he was a Teaching Assistant in the Political Science departments at the University of Kiel, Germany, and the University of Göteborg, Sweden. As of 1996, Wintermann was the departmental Director for the state- and national-level governance boards at the Deutsche Angestellten-Gewerkschaft (ver.di) trade union in Kiel and Hamburg. He joined the Bertelsmann Stiftung in 2002, and works currently as a Project Manager for this foundation. He was awarded his doctoral degree in 2005 for work based on an empirical comparison of the Swedish and German social welfare states. Besides his interests in demographic change, he also focuses on public funding and finance, as well as comparative research in the nonprofit sector.

Summary of the Chapters

The interdisciplinary anthology is composed of chapters by demographers, philosophers, economists, and sociologists. The contributors come from the international scientific community.

Part I Demographic Trends

As a starting point in the first part of the book, *Prof. Dr. Wolfgang Lutz*, Director of the Vienna Institute of Demography, and leader of the World Population Program at the International Institute for Applied Systems Analysis (IIASA), and *Dr. Vegard Skirbekk* draw a general picture of global demographic trends over the past decades, and likely trends in the future in their chapter "Low Fertility in Europe in a Global Demographic Context". They briefly discuss the forces driving this universal process of continuing demographic transition.

In the past, demographers tended to assume that sub-replacement fertility was only a temporary phenomenon, and eventually all populations of the world would converge toward replacement-level fertility. The chapter discusses the possibility that fertility in these countries may actually stay at very low levels, or continue to decline due to self-reinforcing mechanisms of social change. The low fertility trap hypothesis describes three distinct mechanisms (demographic, sociological, and economic) that may lead to such a downward spiral in future fertility.

But it is not only the sheer number of people and their age distribution that matter. The possible consequences of demographic changes greatly depend on the productivity and the skills of the people, something that economists would call the quality dimension. This dimension can be quantitatively approximated by studying the changing distribution of the population by level of educational attainment. Here, the authors present the first global outlook of human capital, i.e., trends in the proportions of people by age, sex, and educational attainment in different countries and world regions.

The authors then deal with the implications of these trends in demographic factors, as well as in changing patterns of human capital for the future global distribution of the population, and for likely economic power and political weight. Special attention is given to the future position of Europe in this changing global context.

Lutz and Skirbekk finally make the case that the positively connoted neologism "demographic sustainability" does not make much sense as a scientific term in demography.

Part II The Impact of Demographic Developments on Key Indicators

Part II starts with the chapter "Demography and Budget Consolidation: An Analysis and Possible Courses of Action", by *Dr. Johannes Meier*, member of the Executive Board of the Bertelsmann Stiftung, and *Dr. Ole Wintermann*, of Action for Demographic Change, presenting results of the "Debt Monitor 2006", and expertise of successful budget consolidation in an international comparison.

The "Debt Monitor 2006" of the Bertelsmann Stiftung gives needed transparency to the public national budgets at the state and federal political levels. At the same time, the Bertelsmann Stiftung supplies solutions for successful handling of increasing national indebtedness.

In the context of financial sustainability, the foundation asserts that investments in education are the crucial factor for retaining the political capacity to act for future generations. Regarding the decrease in the number of employed people due to demographic change, education investments represent a substantial contribution for successful budget consolidation.

Additionally, from the analysis of states with successful budget consolidation, the foundation has found it possible to deduce reform measures it deems necessary for Germany. Thus, the Bertelsmann Stiftung proposes, on the output side, a tightening of entrance rules for social security benefits, as well as stricter control mechanisms of those benefits. On the income side, they recommend fundamental tax revisions, in particular a temporary moderate tax increase for higher-income earners, mainly for political reasons, as well as clear rules for the use of surplus, and a painter release for the reduction of debts. They also suggest changing the budgeting process, with the goal of creating a stronger top-down orientation, rather than the past bottom-up procedure.

The next three chapters discuss the effects of demographic change on the economy. *Prof. Dr. Michael Hüther*, from the Institut der Deutschen Wirtschaft, posits that economic growth, and hence welfare, unfolds by the willingness, the ability, the opportunity, and the incentive to work. If growth and welfare can be ensured by these means in the long run, we can immediately draw a basic conclusion: individuals and their qualifications are the most important drivers of an expanding economy. A shrinking and ageing population leads to a loss in welfare and prospects. It is incompatible with the pursuit of intergenerational justice, which does not only regard the labor force and pensioners, but which also includes the young and the unborn. Without an interference, it is unlikely that the process of population shrinkage will come to an end.

Prof. Dr. Thomas Straubhaar, of the Hamburg Institute of International Economics, counters this position, arguing that a decline in population does not necessarily lead to economic problems. He asserts that fears associated with demographic change have not been empirically proven, and that it is possible that these changes could even be economically positive. In a shrinking population it is possible, for instance, to increase capital intensity per person, leading to increased productivity and per-capita income; human capital can also be increased with a distribution of resources between fewer people. Furthermore, it is aging, rather than shrinking, which presents the biggest demographic challenge. There are most certainly problems to be faced within an aging society, primarily with impediments to growth caused by policies that are designed for a young and growing population, but they can be compensated for through policy changes, especially including incentives for fast technological progress, alterations in the duration of working life, labor force behavior, and intelligent reforms in the pension system in order to make it independent of age structure.

In the next chapter, "Macroeconomics and Age Structure in a Welfare State – Sweden 1946–2005", *Prof. Dr. Thomas Lindh*, Research Director at the Institute for Future Studies, and *Prof. Dr. Bo Malmberg*, Professor of Geography at Stockholm University, demonstrate the effects of changing patterns of age structure on Swedish postwar socioeconomic indicators. In particular, they explain how demographic change has affected the development of saving, growth, investment, current accounts, and the budget balance.

Emphasized by the public-oriented redistribution of the Nordic welfare states, the effects of an aging population are particularly strong on the budget deficit, output growth, and housing demand. These basic age effects suffice to explain most of the variations in the Swedish postwar experience of macroeconomic change, especially the relatively modest performance of the Swedish economy in the 1980s, and its recent recovery.

Part III The Relationship Between Key Sustainability Indicators and Intergenerational Justice

Part III starts with the chapter "Demographic Change and Sustainability: A Generational Balance" by *R. Andreas Kraemer*, *Daniel Blobel*, *Anneke von Raggamby*, and *Doris Knoblauch* of Ecologic Berlin. The four authors evaluate current trends and patterns of environmental and demographic change, in both a global and national context.

It is now common knowledge that we have eroded, and are continuing to erode the Earth's carrying capacity for humans, through rapid growth of the human population, the concurrent urbanization and industrialization, present production and consumption patterns, the inconsiderate use of chemicals, and our use of natural resources and energy. Environmental and sustainability issues can also be compacted by the ageing of society and demographic decline that many countries are now experiencing. These factors and processes are considered in the report "The Bottom Line – Heritage and Legacy for the Germany of Tomorrow: a Generational Balance", on which the chapter is based.

In "Intergenerational Justice in an Extreme Longevity Scenario: Ethical Issues in Biogerontological Endeavours", *Dr. Ulrich Feeser-Lichterfeld*, Research Assistant at the Institute of Science and Ethics in Bonn, examines ethical issues in biogerontological endeavors (dealing with biological mechanisms of ageing).

With newly emerging technologies, the prospect of extreme longevity is perhaps nearing fruition. Such a scenario raises many individual and social issues. This contribution focuses on its intergenerational consequences. The author considers serious questions such as whom these technologies would benefit, and whether they would produce unintended consequences, such as a new type of ageism.

Part IV Intergenerational Justice and Population Policies

The fourth part, on population policies, contains a chapter by *Dr. Joerg Chet Tremmel*, entitled "An Ethical Assessment of the Legitimacy of Anti-natalistic Birth Policies". Dr. Tremmel, the Scientific Director of the *Foundation for the Rights of Future Generations*, first discusses whether or not such policies can generally be considered unethical. Unlike some ethicists, his conclusion is that they cannot be deemed unethical across-the-board. Rather, it is both possible and necessary to distinguish between better and worse types. Whilst it is easy to judge measures that either permit a considerable number of freedoms, or impose considerable restrictions on these, it is the measures contained in the middle of the continuum that are more difficult to evaluate. The four-fifths rule is presented in order to lend substance to the core of the problem, by providing a rule of thumb.

Part V The Implementation of Long-term Thinking

In an innovative last part of the book, *Marco Wanderwitz* (CDU), *Peter Friedrich* (SPD), *Anna Lührmann* (Greens) and *Michael Kauch* (FDP), four young members of the German Bundestag, present a far-reaching, if not revolutionary endeavor to implement intergenerational justice and sustainability in the German Constitution. In November 2006, together with more than 100 of their colleagues in the German parliament, they introduced a proposal to change Article 20 and Article 109 of the Basic Law. The final vote, which needs a two-thirds majority, will presumably take place in 2008. In their chapter "Changing the German Constitution in Favor of Future Generations – Four Perspectives From the Young Generation", each one describes, from his/her perspective (Christian democratic, social democratic, green, or liberal), why he/she supports the proposed change in the Constitution. Their chapter is a good example of how theory meets practice, and science meets politics.

The next chapter, "Demographic Pressure and Attitudes Towards Public Intergenerational Transfers in Germany – how much room left for reforms?", by *Harald Wilkoszewski* of the Max Planck Institute for Demographic Research, highlights the allocation problems in an aging society from a political economy perspective. The German political discussion has focused on reductions of public support for the elderly (e.g., the introduction of a "demographic factor" into the public pension formula), and an increase of public support for families and the younger generation (e.g., higher spending for family policies). However, the implementation of such reforms might not be feasible in the future: the generation of those people aged 60 plus will grow further. Additionally, the senior voting block shows consistently higher political participation rates than the younger generation. Thus, the question arises whether a new political group formed by people of the same age with a common interest is likely to emerge.

This closing chapter tests empirically whether there are characteristics in Germany indicating the emergence of a new political group: Wilkoszewski compares the preferences of different age groups concerning public intergenerational monetary transfers, using the 2003 Population Policy Acceptance Survey (PPAS).

Part I
Demographic Trends

Chapter 1
Low Fertility in Europe in a Global Demographic Context

Wolfgang Lutz and Vegard Skirbekk

1.1 Introduction

There are many dimensions of intergenerational justice, and demography matters for many of these. Traditionally, global population growth has been seen as an important danger in terms of worsening living conditions for future generations through exhaustion of natural resources, and other environmental impacts. More recently, the discussions about global climate change have given these concerns a new urgency (O'Neill et al. 2001). While the concern about unsustainable population growth at a global level, and in particular for countries in Africa and West Asia, which still expect very rapid population growth in the future, remains valid and requires all the necessary attention, a new concern has appeared in the context of very low fertility rates in some countries in Europe, and also increasingly in Eastern Asia. As described in this volume, the rapid population ageing that results from low fertility combined with increasing life expectancy raises a host of new challenges for intergenerational justice. Unfortunately, some people tend to focus only on the challenges associated with rapid growth, while others focus on those resulting from rapid ageing, each downplaying the other. But it is important to understand that both rapid growth and rapid ageing can bring about serious challenges, in some cases for different societies, and in other cases even in the same country. The most prominent example of this is China, where further growth due to momentum, and rapid ageing need to be addressed simultaneously. There are many examples in life where opposing extremes bring problems. Only think of temperature, where we want to avoid both too hot and too cold conditions. Why should our attitude to population dynamics be any less sophisticated than this?

In this chapter, we first discuss recent demographic trends on a global level, and briefly discuss the likely outlook for the coming decades, pointing at the abovementioned heterogeneity in trends. Next, we add a measure of "quality", as economists would say, to the sheer quantity of people, by looking at the

Joerg Chet Tremmel (Ed.) *Demographic Change and Intergenerational Justice*
DOI 10.1007/978-3-540-77084-8 © Springer 2008

changes of human capital, i.e., the distribution of the population by age, sex, and level of educational attainment. In the second part of the chapter, we present a more in-depth discussion of the future of fertility levels in countries that already have very low fertility levels. We challenge the conventional assumption that in these countries, fertility levels will soon recover, and present plausible mechanisms that may lead to further declines and even lock some countries in a "low fertility trap". The mechanisms assumed to cause such a trap are closely linked to the issue of intergenerational justice, and in this sense, intergenerational injustice may be one of the reasons why young people will have ever fewer children, and hence reinforce the speed of ageing and shrinking. The concluding section will put this hypothesis again into a broader perspective.

1.2 The End of Population Growth in a Demographically Divided World

Current global demographic trends and the associated challenges are somewhat confusing to many observers. On the one hand, the "population explosion" about which we have heard so much over the past decades seems to continue in some parts of the world – particularly in Africa and the Arab World – while on the other hand, birth rates have fallen so low in many countries that the populations are rapidly ageing and beginning to shrink (Ehrlich 1968; Ehrlich and Ehrlich 1990, UN 2007). Hence, we live in a world in which for some countries rapid population growth due to a lack of family planning is a problem and a major development obstacle, while in other countries, people start to think that their fertility level is already too low, and the associated rapid population ageing will bring problems for old-age security, international competitiveness, and economic growth in the future. This major demographic imbalance may also be the cause of higher migration pressure in the future.

Throughout human history, population numbers have fluctuated mostly due to changing food and disease conditions. The long-term growth of the human population was minimal until the 18th century. Figure 1.1 shows this pattern of growth for the past millennium, and gives projections to the year 2100. Around the year 1800, modern world population growth started to increase rapidly, driven by a decline in death rates that resulted from better nutrition and improving health conditions in Europe. Over the course of the 20th century, the world population grew from 1.6 to 6.1 billion. This very rapid increase, which some authors have labeled the "population explosion", was a result of falling death rates all over the world caused in particular by the spread of modern medicine after World War II, together with a continuation of high birth rates. But with some delay, birth rates have started to decline, and have already reached very low levels in some countries. Already more than half of the world population has fertility rates below the replacement level of two surviving children per woman (Wilson 2004).

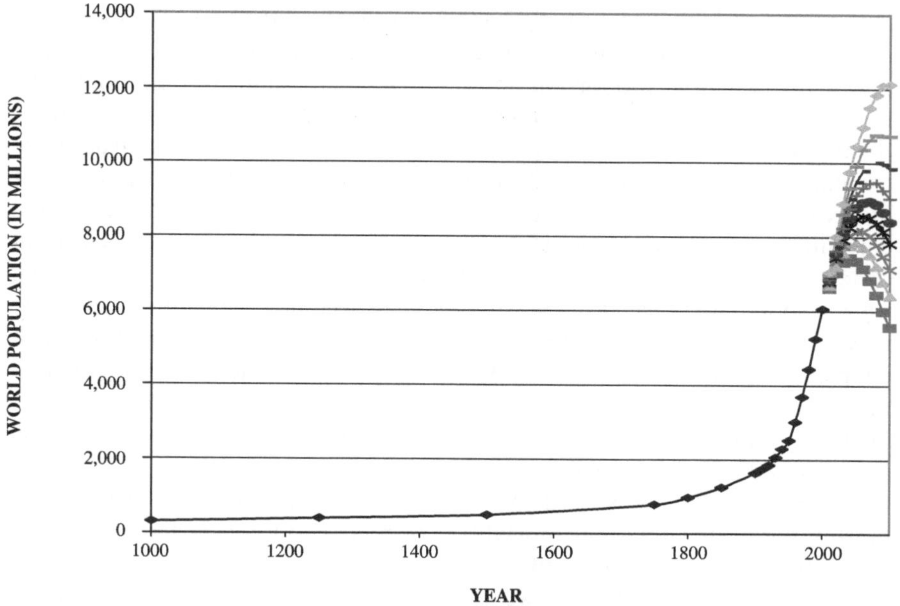

Fig. 1.1 World population growth, 1000–2100 A.D. (after the year 2000, the *lines* represent the deciles of the uncertainty distribution)

On the global level, the population is likely to increase from its current 6.4 billion to somewhat below 9 billion by the middle of the century (Lutz et al. 2001). This significant increase will almost entirely happen in the developing countries, and is due to the rather high fertility in these parts of the world, together with the very young age structure of the population. This so-called momentum of population growth results from the fact that ever more more young women and men will be entering the reproductive ages, and there will be more children born, even if the number of children per woman is at replacement level.

On the right-hand side of Fig. 1.1, the uncertainty range of future population trends is shown. Since the future trends of fertility and mortality are both quite uncertain, population projections also need to reflect the uncertainty around the path that is considered as most likely. The figure gives the likely 80% range of future world population size, which ranges from a world population size of more than 12 billion in 2100 to one of less than 6 billion, i.e., lower than today's size. These data show that there is a high chance that we will experience the end of world population growth in the course of this century. The huge range of uncertainty also tells us that the future path is far from being predetermined, and that it can be greatly influenced by human choice over the coming decades.

These projections also show that the 21st century will bring significant population ageing in all parts of the world. In short, one can conclude that while the

20th century was the century of population growth, with the world population growing nearly fourfold, the 21st century will be the century of population ageing, with the global proportion above age 60 increasing from currently 10% to between 24 and 44% (80% uncertainty interval). Even more significantly, the proportion of the world population that is above age 80 will increase from currently 1% to between 4 and 20%, depending largely on the future course of life expectancy. In Western Europe, this ageing is already more advanced, and currently about 4% of the population are above age 80. Since there is great uncertainty about the future trend in old age mortality – some scientists say that we will soon have reached the maximum life expectancy, while others say there may not even be a limit – there is great uncertainty about the future number of people above the age of 80 years. By the end of the century, the 95% interval ranges from the current level to an incredible 43% of the population, with the median around 20%. Societies with such high proportions of the population above age 80 will clearly be different from today's societies.

The universal process of demographic transition from high fertility and mortality rates to first lower mortality, and then also lower fertility rates is at very different stages in different parts of the world. This is the reason for the demographically divided world we see today. There is an increasing number of countries, not only in Europe but also in Eastern Asia, in which the birth rates have fallen well below replacement level, and the population is ageing rapidly. For these countries, we expect a future of even more rapid population ageing, and in many cases a shrinking of total population size. Simultaneously, in Africa and Western Asia the projections show rapid population growth.

The picture is further complicated by the fact that this demographic divide does not always go along the traditional divide between industrialized and developing countries. Some developing countries have recently seen very rapid fertility declines, and the number of "poor" countries with sub-replacement fertility is increasing. China is the most prominent example, where fertility has recently fallen to an uncertain level between 1.3 and 1.7 (Lutz et al. 2005). For this reason, over the coming two decades, China will have both significant further growth and significant population ageing. It is expected to grow by around 200 million people due to a momentum caused by the very young age structure, with the consequence that more women enter reproductive age. At the same time, the one-child family policy is causing serious problems in terms of the support of the rapidly increasing number of elderly. Surprisingly to some, the USA will also belong to this same group, which will simultaneously experience population growth and ageing, because – unlike Europe – it is expected to grow significantly due to high immigration, and higher birth rates than in Europe.

Table 1.1 gives the trends in the two main drivers of population growth, namely, mortality and fertility. It shows the empirical data for the past half century, and projections for the coming decades as assumed in the medium variant of the UN population projections. Those assume a continued increase in life expectancy, and a universal convergence of fertility rates around a level of 1.85 in the medium run. It shows that over the past half century, life expectancy increased considerably in all parts of the world. Only in Africa has

Table 1.1 Life expectancy at birth, and total fertility rates by selected regions (1950–2050), as estimated and assumed by the United Nations (2005, medium variant)

Region	Life expectancy at birth (both sexes)					Total fertility rate				
	1950–1955	1975–1980	2000–2005	2025–2030	2045–2050	1950–1955	1975–1980	2000–2005	2025–2030	2045–2050
Africa	38.4	46.7	49.1	58.0	65.4	6.72	6.60	4.97	3.39	2.52
Eastern Asia	42.9	66.4	72.6	76.4	79.6	5.68	3.13	1.66	1.82	1.85
South-central Asia	39.6	52.9	63.0	70.9	75.3	6.10	5.11	3.20	2.13	1.95
Western Asia	45.2	60.1	67.8	74.8	77.9	6.48	5.36	3.36	2.36	2.03
Europe	65.6	71.5	73.7	77.8	80.6	2.66	1.97	1.40	1.65	1.83
Latin America & Caribbean	51.4	63.0	71.5	76.8	79.5	5.89	4.50	2.55	1.99	1.86
Northern America	68.8	73.3	77.6	80.5	82.7	3.47	1.78	1.99	1.83	1.85
World	46.6	59.9	65.4	71.1	75.1	5.02	3.92	2.65	2.23	2.05

HIV/AIDS caused a moderate decline at the continental scale over the past decade, with life expectancy having considerably declined in some of the most afflicted countries. In Table 1.1, this is reflected in a very slow overall increase in life expectancy in Africa over the past half century. For the future, a recovery in Africa is assumed, along with a continued increase in life expectancy in all parts of the world.

Fertility rates have also declined considerably around the world over the past decades. With below 1.4 children per woman, Europe has the lowest level, the other extreme being in Africa, where the average is still around 4.9 children per woman. For the coming decades, the UN assumes continued declines in fertility around the world, with the exception of Europe and some very low fertility Asian countries. While the assumed continuation of the fertility transition in developing countries is uncontroversial, the assumption of substantial fertility increases in Europe is more disputed. There are indeed good reasons to assume that fertility may even continue to decline as a consequence of further declining family size ideals, and possibly worsening expected income for the young generations relative to their consumption aspirations. This reasoning has recently been expressed in terms of a consistent "low fertility trap hypothesis" (Lutz et al. 2006). Whether this hypothesis is true, or whether other forces that exert an upward pressure on fertility are stronger, is an open question at this point.

1.3 The Changing Global Distribution of Population and Human Capital

The demographic trends of the past decade, together with those expected for the future, result in major changes in regional population distribution on our planet over the century 1950–2050. Asia, which holds the giant share of the world population, has the most stable proportion (about 55–60%) over this period. The shares of North America, Latin America, and Oceania are also surprisingly stable over time. Big changes affect only Europe and Africa, where over the course of 100 years they fully exchange their positions – Europe's relative demographic weight in the world decreases rapidly. In 1950, Europe (including Russia) was home to some 550 million people, constituting 22% of the world population. At present, Europe has increased to 725 million, but since the world population has increased much more rapidly, Europe's share has declined to only 12%. This is similar to that of Africa, which started at 8% in 1950. By 2050, Europe is expected to shrink to some 630 million, which at that point will be only 7% of the world population. Africa, on the other hand, is likely to continue to grow to around 1.8 billion by 2050, almost three times the expected population of Europe.

As significant as these changes in relative population size are, it is not clear exactly what they will imply for a region's geopolitical standing. The strength and influence of a nation or a continent is not directly a function of its population size. If this were the case, then Africa today should have a similar standing in international politics, economics, or military strength to that of Europe, and this is not remotely the case. What seems to count more than the sheer number of people is the human capital, which can be defined in a simplified way by looking at the people of working age stratified by their level of education. The global distribution of human capital is changing as well, but the pattern looks rather different than that of mere population numbers.

The first global projections of human capital have been recently produced by IIASA (Goujon and Lutz 2004). Figure 1.2 shows the persons of working age by their highest educational attainment. Such data show that in terms of human capital, Europe (including Russia) is still a world power, with well over 350 million working-age people with a higher education – many more than in Africa, and even more than the huge South Asian subcontinent. This helps to put the pure population numbers into perspective. But the figure also shows that significant changes in the global distribution of human capital are to be expected. On a relative scale, gains in today's least developed regions will be strongest partly because the recent improvements in educating the younger generation have already been a significant gain, in comparison to the virtual absence of education for the older cohorts. This is due to the great momentum of educational improvement. Increases in school enrolment today and over the

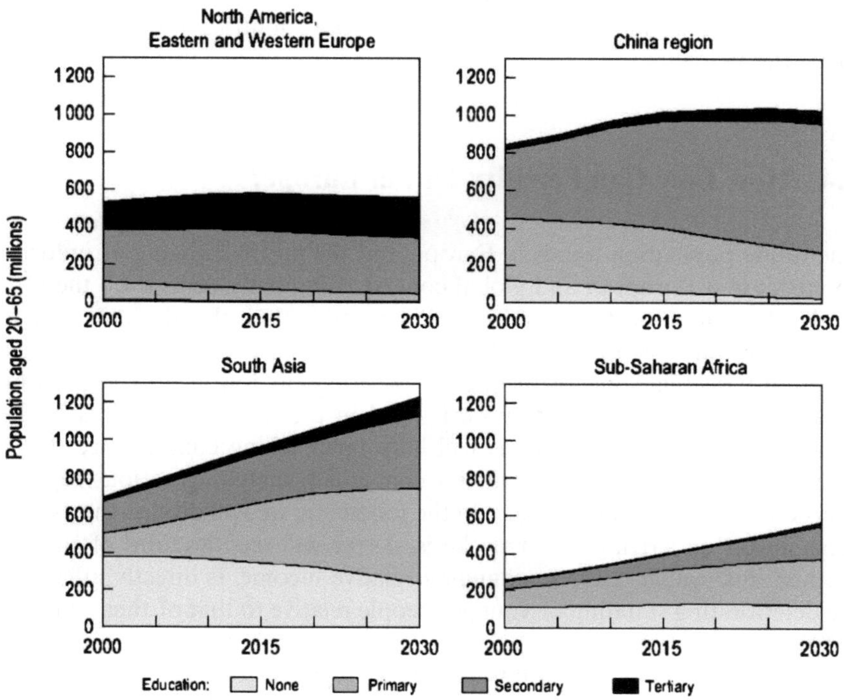

Fig. 1.2 Population (in millions) aged 20–65 by level of education, according to the "ICPD" scenario in four mega-regions, 2000–2030 (ibid., p. 137)

coming decade will only very slowly affect the average educational attainment of the whole working-age population.

Figure 1.2 compares these projections for four "mega-regions". It shows that currently Europe and North America together still dominate the world in terms of human capital, although South Asia and the China region are already bigger in terms of working-age population. The figure also shows the different pathways of China and South Asia (India), which reflects the fact that unlike South Asia, China has invested heavily over the past decades in primary and secondary education, and will see a peaking of its population size over the coming decades. South Asia will soon surpass the China region in terms of population size, but will fall back in terms of human capital.

Even under the most optimistic scenario, Africa will see only very moderate increases in human capital. An interesting point worth noting is that China's human capital is increasing so rapidly that by around 2015, the China region will have more people of working age with secondary or tertiary education than do Europe and North America together.

These global shifts in human capital are likely to result in changing geopolitical and economic weights, and have significant implications for global security in several respects. The changing weights may destabilize current institutional arrangements on the international level when a country's economic and military power is out of proportion with its traditional influence in international politics. This problem of instability of the traditional role may equally apply to the rising superpowers in Asia and the European countries, which are losing in their relative standing.

1.4 How Low Can Fertility Fall in Europe?

The future population trends in Europe, and the future standing of individual countries in a European and global context will greatly depend on the future levels of fertility, particularly in those countries that already have very low levels of fertility. In this context, Lutz et al. (2006) have recently introduced the hypothesis that some of these countries are in a "low fertility trap", which would imply a continued downward spiral in the number of births in these societies. If true, this hypothesis will have far-reaching consequences for the demographic future in the countries concerned, including serious repercussions on intergenerational equity. In the following, we will discuss the assumed mechanisms underlying this hypothesis. As we will see, the third of the three mechanisms, which refers to changing relative income, is directly affected by the deteriorating standing of younger people relative to that of their parents in the countries concerned.

The demographic projections for world regions as discussed above were largely based on the projections of the United Nations Population Division, which until recently assumed that all countries in the world would see fertility converge to replacement level. In 1998, with a rapidly increasing number of countries falling far below the previously assumed magic target level of 2.1 children per woman, the UN (United Nations 1999a) finally abandoned the assumption that all countries of the world would converge to 2.1, and that no country that was still above 2.1 would ever fall below this value. This magic number of children is now assumed to be 1.85. All countries that are now already below 1.3 are projected to recover rather quickly to 1.85; countries that are still above 1.85 are projected to never fall below that level. Eurostat, in its most recent round of national population projections for all 25 EU member countries (Eurostat 2005), makes significantly lower fertility assumptions than the UN in its medium scenario, which is considered to be the most likely one. Eurostat makes its assumptions in terms of cohort fertility, which is a much more stable indicator, and basically assumes that cohort fertility will not decline any further, but rather will stabilize at its current level. In many cases this implies a moderate, near-term increase in period fertility, but much lower levels than assumed by the UN medium variant.

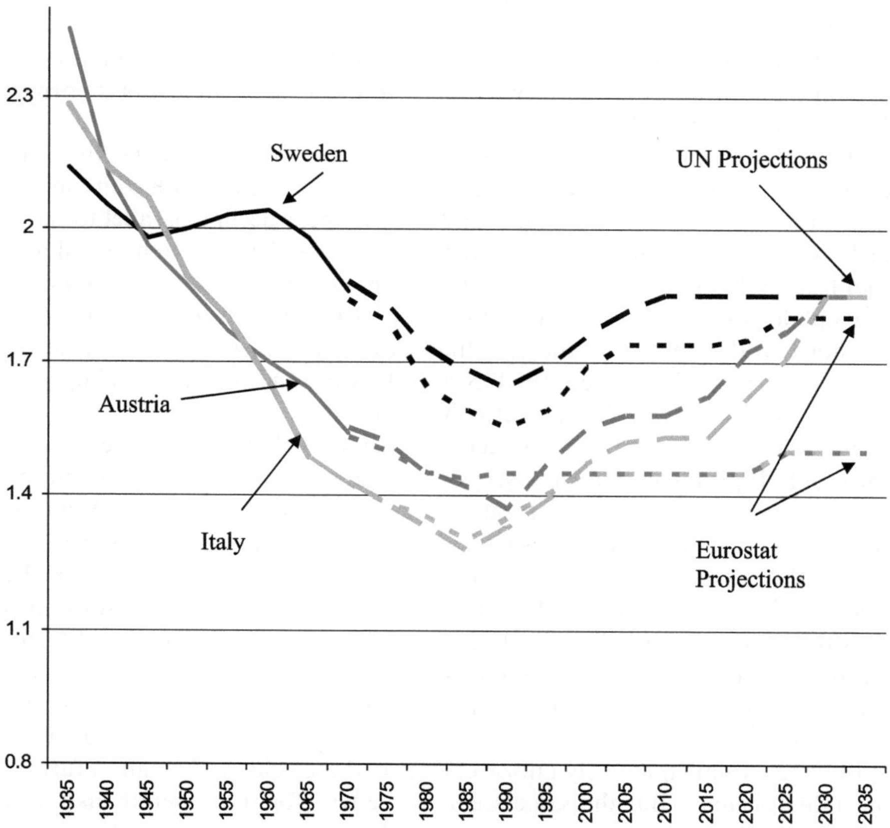

Fig. 1.3 Trends in cohort fertility (empirical, and as assumed by UN and Eurostat projections) for three selected European countries: Italy for Southern Europe, Austria for Central Europe, and Sweden for Northern Europe

Figure 1.3 shows the trends in cohort fertility for three selected European countries: Italy for Southern Europe, Austria for Central Europe, and Sweden for Northern Europe. It gives the empirically observed, completed cohort fertility, followed by the assumed fertility rates according to the UN (United Nations 2005) and the Eurostat (Eurostat 2005) population projections, starting from the birth cohort of 1935, and continuing for 100 years to the birth cohort of 2035. Up to the birth cohort of 1965, the data are entirely empirical; after 1970, they are a mixture of empirical data for the younger ages, and assumed fertility rates for the older ones; from the cohort of 1990 onward, they are entirely assumed data, according to either the UN or the Eurostat projections.

The empirical data for Italy and Austria show an almost linear, steep decline in cohort fertility, from the cohorts born in 1935 to those born in 1985. For these 40 years, each successive cohort had lower completed fertility than the previous one. The fertility trends assumed by Eurostat and the UN imply an abrupt end of the pervasive trend only for the cohorts born after 1985. The UN even implies a significant increase. For Austria and Italy, the UN assumes that cohort fertility would increase with almost the same speed as it decreased over the past decades, and the birth cohorts of 2025 will again have the same level of fertility as the birth cohorts of 1950. The Eurostat assumptions are less extreme, and project only an increase back to the level of the cohorts born in 1965 for Italy and Austria.

The cohort trend was less linear in Sweden. After an initial decline, the birth cohorts of 1945 to 1960 saw a moderate increase in completed fertility levels, which then was followed by a steep and almost linear decline parallel to those in Italy and Austria. But since cohort fertility in Sweden is currently still at a significantly higher level than in the two other countries, Eurostat, according to its philosophy of constant cohort fertility, assumes levels for the future that are not that different from the 1.85 that the UN assumes for all countries in the world. Hence, in Sweden, the UN and the Eurostat assumptions imply an abrupt discontinuity in the trend of cohort fertility.

For what reasons do these projections assume such an unusual reversal in the trend? Typically in trend analysis, one would need to propose a very strong and convincing reason to explain such a deviation from the pervasive trend of the past 50 years of cohort experience. Even more surprisingly, not even the low fertility scenarios produced by these agencies assume a continuation of the trend of the past decades. Furthermore, none of these population projections provide the users with a clear theoretical reasoning for why, in the case of fertility, the declining trend is assumed to reverse, while in the case of mortality it is assumed to continue. When looking at the assumed drivers of mortality decline, ranging from lifestyle factors to medical progress, there are indeed good reasons to assume that likely improvements in these fields will result in further mortality declines. But the same seems to be true for the generally assumed drivers of the fertility decline of the past decades, ranging from the decline of traditional family patterns to more female education, continuing secularization, and increasing uncertainty about the future resulting from rapid social change and globalization. There is no reason to assume a reversal in the trends of many of these determinants of fertility decline in the near future. But why do projections assume a reversal in the trend of the outcome, i.e., fertility?

This deviation from the conventional rules of trend analysis must have to do with a strong belief that somehow there is a powerful force that will stop, and even reverse the trend, i.e., that at the individual level, people will always want children, and that at the aggregate level, human populations would not voluntarily shrink and age to an extent that would be socially disruptive, or in the very long run even lead to extinction. From an evolutionary perspective, these seem to be reasonable assumptions, because a species without a drive to reproduce would not have survived to this day. But there is a strong counterargument, namely, that through the introduction of modern contraception, the evolutionary link between the drive for sex and procreation has been broken, and now reproduction is merely a function of individual preferences and culturally determined norms. Since social norms can change, and in related fields such as the role of women in society, have indeed shown fundamental changes over the recent history, it cannot be ruled out that the social norms about the desire to have children will see similar, fundamental changes over the coming decades. Since such norms tend to change very slowly, and the widespread use of modern contraception is only a rather recent phenomenon in Europe, the current, still apparent desire for children (although already on the decline in some countries) may simply reflect a cultural lag. This lag could be similar in nature to the well-studied lag in desired family size in the process of demographic transition, in which high fertility desires can persist several decades after infant and child mortality have declined.

Whether, after the break of the evolutionary link between sex and fertility, the future of reproduction is entirely a function of potentially instable, individual preferences and social norms, or whether there are other aspects of human nature, such as a caring reflex (at least among women) that may ensure a persistence of a certain desired family size, is a question that needs much further research. Here it is sufficient to conclude that there does not seem to be any "natural law" that would stop fertility from falling further, should preferences and norms change accordingly.

1.5 Three Mechanisms that May Cause a Downward Spiral in Future Birth Rates

Our thinking about the possibility of a low fertility trap was triggered by the recent observation of Peter McDonald, who said that there tend to be two distinct groups of low fertility countries: those where the TFR has stayed above 1.5, and those where it has fallen below the supposedly critical level, and has remained below ever since (McDonald 2005). McDonald also points out that in a recent UN survey about population policy, all countries with TFRs of 1.5 or below have stated that they consider their fertility level as too low. McDonald hypothesizes that, compared to keeping fertility above 1.6, it is more difficult for a country to bring fertility up to, say, 1.6 once it has already fallen to levels of 1.3 or 1.4. From this assumption, he derives the recommendation to governments that they should make efforts to keep fertility above this critical level, and not allow it to fall below.

Whether or not one assumes that there is a specific critical watershed level around a TFR of 1.5 – we do not want to make this point in our chapter – the underlying thinking of a nonlinear dose-response relationship between government efforts and the response of fertility is a welcome contribution to broadening our thinking about the relationship between potential drivers of fertility and the actual fertility change. Because linear regressions have become such a popular analytical tool, we are accustomed to thinking that a unit change in the driver always results in a certain change of fertility, no matter at what level of fertility, and under what side conditions this happens. But there are likely to be all kinds of nonlinearities and possible feedback loops that may result in a bifurcation process. This may include what sociologists might call a change in the demographic regime. For fertility, this may imply that once fertility has fallen below certain levels, and stayed there for a certain time, it might be very difficult, if not impossible, to reverse such a regime change. Recent work by Rindfuss et al. (2004) on social transitions in Japan supports this assumption of nonlinear, self-reinforcing processes in social change, with thresholds and tipping points.

Is it justified to call this possible mechanism of irreversible (or hardly reversible) regime change a "trap", a notion that neither McDonald nor Rindfuss use? If a trap is defined as an unpleasant situation (governments would rather see higher fertility) into which one enters unintentionally, and from which it is very difficult to escape, then indeed the described demographic regime change may be called a trap. But in addition to postulating the possibility of such a tipping point in fertility, it would be good to be able to identify and describe the possible mechanisms that would constitute such a self-reinforcing process toward lower birth rates, and consequently accelerating the ageing and shrinking that are difficult to escape. In the following, we will describe three such mechanisms: a demographic one, another related to social norms, and yet another an economic mechanism.

The low fertility trap hypothesis (LFTH) consists of these three independent elements that all work in the same direction, and can reinforce each other. While the first is a demographic accounting truism, the two others are testable sub-hypotheses. One may classify the three mechanisms as demographic, sociological, and economic. To better distinguish between these three independent forces, we call these LFT1 to LFT3. Figure 1.4 shows how they independently influence the birth rate.

On the left-hand side of Fig. 1.4, we see the different measures of fertility. Since the different assumed mechanisms influence these different aspects of fertility in different ways, it is important to clearly distinguish between these. At the bottom we have the end result of this chain of influences, which is the absolute number of births in a population. This is what matters for population growth, and for the change in the age structure; therefore, it is seen as the final explanandum in our analysis. If populations of different sizes are to be compared, then the absolute number of births can be replaced by the crude birth rate, which is an equivalent measure, the only difference being that it is standardized in terms of total population size. The absolute number of births is, in turn, a direct function of the age pattern of period fertility, and the age structure of the population. Period fertility, in turn, results from a combination of cohort fertility and shifts in the timing of fertility, which can have different determinants. Finally, we assume that the level of cohort fertility is also influenced by norms indicating the ideal personal family size. These norms are subject to changes, as will be described. In studies dealing with the determinants of birth rates, it is not yet common to clearly distinguish between these four different levels of measuring reproduction. If it were to be used more consistently, it could help avoid unnecessary confusion.

As described in Fig. 1.4, LFT1 operates at the level of *population dynamics*, and refers to what demographers sometimes call the negative momentum of population growth. It is based on the well-known demographic mechanism

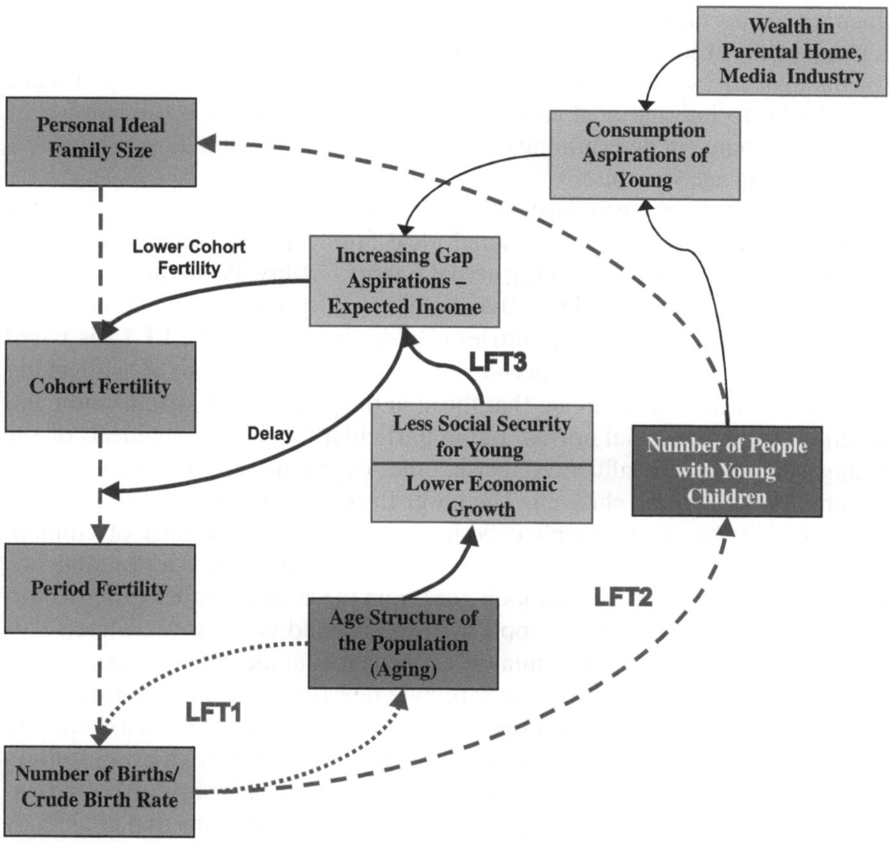

Fig. 1.4 The demographic (*LFT1*), sociological (*LFT2*), and economic (*LFT3*) mechanisms that constitute the low fertility trap hypothesis

that the age distribution of a population exerts an independent influence on the number of births or the crude birth rate, which is not a function of the fertility level of that period, but rather results from past fertility, mortality, and migration. This momentum can be a force toward shrinking in the case of a history of very low fertility that has modified the population age structure to such an extent that ever fewer women enter the reproductive age, and hence the number of births decline, even in the hypothetical case that fertility instantly "jumps" to replacement level. This process in itself causes a downward spiral in the number of births. If there are fewer births today, there will be fewer potential mothers "down the road", which in turn will further decrease the number of births.

This purely demographic mechanism (LFT1) is shown in the lower left corner in Fig. 1.4. It shows the absolute number of births in a given year as a function of the level of period fertility and the age structure of the population. While the level of period fertility is determined by the rest of the model, the two solid lines give the feedback mechanism that is part of LFT1: the number of births influences the age structure of the population, and some three decades later, this modified age structure determines how many births will result from a given level of period fertility. Of course, the age structure can also be influenced by mortality and migration, but this is viewed as exogenous in LFTH. Instead of the absolute number of births, one may consider the crude birth rate (births divided by the total population size) as an output variable that lends itself better to international comparisons. But in the end, it is the number of births that counts in determining the age structure, and hence all consequences of a changing age structure.

LFT2 refers to a mechanism based on sociological reasoning. It is structured around the concept of personal ideal family size, which is assumed to be one of the factors determining actual cohort fertility. Personal ideal family size tends to be markedly higher than actual fertility, but it seems to be on the decline in several European countries (Goldstein et al. 2003). LFT2 is based on the hypothesis that such a decline is triggered by declines in actual fertility some time earlier. It is assumed that through the processes of socialization and social learning, the social norms, and in particular the family size ideals of the young generation, are influenced by what they experience around them in terms of families with young children. The fewer the children belonging to the environment that the young people experience, the lower the number of children that will be part of their normative system in terms of what is a desirable life. Hence, in Fig. 1.4, the feedback loop goes from the actual number of births in a population, to the number of people with young children a few years later. This in turn is viewed as a key determinant of the personal ideal family size.

LFT3 is based on an economic rationale referring to the gap between personal aspirations for consumption and expected income, which is assumed to result in fewer births. This argument is directly derived from Richard Easterlin's relative income hypothesis, which claims that it is not the absolute (expected) income that matters, but rather income relative to the aspirations that are largely formed in one's youth, and greatly dependent on the standard of living in the parental home (Easterlin 1980). This first element of Easterlin's hypothesis has always been in the shadow of the second, much more controversial element, namely, that small cohort size will result in higher expected income. In this hypothesis, we will refer only to the first element, which is the less problematic one and has given the relative income hypothesis its name. In the more detailed discussion below, we will elaborate somewhat on the second part, which does not seem to be a dominant force prevalent in Europe today.

In Fig. 1.4, LFT3 is represented by the solid lines. The gap between aspiration and expected income is a result of distinct changes affecting these two factors. As to expected income, a declining number of births is shaping the age distribution in a way that will result in more rapid ageing, which in turn triggers necessary changes in the current social security system, which typically means cuts that will affect mainly today's younger cohorts, while being less severe and more gradual for the older ones. In addition to this rather evident deterioration of expected social security benefits for the younger cohorts, rapid population ageing may also result in lower productivity, and consequently in a globalized economy, less investment, and lower economic growth in the future. Both factors result in a more pessimistic economic outlook for today's younger generations, which is widely documented in opinion surveys. On the other hand, aspirations for material consumption are probably higher today than they ever were before. Today's youngsters are not only experiencing an unprecedented degree of exposure to advertising aimed at further raising the aspirations for consumption, but they also tend to come from relatively wealthy homes, their parents having fully benefited from the economic boom of the past decades. There is also a demographic factor: due to the fertility decline, since the 1970s children have had to share parental wealth with fewer siblings, a factor that helped to raise the standard of living to which they have become accustomed.

In terms of the effect of this widening gap between aspirations and expected income (in the left column of Fig. 1.4), we may assume two different effects of fertility. First and foremost, the decline in relative income would (according to Easterlin) affect the quantum of fertility, i.e., cohort fertility. But the extensive recent literature on the postponement of fertility, and the resulting increase in the mean age of childbearing, which has an independent effect on depressing period fertility (the tempo effect), suggests that such a gap would also result in postponement. Young people are not yet certain how their future income will develop. Therefore, a likely reaction is to postpone the decision to have children until a later date when the future may look clearer. Hence in Fig. 1.4, we have two effects of declining relative income, one on the translation of personal ideals into actually wanted cohort fertility, and the other in the process of the timing of fertility, i.e., the translation of cohort into period fertility.

1.6 Conclusions

At the European level, population projections usually assume a convergence of fertility and mortality trends among all European societies. This is understandable under a European integration perspective, and under conditions of increasing communication, travel, and economic interdependencies. On the other hand, the hypothesis discussed above suggests that there may indeed be diverging paths with respect to the future levels of fertility. Those societies that have experienced relatively stable fertility levels not far below replacement for the past decades may continue to do so, while the ones that have seen rapid declines may even experience further declines. But such diverging trends may not only be observed at the level of countries, but could also refer to other social groups such as specific ethnic or religious sub-populations within or across countries. Diverging age structures between different population groups within Europe are likely to provide further complexity to intergenerational equity, and may further challenge social security systems.

It cannot be ruled out that, even within the same social groups, there may be increasing "divisions of labor" for a society's reproduction, with significant segments of the group having fewer or no children, while others have a larger number of children, whether or not they receive financial compensation for this extra effort for societal continuation. These are clearly highly contentious subjects, but they illustrate that even in the narrow field of fertility, the issue of intergenerational justice cannot be discussed independently from the issue of intragenerational justice.

On the global level, we may be heading toward a future of continued heterogeneity, and even further diverging conditions in terms of demographic trends, health, and economic wellbeing. For all we know, global warming is likely to most strongly affect those regions that already have high vulnerability partly due to unstable demographic conditions and rapid population growth that have made it more difficult to expand educational coverage, and build the necessary infrastructure to protect against natural disasters as well as diseases. We need a more general framework, such as the recently proposed framework of "population balance" (Lutz et al. 2004) that integrates the demographic issues of growth and ageing together with human capital and environmental challenges in a common model, so that we are not discussing the one while forgetting about the other. A rapidly ageing, and even decreasing European population may be associated with many challenges for the younger generation of Europeans, but it also has to be seen in the global context, where population growth and increasing energy consumption aggravate the environmental risks for coming generations. An assessment of the net effects is very difficult, and greatly depends on values taken into account. But this dimension cannot be disregarded when discussing intergenerational justice.

References

Easterlin RA (1980) Birth and fortune: the impact of numbers on personal welfare. Basic Books, New York

Ehrlich and Ehrlich 1990, UN 2007. World Economic and Socal Survey 2007. United Nations: New York.

Ehrlich PR (1968) The population bomb. Ballantine, New York

Ehrlich PR, Ehrlich A (1990) The population explosion. Simon & Schuster, New York

Eurostat (2005) http://epp.eurostat.cec.eu.int/portal/page?_pageid=1996,45323734&_dad=portal&_schema=PORTAL&screen=welcomeref&open=/Popula/proj&language=en&product=EU_MASTER_population&root=EU_MASTER_population&scrollto=0

Goldstein J, Lutz W, Testa MR (2003) The emergence of sub-replacement family size ideals in Europe. Popul Res Policy Rev 22(5/6):479–496

Goujon A, Lutz W (2004) Future human capital: population projections by level of education. In: Lutz W, Sanderson WC, Scherbov S (eds) The end of world population growth in the 21st century: new challenges for human capital formation and sustainable development. Earthscan, London, pp 121–157

Lutz W, Sanderson W, Scherbov S (2001) The end of world population growth. Nature 412:543–545

Lutz W, Sanderson WC, O'Neill BC (2004) Conceptualizing population in sustainable development: from "population stabilization" to "population balance". In: Lutz W, Sanderson WC, Scherbov S (eds) The end of world population growth in the 21st century: new challenges for human capital formation and sustainable development. Earthscan, London, pp 315–334

Lutz W, Scherbov S, Cao GY, Ren Q, Zheng X (2005) China's uncertain demographic present and future. International Institute for Applied Systems Analysis, Laxenburg, Austria, IIASA Interim Rep IR-05-043

Lutz W, Skirbekk V, Testa MR (2006) The low fertility trap hypothesis: forces that may lead to further postponement and fewer births in Europe. In: Philipov D, Liefbroer AC, Billari FC (guest eds) Vienna Yearbook of Population Research 2006. Special issue Postponement of Childbearing in Europe. Verlag der Österreichischen Akademie der Wissenschaften, Vienna, Austria, pp 167–192

McDonald P (2005) Low fertility in Singapore: causes, consequences and policies. Paper Forum on Population and Development in East Asia, 16–17 May 2005, Beijing

O'Neill BC, MacKellar FL, Lutz W (2001) Population and climate change. Cambridge University Press, Cambridge, UK

Rindfuss R, Choe MK, Bumpass LL, Tsuya NO (2004) Social networks and family change in Japan. Am Sociol Rev 69(6):838–861

United Nations (1999) World Population Prospects. The 1998 Revision. United Nations, Department of Economic and Social Affairs, Population Division, New York

United Nations (2005) World Population Prospects. The 2004 Revision. United Nations, Department of Economic and Social Affairs, Population Division, New York

United Nations (2007) World Economic and Social Survey 2007. United Nations, New York

Wilson, C. (2004) "Fertility below Replacement Level", Science, 566:207–209, 9th of April

Part II
The Impact of Demographic Developments on Key Indicators

Chapter 2
Demography and Budget Consolidation: An Analysis and Possible Courses of Action

Johannes Meier and Ole Wintermann

2.1 Introduction

Demographic trends pose a major challenge to political decision makers in Germany. German society is facing the combined trends of aging, increasing diversity, and shrinkage – with the added complication that these fundamental shifts are occurring in highly differentiated patterns in different regions. This calls for major adjustments to policies, systems, and planning on a national, regional, and community level.

While there is an increasing consensus that some action needs to be taken, it is less clear where the more fundamental changes should begin, and how a broad consensus can be achieved for implementing difficult adaptation strategies. In particular, the country's baby boomers both pose a challenge and present an opportunity. As for the challenge: baby boomers have considerable earning power, and therefore constitute a major source of financing for the social welfare state. Within 25 years, however, the majority of the baby boomers will have retired, and will be drawing benefits. Given the welfare state's current pay-as-you-go systems, this will put a major burden on subsequent generations, which are significantly smaller, and thus require considerable increases in productivity. The situation is complicated by increasing debt levels that limit policymakers' freedom to take action. With regard to the opportunity that baby boomers provide, it should be noted that this generation can be characterized not only by its size, but also by its ability to shape new trends and to introduce new patterns of behavior.

In this chapter, we argue that the demographic changes impacting Germany call for differentiated adaptation strategies that anticipate the country's age structure in the coming decades. However, as many of these adaptation strategies are still to be specified, special attention needs to be paid to ensuring that future generations have sufficient room to maneuver. This requires that public

Joerg Chet Tremmel (Ed.) *Demographic Change and Intergenerational Justice*
DOI 10.1007/978-3-540-77084-8 © Springer 2008

budgets have to be consolidated as a critical first step in a short-term, one that must be taken without further delay.

A successful consolidation strategy tends to require a clear understanding of underlying principles and goals, which need to be upheld over a longer time span by all constituents. As political rationales do not necessarily follow technical rationales, it is important to discuss how such principles and goals can be upheld by a critical mass of actors over the long term.

We believe that – as is true of any major reform effort – it is crucial to invest heavily in the explanation of why consolidation of public budgets is necessary. Usually the best explanations in major reform programs have a principle-based or moral quality, and make reference to the "light at the end of the tunnel". In addition to such an explanatory framework, clear goals need to be set. These goals provide the basis for tracking progress, and communicating intermediate success during the long and arduous journey. Finally, credibility needs to be established continuously by executing measures that are understandable, consistent, and well prioritized.

In this context, the Bertelsmann Stiftung has recently conducted two studies: the Public Debt Monitor update, and an international comparison of successful consolidation policies. The Public Debt Monitor provides an understanding of sensible and necessary consolidation goals by making implicit debt visible over the medium term, and demonstrating the impact of recent consolidation initiatives. The international comparison of successful consolidation strategies identifies success factors and policy patterns as a reference point for strategy definition and communication.

In this chapter, we introduce key results from both studies.

2.2 Public Debt Monitor

The only way to determine whether the 16 states and the federal government are gaining or losing ground in their efforts to consolidate their budgets is to constantly monitor and analyze their fiscal policies. The Bertelsmann Stiftung's Debt Monitor is designed to do exactly that. The project tracks the budgets of the federal government (including allocations to the public pension system) and the states (including municipalities and local government associations). Developed by economists and public policy analysts, the program uses clearly defined assumptions and calculations to quantify the need for consolidation in each budget. It also takes current debt levels into account. The Debt Monitor is intended to make the consequences of fiscal policy more transparent, permit closer oversight of public funding, and – through publication of its findings – bring greater discipline to fiscal policymaking.

In the year 2020, Berlin is projected to have the highest debt level, followed by Saxony-Anhalt and Bremen, assuming that fiscal policy remains unchanged, and without taking into account the increase in value-added tax (Fig. 2.1).

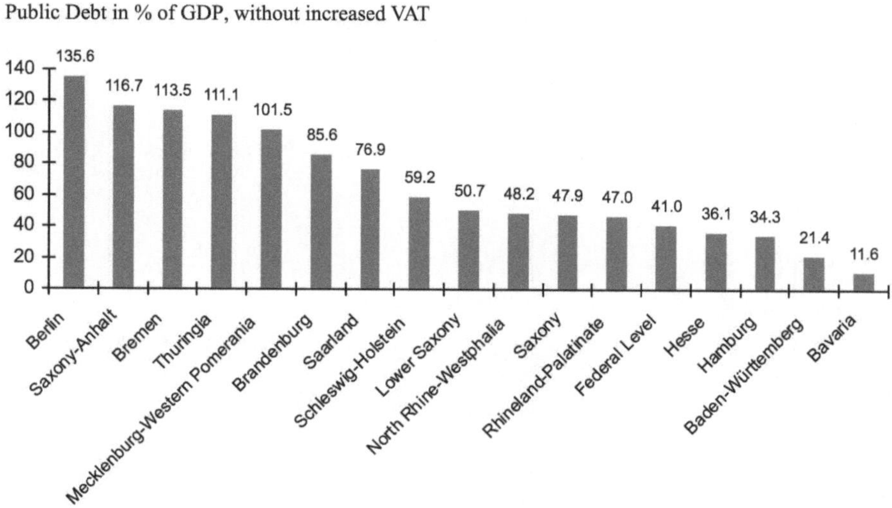

Fig. 2.1 Public debt level in relation to GDP in 2020, without increased value-added tax (VAT)

If the increase in value-added tax is taken into account, then Berlin's debt level will still be highest, with Bremen next, then Saxony-Anhalt (Fig. 2.2).

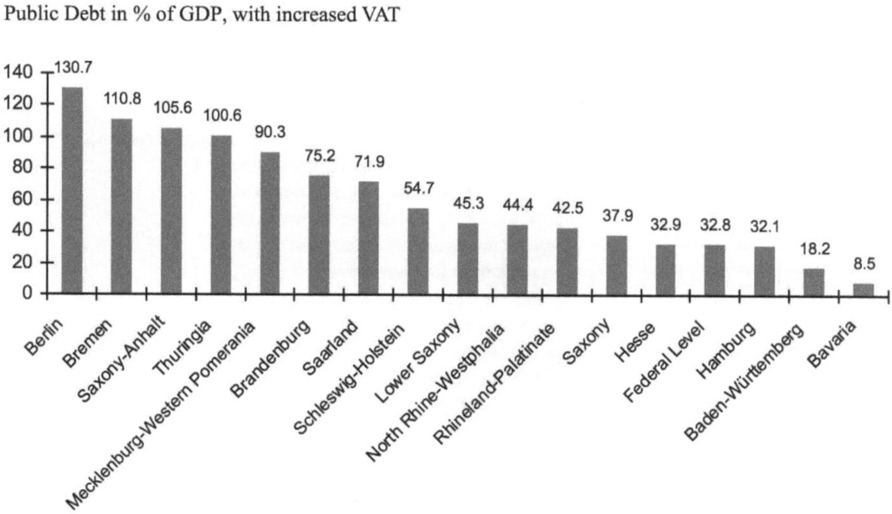

Fig. 2.2 Public debt level in relation to GDP in 2020, with increased value-added tax (VAT)

If we take into account the increase in value-added tax, in 2020 predicted per-capita debt will be highest in Bremen, followed by Berlin and Saxony-Anhalt (Fig. 2.3).

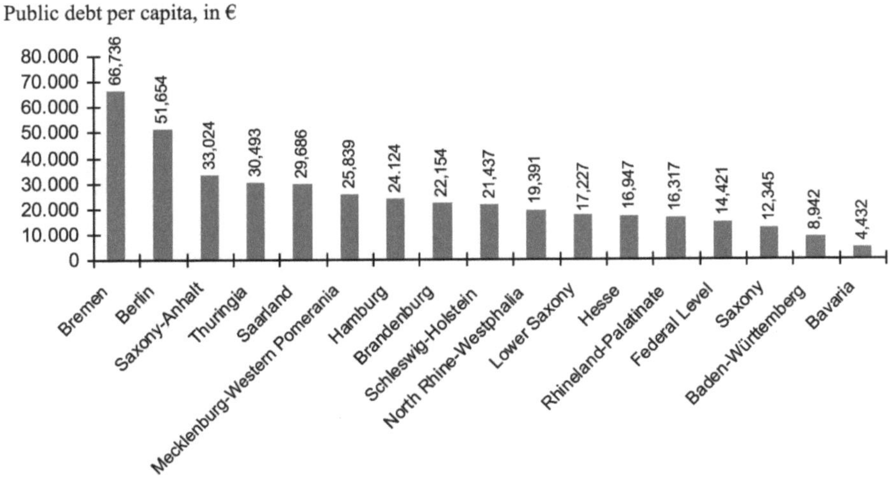

Fig. 2.3 Predicted per-capita debt in 2020, in €

Figure 2.4 shows the need for consolidation of primary expenditures in each state, taking into consideration the value-added tax.

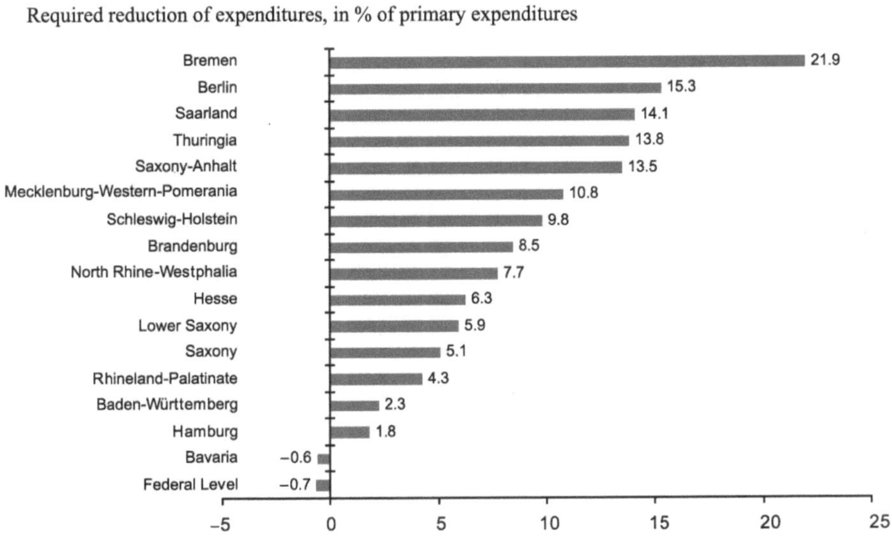

Fig. 2.4 Percentage of required consolidation in cutting primary expenditures

Bremen, with a required cutting of 21.9% of primary expenditures, leads the list of the states in need of budget consolidation, followed by Berlin and Saarland. Bavaria is the only state to have a negative level of new debt, at –0.6%. The relevant percentage for the federal government is –0.7%.

It is remarkable that, on the one hand, changes in interest rates and productivity lead to hardly any effects in the development of public debt in 2020 or 2030. Lower rates of interest and higher rates of productivity are merely a marginal determinant of the absolute level of debt in the future.

On the other hand, the rise of the German value-added tax at the beginning of 2007 leads to a significant lowering of future debt levels. If, and only if the higher tax income is "invested" in the consolidation of public budgets will it be possible to achieve the better result shown in Fig. 2.2. These sensitivities are in line with a key finding of the international consolidation analysis: a successful consolidation strategy tends to simultaneously raise taxes and lower social expenditures. This stands in contrast to core beliefs often espoused in everyday politics, whereby politicians want to either raise taxes or lower social expenditures, but seldom both.

2.3 Successful Consolidation: An International Comparison

As part of a transparent presentation of the budget situation at the federal and state level, the Bertelsmann Stiftung has cooperated with Prof. Uwe Wagschal of Heidelberg University in publishing a report laying out options derived from a comparison of successful budget consolidation efforts in other countries.[1]

2.4 Reform Measures on the Expenditure Side

The following reforms on the expenditure side are recommended as methods for achieving successful consolidation.

1. First, the indexing of social benefits should be suspended or adjusted. In concrete terms, this could be done by introducing a certain commitment (*Regelbindung*) governing changes in wages and transfers in the public sector (including remuneration for members of parliament). Full adjustment to changes in economic indicators would be permitted only if the national deficit is limited, and the amount of debt remains under a certain level.
2. Second, overall growth in expenditures should be linked to the budget situation and economic developments. The aim should be to ensure that long-term growth in expenditures remains under the average growth level (roughly 0.5% below real economic growth), in order to support positive growth in the private sector.

---

[1] All studies can be downloaded from http://www.aktion2050.de

3. It should also be noted that other countries have restricted access to social services, and tightened control mechanisms as part of their budget consolidation processes. In addition to carrying out the Hartz IV reforms, it is important to review and adjust other branches of Germany's social insurance system, such as long-term care insurance and the healthcare system.

2.5 Reform Measures on the Revenue Side

1. First, surpluses and one-time revenues (e.g., from gold, licenses, privatization) need to be invested in Germany exclusively in debt reduction, as successful consolidators have done. There is no way to avoid establishing clear rules in this context, as the controversy over the German Federal Employment Agency surpluses has shown.
2. Moreover, in certain countries moderate tax increases, particularly for those with higher incomes, have helped to achieve consolidation from the political-economy perspective. This kind of tax policy would help distribute the costs and benefits of consolidation more equitably, and it would be easier to communicate such a policy to the public.
3. The option of fundamental tax reform should be reconsidered. We are currently seeing a gradual dismantling of tax breaks and financial supports, which broadens the income-tax assessment basis. Comprehensive tax reform, eliminating all deductions while at the same time substantially lowering tax rates, would be a clear and growth-friendly alternative. Some countries that have undergone consolidation, such as a number of Scandinavian countries ("dual income tax") and The Netherlands, as well as transition countries like Slovakia and Russia, have had good experiences implementing fundamental reforms. In most cases of sustained consolidation, in the short term revenues have declined during the consolidation phase, which has had in a mid- and long-term perspective a positive effect on economic growth and employment, while simultaneously rehabilitating the budget.

2.6 Institutional Changes in the Budget Process

While consolidation can be achieved over the short term by taking steps on the revenue and expenditure sides simultaneously, it is more likely to be sustained over a longer period of time by making institutional changes.

1. First, a look at other countries indicates that the budget process should be changed in favor of a stronger top-down orientation, rather than the existing bottom-up process.
2. Second, the budget should be built on cautious estimates of future developments, generated, for example, through systematic underestimation, to remain on the safe side in determining the benchmarks on which the budget

is based. Over the past 15 years, economic growth has been systematically overestimated.

3. In addition, the experiences of other countries indicate that a policy of "laying back the money for bad times" should be introduced, stipulating that any unforeseen surpluses are to be used to alleviate the national debt.
4. Furthermore, expenditure and deficit goals should be announced at the beginning of each legislative period, with the goal of enhancing discipline. In Germany, this should be emphasized in the coalition agreement and the government policy statement.
5. Finally, changing to multiyear budgets would result in a stronger future orientation, and provide a more solid foundation for medium-term fiscal planning.

2.7 Drawing Conclusions from "Soft Factors"

1. Leadership is crucial for consolidation. Moreover, it is clear from initial experiences at the state level that voters would respond favorably if politicians were to commit to consolidation, voice their support for it publicly, and make consistent efforts to achieve it.
2. In addition, far-reaching reforms should be carried out as soon as a change in power or government has taken place, in order to enhance political credibility and take advantage of the "honeymoon effect".
3. Because of their large majorities, grand coalitions have a good chance of success in putting the budget back onto solid ground, particularly in states where a variety of players have veto power.
4. It should be noted that consolidation depends largely on overall economic conditions, and on developments in the financial and capital markets. Declining economic growth significantly affects the chances of consolidation, as does an increase in interest rates. Here too, however, governments can build trust by pursuing credible policies, and a sustained economic policy can ultimately help to achieve both goals.

While the Public Debt Monitor has provided more transparency on the variance of debt at the state level, the international comparison of consolidation strategies suggests key success factors for setting the proper agenda.

2.8 Summary and Outlook

In view of demographic trends, consolidation will present a growing challenge to society and the political sphere. The 2006 Public Debt Monitor has provided insight into the situation to be expected at the federal and state level in 20 years. The international comparison of successful consolidation efforts shows determinants and realistic measures for achieving lasting budget consolidation. Consolidation is clearly possible, but very hard to manage from a political point of view. In Germany, this management challenge is complicated by the highly interlinked financial flows between the federal, state, and community levels within the country's federal system. For consolidation to be successful, it is critical that an integrated view of the absolute debt at all levels has to be taken into account, and clear accountabilities be assigned.

Looking beyond the need to maintain a degree of financial leeway by consolidating public budgets, emphasis must be placed on the critical role that productivity levels play for the robustness of the German welfare state. A low rate of reproduction, and the aging of the population could potentially contribute to a serious weakening of Germany's viability as a business location, since growing social burdens are enhancing non-wage labor costs, while the number of workers is declining. That is why action is required both to improve infrastructure, and to make effective use of the potential within the existing labor force.

We believe that this can best be achieved by using the available leeway to focus attention on increasing human capital, by increasing investment in education and R&D. This is not at odds with the call for consolidating public budgets: each Euro that is not spent on education tends to result in long-term costs that are an order of magnitude higher than the unspent funds. Current bookkeeping methods, however, do not adequately account for these "preprogrammed" social expenditures, and for reduced productivity.

Thus, an effective strategy for consolidating public budgets needs to be complemented by a strategic vision for ensuring productivity in an aging, diverse, and shrinking society.

Chapter 3
Intergenerational Justice and Economic Growth. A Challenge for Economic Policy

Michael Hüther

3.1 Economic Theory and the Theory of Justice

Economic theory and the theory of justice entail a common feature: both are traditionally subject to a limited time horizon – the perspective of the present generation. Under such premises, efficiency and justice can easily be discussed and balanced. Neglecting a historical perspective, i.e., the long-term development under real-time conditions, significantly reduces the set of variables, and makes redundant the answers to questions like the following.

- Where do the rules for analysis of incentive effects come from? Who formulates the "good constitution"?
- How can individuals' different sets of values be explained?
- Why do different social subsystems occur for identical regulation systems?
- How relevant is the intertemporal shift of scarcities – especially between physical capital and human capital – for the growth perspectives of future generations?

Homo oeconomicus lives in a theoretically defined world of unlimited competition. That makes him attractive. We define, but rarely question the conditions of his behavior. This approach has persisted throughout the progress of macroeconomic analysis, starting from the fundamental assumption of an equilibrium in neoclassic theory, over the fundamental assumption of a disequilibrium in Keynesianism, to the growth of theoretical questioning concerning the conditions of intertemporal stability of capital accumulation. Finally, the discussion on the sustainability of fiscal policy issues that occurred during the last two decades has altered this approach. Especially Alan Auerbach and Laurence Kotlikoff have, under the scope of fiscal policy, added a link between the claims and the living conditions of different generations, with the means of generational balancing (for an overview, see Auerbach et al. 1999). With the help of these models, intertemporal effects of distribution in fiscal policy and

Joerg Chet Tremmel (Ed.) *Demographic Change and Intergenerational Justice*
DOI 10.1007/978-3-540-77084-8 © Springer 2008

the social security system can be analyzed. The results of these studies have meanwhile attained an important place in policy consulting (see Sachverständigenrat 2001, and later editions thereof).

For a long time, an original generational perspective has been adopted in the environmental debate. To the degree to which neoclassical considerations of an emission-oriented environmental protection with the aim of eliminating pollution have been complementing the concept of sustainability, claims of future generations have systematically been incorporated (see Bardt and Hüther 2006). Since then, environmental goals have been balanced against social and economic targets. Prevention has taken the place of cure in environmental policy.

These long-term-oriented, multigenerational approaches are gradually complemented by questions of demographic change – for Germany in particular, a shrinking and ageing population. Economic prosperity and justice cannot be regarded independently from the population development, and just as important, human capital accumulation (see Berkel et al. 2004). This required mental progress such that we do not merely regard the impacts of the demographic trend as a subject to be modified by policy measures, but also the trend itself.

Every line of argumentation concerning the link between interests of different generations rests on the insight that the market economy system does not contain a guarantee for expansion in time. Scarcities vary not only between shrinking and expanding markets, which is a vital feature of the ordinary structural change, but also between different economic states of generations. The commons – an image that is often cited in the theory of public goods – is the location of conflicting interests not only within a generation, but also between different generations – generations whose size and structure are still unknown. Hence, scarcity becomes important in matters that are evaluated as stable, or at least sufficiently inertial. Therefore, the potential of human capital accumulation is defined primarily by a process of path dependency. In the case of a continuously shrinking population, the necessity of disinvestment that is ordinarily relevant only in specific single markets occurs on an aggregate level. Economic theory, having inherited from the classic model the optimism of expansion, needs to focus contraction. The fact that no symmetric property rights exist between generations – as opposed to within a generation – adds some complexity to the issue. Due to factual irreversibilities or prohibitively high costs for revisions, compensation strategies between generations are hardly feasible.

The aspect of long-term implications of present economic action has profoundly changed and amplified. However, the subject lacks valuable content if it cannot be measured with a commonly accepted norm. As much as the valuation of economic action within a time frame needs to be oriented along certain norms, this is true also for an intergenerational perspective. Even though efficiency and justice exhibit a relationship of conflict, they cannot be regarded separately. Economics simply is a normative science. Or, to echo Herbert Giersch, former president of the Kiel Institute for the World Economy (Kieler Institut für Weltwirtschaft): "Value judgements in questions of economic policy are inevitable. It would be a mistake to conceal them in an open discussion.

They will be detected anyway. Therefore it is better to show one's colors in the first place and to explain where one is located within the field of conflicting values" (Giersch 1999).

The contribution of the theory of justice was to abandon its primary focus on individual ethical problems, and to broaden its range of topics to social aspects (see Horn and Scarano 2002). Philosophers of the ancient world and the Middle Ages interpreted justice primarily as a guideline for people's behavior. However, the discussion of justice with regard to proceedings, laws, rules, social regimes, economic systems, opportunities of participation, and results of individual action in the social context imply that these concepts can be influenced. Consequently, 18th century economics has produced a modified expression along with conceptual consequences, abandoning the narrow view of the "economics of the house" ("Hausväterliteratur"; see Landshut 1973), and providing for a broad view of the division of labor according to Adam Smith.

Hence, concepts of justice were called for, debating the participation opportunities of an anonymous economic system, as well as the question of an appropriate yield of economic action. The consideration of future generations – on the one hand, through the formulation of claims regarding the actions of the present generation, on the other hand as a target group for the definition of constitutional rules – arose from the question of long-term stability of social and economic regimes. In institutional economics, such considerations meet the questions of how incentive structures can be defined within constitutional regimes, and how the creation of such regimes takes place.

Intergenerational justice and economic growth beyond the accumulation of physical capital are – that should have become obvious – unambiguously two sides of the same coin. Hence, the preconditions of their discourse are given. Yet, their conceptual conjunctions are rudimental. They are the subject of the following discussion. After a glance at the empirics of demographic change in Germany, the consequences of a shrinking population for economic growth will be analyzed with a supply-sided view. Then, the concept of intergenerational justice will be discussed, in order to finally formulate a national strategy for long-term growth.

3.2 Germany: Facing Demographic Change and the Need for Education Reform

The development of the population and the formation of human capital should be discussed jointly. While population growth defines the potential of human capital formation, the latter determines the original income perspective of each cohort. Hence, an empirical observation needs to reflect both aspects.

Describing demographic change resembles the analysis of the global climate change: the debate easily slides onto an emotional or dramatic level. Horror scenarios may have pedagogic effects. But oftentimes they generate a fatalistic attitude that implies the nonexistence of effective solutions, suggesting that solely an adaptation strategy appears promising. However, rather than painting catastrophe scenarios, the analysis of the problems at hand should be driven by reason, not by emotion.

We will at first address the empirical facts as stated in the 11th coordinated population forecast of the Federal Statistical Office of Germany (11. koordinierte Bevölkerungsvorausberechnung; see Statistisches Bundesamt 2006). Demographic change is driven by three factors: fertility, life expectancy, and migration. The forecast is based upon the perception of historical changes, and therefore – under a somewhat secular view – draws upon plausible assumptions regarding the future trend. The population forecast can hence be interpreted as a reflection of alternative scenarios presuming varying conditions, and thus identifying the sensitivity of differing assumptions with respect to the outcome. Clearly, a demographic equilibrium – defined as a state without permanent growth or shrinkage, and a steady age distribution – is not a realistic pattern. Globally, a demographic disequilibrium can be regarded as the normal state (see Birg 2003a, p. 6).

Since the mid-1970s, fertility in Western Germany, and lately also in Eastern Germany has settled to a rate of 1.4 births per woman (cf. Fig. 3.1). With this birth rate, Germany is located in the lower part in an international comparison. However, generative behavior in Germany is anything but stable. Whilst fertility of women 30 years and younger is decreasing, the birth rate of women older than 30 has been rising in the same proportion. The underlying cause consists in the fact that both the marriage decision and the family decision have decelerated within the last decades.

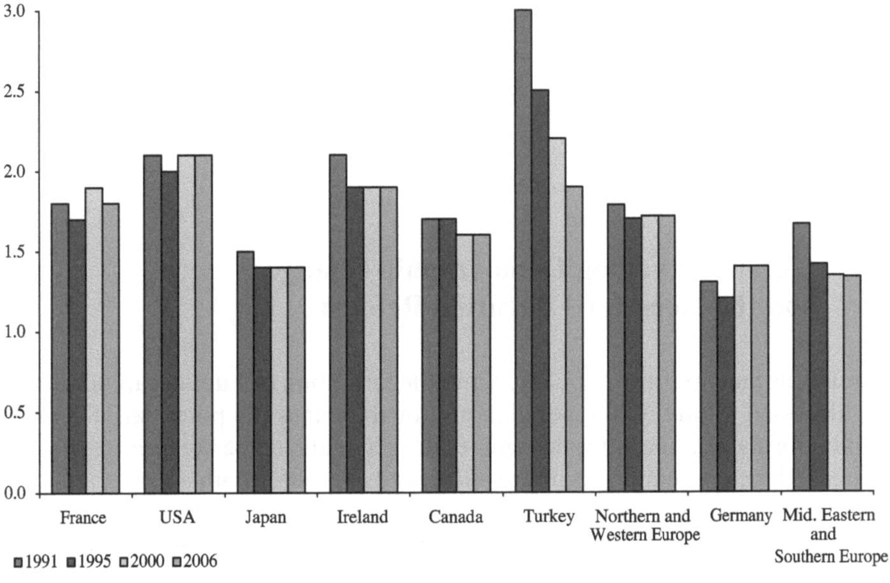

Fig. 3.1 Fertility rates in selected countries (source: Census Bureau USA)

Interestingly, the composite birth rate of female immigrants has decreased due to altered migration flows, namely by 17% since 1991. The share of female immigrants from Eastern Europe, where fertility constitutes a low level, has increased substantially. Contrarily, the proportion of Turkish women relative to all female immigrants has decreased from 30% in 1990 to 22% in 2004. Overall, the average age of female immigrants at the time of birth rose as well.

Germany is the only country displaying a very low fertility for 30 years. However, the drop in birth rates clearly appears to be a European phenomenon. With the exception of France, which has recently been approaching the replacement rate of 2.1, no European country reaches this level. Three groups of countries can be differentiated (Fig. 3.1): the Scandinavian countries and Benelux with a birth rate of roughly 1.7, Mid, Eastern, and Southern Europe with a fertility rate around 1.3, and France and Ireland with a rate of approximately 1.9. Internationally, a similar structure can be observed: Japan's fertility rate equals 1.4, Canada's 1.6, Turkey's 1.9, and the USA has a birth rate slightly over 2. In all likelihood, these differences reflect not only varying political frameworks, but also culturally determined patterns of behavior and approval.

In other words: with the exception of the USA, "modern societies obviously benefit from children that are not born. They do not need children" (Hondrich 2006, p 34; see also Birg 2003a, p. 7). In the short run, observers such as the sociologist Karl Otto Hondrich suggest that children compete with economic and career prospects for high-skilled women.[1] Hence, the economy would simply require open labor markets for young adults. Due to its limited time horizon, this view is to be perceived as a provocation, which sharply describes a conflict that is primarily found in industrial economies. If it is true – as Hondrich claims – that fertility "is not an individual but a collective variable", then it follows that there is a need for a collective commitment to resolve this conflict (Hondrich 2006).

For the fertility level, complex decision structures are to be analyzed that regard individual living conditions, as well as social and group-specific preference patterns. An empirically evident aspect is the financial situation of families, compared to not having children (see Hülskamp 2006). Only couples with children in Germany – and Great Britain – dispose of significantly less income than those without children. Since, compared to Germany, a substantially higher financial support through public transfers in countries like the USA, Canada, Sweden, and Finland can be ruled out as a reason, the deviating labor force participation rate of childless women and of mothers becomes a central factor for explaining this observation.

Concerning the question of which behavioral patterns determine the development of the fertility rate – the growing childlessness, or the disappearance of multi-child families – the answers differ between nations. For Germany, the polarization hypothesis was developed (see Dorbritz 2005) according to which

---

[1] This is supported by a newly published study on the incentive effects of income-differentiated childcare costs: see Bütler (2007). For an overview, see Dickmann and Seyda (2005).

childlessness rose at the expense of the one-child family, while the share of women with two or more children decreased by a lower rate. Childlessness in Germany amounts to a little over 25% for the relevant age groups. While this development can be observed throughout Europe, Germany took the lead in this development, displaying particularly high values.

Therefore, an essential factor of changing the fertility rate is the alteration of the labor market orientation, as well as the creation of opportunities for women in the labor market that began to emerge especially since the middle of the last century. This alteration has occurred in three dimensions (see Goldin 2006). First, the time horizon for the occupation of women has changed. Whereas it used to be short and limited to certain phases of life or family situations, it has continuously been extended to the complete time span of employability. Second, occupation increasingly becomes a matter of individual planning and preferences. Third, a woman's employment decision has altered from a derived one with regard to her spouse's occupation, to a cooperative decision within the household. Insofar, women's labor market behavior can be characterized as "a change from "jobs" to "careers" (see Goldin 2006).

Beside the fertility rate, life expectancy is an important factor for population growth. Life expectancy, which is continuously rising in a long-term perspective, increases the share of old people even in case of a fertility rate on the replacement level. As opposed to the findings for fertility rates, this is true for all industrial countries that have been considered, albeit with different paces of the ageing processes. This development especially results from progress in medical care, hygiene, nutrition, and living conditions, as well as improved working conditions and an increased material prosperity. The substantial rise in life expectancy by the middle of the 20th century is caused mainly by a drop in infant mortality. Since then, the increase in life expectancy has slowed down.

Germany does not hold a leading position in life expectancy in an international comparison. The Federal Statistical Office of Germany calculates life expectancy with two different assumptions. The first scenario examines both the long-term development since 1871, and the short-term development since 1970. The first scenario yields an increase in life expectancy by 2050 of 7.6 years for men, and 6.5 years for women (each from the point of birth), i.e., the gender difference is reduced by a little more than a year. The second scenario is based upon the short-term trend, and presumes an increased gain in life expectancy, depicting a ceiling of 9.5 or 8.3 years from birth, respectively.

Finally, a third driver of demographic change is migration. In a long-term-oriented comparison, its influence is less distinct, and hence less significant than that of the other two factors. In the 20th century, Germany's net migration displayed substantial variations due to political influence (1955 to 1968 recruitment of migrant workers, the 1973 recruitment ban, the 1983 Repatriation Act, the 1993 Asylum Procedure Act). During the last decade, net migration has stabilized. In an international comparison, Germany is among the high immigration countries. The annual immigration surplus is likely to remain between 100,000 and 200,000 persons. Accordingly, the Federal Statistical Office of Germany presumes two different scenarios for the population estimation. Hence, extreme scenarios that approximate a compensation of the endogenous population development by migration are – justifiably – excluded. If, for example, a rise in the share of old people were to be avoided, a net immigration of 188 million young people by 2050 would be required, according to the United Nations (see Birg 2003a, p. 12).

Overall, a fluctuation band for population development can be established (Fig. 3.2). In each scenario, the population will drop by 2050, compared to today. Contrary to historical situations of former centuries, this fact – taken by itself – does not appear as a problem. Having people live everywhere is not a mandatory condition. Within the scope of scenarios under today's non-Malthusian conditions, no economically optimal population size exists. However, something else has to be borne in mind: the population estimation suggests, in the sense of comparative statics, the end of all adjustment processes in 2050. In fact, however, the situation is that of a continuously shrinking population. Hence, the scope of the analysis has to be the process of continuous contraction, rather than a snapshot of a certain year, based on an endogenous compensation as opposed to political interference.

To which degree population development can be associated with an increase in income depends centrally upon human capital formation of the different

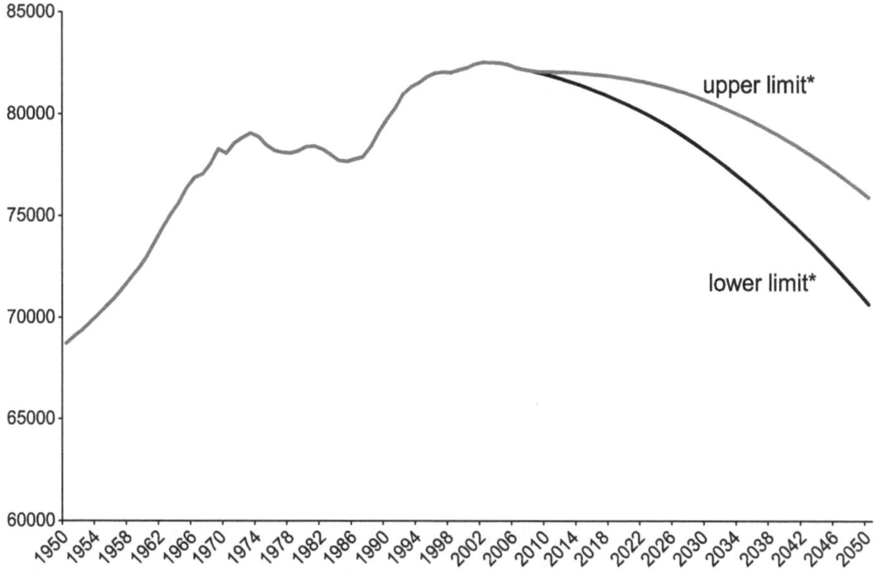

* Upper limit: Scenario 2-W1 (fertility rate: 1.4, immigration: 100,000/year, life expectancy: high); lower limit: Scenario 2-W2 (fertility rate: 1.4, immigration: 200,000/year, life expectancy: high)

Fig. 3.2 Scenarios of population development (in 100,000s; source: Statistisches Bundesamt, Federal Statistical Office of Germany)

cohorts. Human capital formation – or its correlative educational poverty – can be captured empirically with different concepts according to different age levels (see Anger et al. 2006, p. 7). For adolescents in secondary education (aged 15 years), the absolute and relative degree of educational poverty is determined by means of standardized tests like PISA, which measure competencies. For persons aged 25 to 64, the acquired certificates reported in official statistics are taken into account.

In both categories, Germany attains at best average results, despite great efforts and fairly substantial expenditures, which in some categories lie above the OECD average. As for the category "reading", 22.3% of the students do not attain competency level 2 (see PISA-Konsortium Deutschland 2005). These adolescents are virtually predetermined to belong to a disadvantaged group in the labor market, since their reading competencies are insufficient to be qualified for skilled employment. The dual system of vocational education and training, which Germany can be proud of, does not come into effect for these persons. In contrast to the value mentioned above, only 8.5% (in 2004) of each class leave the school system without any degree. This divergence demonstrates the different explanatory content of certificates and competencies.

A similarly unpleasant finding is that Germany cannot keep up with the dynamics of other industrial countries with respect to the trend toward higher qualification – measured as the share of persons with a tertiary degree. With regard to the OECD average, it can even be argued that the educational expansion has come to a halt (Fig. 3.3).

A lack of human capital accumulation has serious impacts on the individual level, as well as on the welfare level (see Anger et al. 2006). For the individual, employment and income perspectives are significantly impaired. The global structural change entails a deepened division of labor and an intensi-

Fig. 3.3 Higher qualification in an international comparison, persons with a tertiary degree (ISCED 5 A/6) in percent of each cohort (55 to 64, 45 to 54, 35 to 44, 25 to 34 years), 2003 (source: OECD)

fied competition on the commodity and factor markets. It is also characterized by an accelerated knowledge intensification and labor-saving technological progress. It is therefore hardly astonishing that low-skilled unemployment has risen substantially in nearly all industrial countries. Among persons without a vocational education, the unemployment rate in Germany amounts to approximately 20%, and hence occupies a top position in an international comparison. Consequently, the hourly gross wage of low-skilled labor has performed below average.

The welfare effects of educational poverty are determined on the one hand by the constraints to technological competitiveness, and the innovative ability of an economy, and on the other hand by the direct and indirect costs of public budgets. According to an OECD analysis, human capital no longer yields a positive contribution to economic growth in Germany (see OECD 2003). Direct fiscal costs already amounted to 3.5 billion Euros in 2004 (see Klein 2005).

3.3 Driving Forces of Economic Growth

The observations on demographic change and human capital formation demonstrate that Germany is at best average in both dimensions. This finding raises concerns regarding future economic development. Yet, arriving at sound conclusions on which to base policy requires a systematic economic analysis of the observations mentioned above. Growth theory can be employed as an appropriate framework. As established above, the center of analysis is the inspection of adjustment processes, rather than a steady-state equilibrium.

In its early stages, the growth theoretic debate was determined by the question of whether population growth – the continuation, or even amplification of which was out of doubt – might overstrain real economic possibilities. This is exemplified by the Malthusian "Population Act" (Malthus 1798). Later on, Solow established population growth as a pivotal function for economic growth within the framework of neoclassic growth theory (see Frenkel and Hemmer 1999). The development of gross domestic product is assumed to be determined by population growth and the rate of technological progress. The central relation is defined in terms of the growth rate of capital intensity:

$$\Delta k = sy - (d + g + n)k \tag{3.1}$$

An increase in the growth rate of capital intensity (k) – i.e., the capital endowment per worker – results from a decrease of the savings rate per capita (sy), and a decrease in the capital depreciation rate (d), the rate of technological progress (g), or the population growth rate (n). Capital intensity rises to the degree to which savings exceed the required capital extension. In a long-term equilibrium (steady state), a further capital intensification is not necessary ($\Delta k = 0$):

$$sy = (d + g + n)k \tag{3.2}$$

This equilibrium is characterized by a constant production per worker. The absolute growth of gross domestic product is subject to the rise in technological progress and population growth.

This leads to the question of the effects of a shrinking population in the neoclassical framework (see Grömling 2005, pp. 70 ff.). During the transition to a new equilibrium – which is the relevant aspect of the analysis – capital intensity rises, because a reduced part of the current savings is required for capital extension (i.e., the endowment of new workers with capital). Hence, a shrinking population directly increases production per inhabitant. The new equilibrium displays a higher output level per inhabitant as well. Only the growth rate per capita during transition exceeds the growth rate in the initial equilibrium. Whether the absolute gross domestic product can be maintained is dependent on the question of whether technological progress can compensate for the contraction of the population.

According to these results, a shrinking population is not a problem, and per-capita income even rises during the period of transition. However, this finding applies only under three conditions: first, the shrinking population, and the associated ageing of society, does not slow down technological progress, and hence factor productivity is not reduced. Second, the relative development of the population, and the labor force participation rate do not diverge. Third, capital remains in the country, despite its reduced marginal productivity (which necessarily results from an increased capital intensity in the Solow Model), and hence does not react to global differences in growth paths.

Furthermore, neoclassical growth theory features critical assumptions (exogenous population growth, exogenous technological progress, decreasing marginal products of capital) that have lead to the development of the new or endogenous growth theory (see Grömling 2005, pp. 74 ff.; also see Hemmer 1999). Via a special analysis of human capital and its relevance for technological progress, the possibility of endogenous growth is described – based on external effects and economies of scale. Innovation processes hence become particularly important. Additionally, the neutrality of savings and investment decisions for the growth rate of the gross domestic product are challenged, and the significance of infrastructure investments as inputs are analyzed.

Taking a closer look at the different critical aspects concerning the neoclassical results leads to the following conclusions for labor force, capital stock, and technological progress (see Grömling 2005, pp. 78 ff.).

- The assumption in neoclassical growth theory of a parallel development of population and labor force cannot be maintained. The share of the labor force potential in Germany's total population, which presently equals about 51%, will decrease to 42.5% by the year 2050. The age structure of the labor force potential will alter substantially. The share of 15- to 45-year-olds of over 62% will drop to 55%, and the average age will rise from 40.3 to 42.5 years (see Schäfer 2005). Therefore, the shrinking population becomes a growth handicap.
- The presumption of a capital intensification via a contraction of the population is based on the hypothesis that investment activity – regarded in relative terms – will not weaken. The modernization of the capital stock due to a

shrinking population might even lead to more than proportionally reduced replacement investments, because of the necessary adjustment of the capital stock. This may become a burden on domestic investment in global competition, due to superior options of growing societies, and it may result in a reduction of capital intensity. Yet, relative scarcity of labor may induce additional substitute investment.

- The assumption of an exogenously given and constant technological progress is also more than questionable. The propensity to innovate will be reduced significantly in a shrinking, and hence ageing, society if no preventive measures are taken, because the technological renewal of the economy is slowed, and risk propensity, the open-mindedness with respect to technological innovations, and the propensity toward entrepreneurship are reduced. Furthermore, a reduced market size impairs entrepreneurial investment conditions. This process is carried by a declined relevance of the generation aged 30 to 40 years (see Sinn 2003). This would imply a weakened future development of total factor productivity and labor productivity. However, this aspect is not necessarily as dominant as other studies show – especially if different educational orientations are considered (see Krey and Meier 2005). A differentiated examination of the ageing process, and distinction between "young seniority" – starting around the age of 60 – and "high seniority" – beginning with the age of 80 – reveal that compensation strategies are feasible (see Baltes 2001). However, this presupposes well-directed political action, especially by means of age-corresponding life and employment concepts. At any rate, the rising share of old people requires an increased per-capita spending in the social security systems that is hence not disposable for investment purposes, and therefore establishes disadvantages in comparison with younger societies (see Birg 2003b, p. 160).

Altogether, there is strong evidence for the argument that population shrinkage due to an altered fertility behavior, in combination with a thus inevitable ageing of society, establishes a burden on economic growth perspectives.[2] Accordingly, an OECD analysis reveals that economies have experienced different growth performances especially due to different patterns of labor force participation, and differences in the skills of their labor forces (see OECD 2003, p. 28 ff., here p. 53): "In particular, most of the countries that experienced an acceleration of GDP per capita growth also recorded an increase in labour utilisation, while most of those where employment stagnated, or even declined, saw a deterioration in their growth performance. This is because in these countries, labour productivity growth has not been able to offset the negative contribution to growth coming from poor employment performance".

A decomposition of the growth factors reveals the different demographic conditions in an international comparison (Table 3.1). Evidently, the favorable

---

[2] Hondrich's hypothesis (Der demographische Wandel, p. 36) – that fertility decline does not exhibit an economic problem concluding an exclusive concentration on productivity increases – can therefore not be maintained.

Table 3.1 Decomposition of growth factors (possible rounding differences; source: Sachverständigenrat zur Begutachtung der gesamtwirtschaftlichen Entwicklung, Jahresgutachten 2004/05, p. 493)

	Gross domestic product (Y)	Labor productivity (Y/H)	Volume of labor (H)				
			Total	Annual working hours per employee (H/E)	Labor force participation rate (E/B*)	Share of workforce in total population (B*/B)	Population (B)
USA							
1991 to 2003	3.2	1.8	1.4	0.0	0.1	0.0	1.2
1991 to 1997	3.5	1.6	1.9	0.2	0.6	0.0	1.0
1997 to 2003	3.0	2.1	0.9	−0.2	−0.4	0.0	1.4
European Union (EU-15)							
1991 to 2003	1.9	1.9	0.0	−0.4	0.2	−0.1	0.3
1991 to 1997	1.7	2.1	−0.4	−0.2	−0.5	−0.1	0.3
1997 to 2003	2.1	1.6	0.5	−0.6	0.9	−0.1	0.3
Germany							
1991 to 2003	1.2	2.1	−0.8	−0.6	−0.3	−0.2	0.3
1991 to 1997	1.2	2.4	−1.2	−0.5	−1.0	−0.2	0.4
1997 to 2003	1.3	1.7	−0.4	−0.6	0.4	−0.3	0.1

growth performance in the USA results from population growth, the expansion of the volume of labor, and labor productivity. Contrarily, the European Union, and even more so Germany must compensate the shrinking volume of labor that results from the weak population development, and a declining labor force participation rate as well as reduced working hours.

The expectation – prevalent especially in Germany a few decades ago – that a diminished volume of labor due to reduced working hours could be more than compensated by an increase in productivity has been mistaken. Especially in times of an intensified international division of labor, it is unlikely that an economy will permanently and comprehensively be able to realize a technological advantage. However, the high-tech-carried insular growth that is necessary for such a position can be expected only sporadically for closely defined regions with outstanding conditions (see Grömling and Lichtblau 2006).

The decomposition of growth factors discloses the basic approaches for policy measures in Germany with respect to demographic change:

- Factor B: demographic policy directly aims at governing demographic change, employing fertility and migration as target variables.

- Factor B*/B: by varying the access rules to the pension system, the age span of employment can be extended.
- Factor E/B*: positive contributions to economic growth are an increased labor market participation of women as well as of young people, by the means of a shorter duration and a more modular design of university studies, and an increased labor force participation rate of the elderly that is extended to the legal retirement age.
- Factor H/E: similar effects can be attained by extending the hours worked per week, abolishing holidays, or reducing vacation time. Contrarily, expanding part-time employments entails a burden.
- Factor Y/H: finally, human capital formation positively affects labor productivity, and indirectly promotes technological progress.

A family policy, for example, which is directed to these factors improves the growth perspectives of an economy in various ways: by increasing fertility, improved participation opportunities for women in the labor market, or a higher educational level for children. By these means, the German gross domestic product could be increased by the year 2050 by 24 percentage points more than without such a population-oriented family policy. The difference in per-capita income growth would amount to 9 percentage points (see Bundesministerium für Familie, Senioren, Frauen und Jugend 2006). It follows from this that different growth structures can be explained by such policy strategies with respect to the OECD results. According to an OECD analysis, different investment strategies and varying regulations have an impact on growth contributions such "that observed cross-country differences in GDP per capita levels may be largely the result of differences in long-run equilibrium levels rather than different positions of countries along a similar growth path" (see OECD 2003, p. 28 ff., here p. 89). In this context, family policy in combination with education policy can be viewed as a strategy for long-term investment. However, in the light of individual as well as social values and traditions, such altered policy measures can be successful only within a long-term process.[3]

3.4 The Concept of Intergenerational Justice

Even though there are good economic reasons for population-oriented policy measures, they are subject to an intensive controversy. The different lines of criticism regarding an active population policy are the following.

- A common argument is that such policy measures would compromise freedom of choice of a highly personal decision, presuming that existing policy arrangements have neutral effects, and that the individual decision for, or against children is not associated with social implications. Both arguments are objectively questionable.

---

[3] For the determinants of demographic change, see Birg (2003c).

- Others support the hypothesis that a shrinking population is not to be regarded as economically or ecologically precarious, because it would protect nature and save natural capital. This argument is based upon an environmental perspective simulating the environment that is to be protected as one without human influence. Demographic change as a process of contraction, implying the rejection of economic growth, is welcomed. Hence, no policy measures would be necessary. This position is questionable on a normative basis.
- A third line of criticism is associated with specific historical bearings of our nation. After the experiences with the nation- and race-oriented national socialist despotism aiming at, on the one hand, population growth, and on the other hand spatial expansion, Germany for a long time was not able to objectively approach matters of population development. This has changed.

One may regard population shrinkage as a result of individual decisions, and hence as an underlying condition. However, this implies a systematic disregard of a constitutive factor for economic welfare and social progress: the mutual commitment within a family. The market system, state intervention, and the family define the economic system and carry its development. A libertarian economic system requires for its permanent success not only an adequate coexistence of market system and state intervention, but also the continuance of the family as a tie between generations. "The market system is tied by DNA chains", as the economic historian Harold James puts it (James 2005). The intertemporal tie that we use to describe the concept of intergenerational justice emerges from the family. Even though the multigenerational family may still function – possibly better than in former times – "those who deny the strong bond between capitalism and the family do not know anything about the historical development of this tie" (James 2005).

The phenomenon of the family has lost much of its meaning. The sustainability of a social system becomes obvious only with regard to intergenerational justice. Malfunctioning markets and ill-governed public institutions overwhelm and overstrain us in the short term, if they exhibit a long-term quality in the sense of intergenerational aspects. Thinking for the long term, the family is to be regarded as the pivotal stabilizing element of such a system. For a sustainable design of such systems, an assumption on the relative weight of generations has to be made, based upon a concept of intergenerational justice.

The concept of intergenerational justice is rather dazzling, and therefore a particularly suitable target of overstatement as well as fundamental criticism.[4] The need for clarification applies to both parts of this term.

- A suitable definition of the term "generation" clearly separates groups of a society according to a time-invariant characteristic, and at the same time

[4] See Börsch-Supan (2003), who denotes intergenerational justice a chimera being "no scientifically maintainable – i.e., verifiable – concept" (p. 221, translated into English). Granted that intergenerational justice is a concept of normative nature, it is not verifiable, just like any normative concept.

establishes a link due to stability of political jurisdictions. Therefore, the definition of a generation must be chronological, although incorporating several birth cohorts. With the term "intergenerational", those living today can be separated from future generations. The identical political framework establishes a tie between generations that results primarily from historical bearings and cultural traditions.

- The claim for a concept of justice with regard to generations poses a much greater problem. As opposed to within a generation, intergenerational justice implies confronting two different groups, which – due to the lack of information on the future generation's preferences – cannot be subjected to a common norm of justice. The two generations are not able to exchange arguments in a common debate forum. Any definition of justice is necessarily established by living at present.[5]
- In fact, the responsibility of the present generation with respect to the future has expanded – on the one hand, due to the given degree of technological competence for a deliberate or unconscious influence of future living conditions, and on the other hand with regard to the possible prediction thereof (see Birnbacher 2006). Similarly, burdens and negligence from predecessors can substantially restrain the potential for economic action of the present generation, as certain decisions are neither revisable nor compensatable.

It has become apparent that intergenerational justice refers to the relationship between two sets of living conditions – those of the present, and of the future generation. Conceiving intergenerational justice as a dynamic concept that is applicable in a long-run perspective entails the problem that the present generation is confronted with a strained relationship toward the legacy of their parent generation. As opposed to considerations of justice within a generation, this fact cannot be ignored. Insofar, the concept of intergenerational justice can be conceived simultaneously as a contingent and as an open concept: the concept of justice is defined by the present generation, though limited in its autonomy by path dependencies. The required balancing of interests is always twofold – on the one hand, within the presently acting generation, and on the other hand between those living at present and in the future. Whereas the balancing of interests within a generation can be substantiated by employing the concept of participational justice, for the intergenerational balancing an equalization of interests appears appropriate. Compared to the preferences and conditions of presently living generations, there is little reason to attach less value to those of future generations, with respect to economic, social, and environmental objectives, and vice versa (see Bardt and Hüther 2006, p. 21). This hypothesis is supported by the theory proposed by Rawls. The concept of the veil of ignorance can be applied to a multigenerational approach. According to this concept, the welfare of all generations would be equalized, because "no one knows his place

[5] It is not the hardly definable formal rights of unborn generations that is subject of the debate, but a general and anonymous future commitment, as discussed below. For the discussion on the existence of the rights of future generations, see Beckerman (2006).

in society, his class position or social status; nor does he know his fortune in the distribution of natural assets and abilities, his intelligence and strength, and the like" (Rawls 1999, p. 118, and pp. 259 ff.).

A future commitment is – due to the extended impact duration – derived from the competency of the present generation to influence future living conditions, rather than from a failure or guilt of the presently living. It is subject to the following conditions (see Birnbacher 2006, p. 24 f.).

- First, the postulation of a common and anonymous commitment for the future is contrary to the conventional notion that commitment refers to certain actions under specific conditions with implications for certain individuals. Thus, the opportunity costs for each individual are increased. This is especially true if time preference is high, and a diminishing marginal utility of future consumption can be expected (see von Böhm-Bawerk 1889).
- Second, bearing responsibility for the future is limited by individually bounded options. Individual influence is an essential condition. At the same time, the willingness to correct the omissions of former generations is necessary.
- Third, limited foresight is a restriction despite technological possibilities. This becomes apparent with respect to climate change, the dimensions of which – according to the latest report by the UN Commission (IPCC) – still establish the need for action, but do not give reason for fatalism or hysterical dramatization. The uncertainty in diagnosis must be adequately considered if commitment is to be mobilized.

In analogy to the ordoliberal vision of a social market economy, two lines of action can be differentiated that do not exclude one another: on the one hand, precautions for the future can take the form of the best possible mobilization of growth dynamics in order to extend the options of future generations to a maximum possible degree. This corresponds to a general insurance against unforeseeable events. On the other hand, pathological developments that are anticipated today can be cured with the help of long-term-oriented measures aimed at their underlying causes. However, experience teaches us that our knowledge of problems is always merely preliminary, because of which decisions based upon these hypotheses must always be revisable (see Bardt and Hüther 2006, p. 7 f., 21 f.). The first approach entails the advantage to not imperatively view today's and future interests as an antagonism that interprets precautions for the future as a burden and constraint on present generations. The conditions of specific problems, which the second approach is subject to, can be considered as elements of the framework for structural change. Hence, defining the temporal dimension, social reality, and factual reference with respect to the adoption of future commitment can be avoided. Intergenerational justice needs to formulate realistic claims (see Lumer 2006):

- The neutrality between the preferences and conditions of different generations gives rise to the principle of limited (moral) commitment. It avoids excessive demands on the present generation, and reflects the restrictions with respect to future responsibility. In the words of John Rawls: "The correct principle, then, is one the members of any generation (and so all generations) would adopt as the principle they would want preceding generations to have followed, no matter how far back in time. Since no generation knows its place among the generations, this implies that all later generations, including the present one, are to follow it. In this way we arrive at a savings principle that grounds our duties to other generations: it supports legitimate complaints against our predecessors and legitimate expectations about our successors." (Rawls 2001, p. 160).

- The consideration of future living conditions must obey the principle of efficiency. The moral declamation for the far and infinite future entails the risk of discarding economic reasoning, and of overstretching the economic mechanism. In this respect, different relative scarcities are affected. Therefore, the claim of efficiency with regard to political solutions must not be compromised.

Taking these considerations together, a concept of intergenerational justice that appears sustainable and helpful requests the present generation – under the notion of path dependencies – not to exploit the options of future generations. Hence, safeguarding the perspective of a restricted growth requires a positive intergenerational savings rate.[6] This principle must refer to the future, and operate from the past by providing that "each generation receives its due from its predecessors and does its fair share for those to come" (Rawls 1999).[7] Hence, the required investment – in human capital, in physical capital, and in the sustainability of natural capital – can be provided for (see Rawls 1999, pp. 118, 252), while simultaneously rejecting an extreme time preference. The avoidance of observable risks to future growth needs to be provided for.

3.5 A National Strategy for Long-term Growth

Intergenerational justice in the sense outlined above must be incorporated into the strategic orientation of policy measures as well as their implementation, rather than remaining a virtual concept. The government needs to correct individual rationality where it jeopardizes – due to limited factual or temporal horizons – the long-term stability of society and its living conditions. Our considerations have pointed out that the introduction of an infinite time horizon – in consideration of generational neutrality and a general claim of efficiency –

---

[6] This also implies the restriction of public debt (the explicit as well as the implicit debt in the social security systems), in order to not exploit future generations.

[7] Rawls (1999, p. 254). "In arriving at a just saving principle [...], the parties are to ask themselves how much they would be willing to save at each stage of advance on the assumption that all other generations have saved, or will save, in accordance with the same criterion" (p. 255).

exerts a twofold challenge on politicians: first, in the sense of a general commitment, a long-term promotion of an economic dynamic must be organized. This requires supply-oriented economic policy measures. Thus, options for future generations can be extended (see Institut der deutschen Wirtschaft Köln 2005). Second, several measures can be applied to define appropriate lines of orientation for economic development. In this respect, the balancing of intergenerational opportunities is a claim to be met. The long-term stability of society hence becomes an independent value, and the commitment of the present generation is extended. The following policy areas for precautionary measures can be derived with an ordoliberal view (see Hüther and Straubhaar 2007).

- Providing for functioning markets implies a precautionary competition policy that prohibits raising market power, rather than the ex post abuse of market power. The openness of markets, and the contestability of economic power are pivotal conditions for economic dynamics. This is one of the most important tasks where policy measures in the form of defining a framework as well as interventions are called for.
- If the natural development of the population, as stated above, entails a dynamic such that the sustainability of society is in question, then policy measures to provide for intergenerational justice in the areas of family policy and migration must be introduced. Hence, the interests of future generations can be balanced equally with the interests of the present generation. The costs of idleness are greater than the costs that derive from the risk of inaccurate action. Therefore, the claim for reversibility of political measures and its results is not applicable here.
- The protection of intellectual resources constitutes a great challenge to society. Sustainable growth perspectives can be provided only by a combination of education policy and population-oriented family policy, as well as migration policy. These policy areas exhibit manifold interdependences with regard to individual life concepts, and hence with respect to attaining knowledge and skills.
- These conclusions are also applicable for the protection of natural resources. In this area, policy measures are called for as well. The commandment "Thou shalt not steal" also holds with regard to future generations (in the sense of a sustainable environmental policy and weak sustainability). However, the criterion of reversibility of decisions is particularly important in this respect, because environmental knowledge must be regarded as preliminary, rather than final knowledge – even though the latter may oftentimes be suggested. A glance into Germany's history in environmental policy since 1971 provides evidence for this conclusion, with its modification of theories and concepts as well as the employment of instruments.

Very few countries currently treat the concept of intergenerational justice strategically and with high political priority (see Bertelsmann-Stiftung 2006). Prominent examples are Australia, Finland, Great Britain, and The Netherlands. Each of these has introduced comprehensive governmental initiatives that are concerned with the implications of demographic change, especially for the labor market. Particularly Australia managed to develop a "whole-of-government approach" in a collective ministerial effort with the participation of important groups of society (see Barth et al. 2006). The "National Strategy for an Ageing Australia" comprises different policy areas including the pension system, the ageing workforce, the attitude toward ageing, healthy ageing, and the nursing system, and was institutionalized as a cross-ministerial topic. In the other countries mentioned above, the political implementation concentrates primarily on particular topics, especially on the aspect of older people's employment opportunities. Even though our argument in the analytical part has focused on demographic change, the view can be expanded to the provision of growth in the other areas mentioned above. Therefore, the task is not only to consistently formulate for these policy areas strategic goals for sustainable growth under consideration of the concept of intergenerational justice, but also to establish the institutional conditions for their implementation.

In this respect, the federal order is concerned, the sustainability of which has not been analyzed with regard to the concept of intergenerational justice and long-term growth. The agenda of long-term growth must be defined by a central authority. Both criteria in the theory of federalism – homogeneity of the citizens' preferences, and spillover effects – support this conclusion (see Institut der deutschen Wirtschaft Köln 2007):

- For the two orientations within the concept of intergenerational justice, homogeneous preferences can be assumed for the Federal Republic of Germany. First, time preference should not vary by regional conditions. Second, due to an increasing mobility of individuals between federal states, measures aiming at sustainability must be adopted for Germany's complete future generation, rather than for a generation specified by its affiliation to a federal state.
- Furthermore, the adoption of specific, uncoordinated strategies by an individual federal state would be associated with significant efficiency losses due to substantial spillover effects over federal borders. Such cross-border effects can be expected due to the mobility of the factors of production in all policy areas. Hence, a central framework for education policy needs to be established, as already exists for competition policy, migration policy, and family policy. For environmental policy, the deviation legislation ("Abweichungsgesetzgebung") that was introduced with the latest reform of federalism should be reviewed, as far as it is not restricted to regionally limited environmental issues.

A "national strategy for sustainable growth" must be established strategically on the federal level, defining targets and minimum standards. The implementation needs to be reviewed and made transparent with the means of a federal evaluation. Within the scope of their jurisdictional autonomy, the federal states can then decide upon the employment of instruments. Interjurisdictional competition is hence carried out through the pace, quality, and sustainability of meeting the targets and standards. Such a concept requires the courage to address delicate policy issues, i.e., aspects beyond competition policy and environmental policy, by defining strategic targets, rather than taking blindfolded action.

- This requires the definition of quantitative goals for family policy, for example, in order to attain a demographic equilibrium.
- It also requires clearly defined criteria for migration policy – for example, by focusing on economically successful integration.
- Finally, it requires targets for educational policy – for example, by an age group-specific definition concerning on the one hand the reduction of educational poverty, and on the other hand an increase of the ability to study.

The implementation should be assigned to a ministry with cross-departmental competence consisting of parts of the ministries of economics, education, family, and environment, and furthermore assuming responsibility for the coordination and evaluation of the federal states.

It can be concluded that there is no reason to believe in catastrophe scenarios with regard to a shrinking and ageing society. But a systematic and comprehensive approach as described in this paper is necessary to solve the problems associated with this phenomenon.

References

Anger C, Plünnecke A, Seyda S (2006) Bildungsarmut und Humankapitalsschwäche in Deutschland. In: IW-Analysen 18, Cologne, pp 27 ff.

Auerbach AJ, Kotlikoff LJ, Leibfritz W (eds) (1999) Generational accounting around the World (NBER). Chicago

Baltes PB (2001) Das Zeitalter des permanent unfertigen Menschen: Lebenslanges Lernen non-stop? In: Aus Politik und Zeitgeschichte 36, pp 26 ff.

Bardt H, Hüther M (2006) Angebotsorientierte Umweltpolitik. Positionsbestimmung und Perspektiven. Cologne

Barth HJ, Heimer A, Pfeiffer I (2006) Von Vorbildern lernen – »Best practice»-Strategien und Initiativen aus zehn Ländern. Bertelsmann-Stiftung, Gütersloh, pp 161 ff.

Beckerman W (2006) The impossibility of a theory of intergenerational justice. In: Tremmel JC (ed) Handbook of intergenerational justice. Edward Elgar, Cheltenham, UK, pp 54 ff.

Berkel B, Börsch-Supan A, Ludwig A, Winter J (2004) Sind die Probleme der Bevölkerungsentwicklung durch eine höhere Geburtenrate lösbar? In: Perspektiven der Wirtschaftspolitik 5(1/2004), pp 71 ff.

Bertelsmann-Stiftung (ed) (2006) Älter werden – aktiv bleiben. Beschäftigung in Wirtschaft und Gesellschaft. Carl Bertelsmann-Preis 2006, Gütersloh

Birg H (2003a) Dynamik der demographischen Alterung, Bevölkerungsschrumpfung und Zuwanderung in Deutschland. Aus Politik und Zeitgeschichte 20

Birg H (2003b) Demographische Zeitenwende. In: Hessische Staatskanzlei (ed) Die Familienpolitik muss neue Wege gehen! Wiesbaden

Birg H (2003c) Strategische Optionen der Familien- und Migrationspolitik in Deutschland und Europa. In: Leipert C (ed) Demographie und Wohlstand, p 30

Birnbacher D (2006) Responsibility for future generations – scope and limits. In: Tremmel JC (ed) Handbook of intergenerational justice. Edward Elgar, Cheltenham, UK, p 24

Böhm-Bawerk E von (1889) Positive Theorie des Kapitals. Innsbruck, pp 262 ff.

Börsch-Supan A (2003) Zum Konzept der Generationengerechtigkeit. Zeitschr Wirtschaftspolitik 52

Bundesministerium für Familie, Senioren, Frauen und Jugend (ed) (2006) Wachstumseffekte einer bevölkerungsorientierten Familienpolitik (Gutachten des Instituts der deutschen Wirtschaft Köln). Berlin

Bütler M (2007) Arbeiten lohnt sich nicht – ein zweites Kind noch weniger. Zu den Auswirkungen einkommensabhängiger Tarife auf das (Arbeitsmarkt-) Verhalten der Frauen. In: Perspektiven der Wirtschaftspolitik 8(1/2007), p 1 ff.

Dickmann N, Seyda S (2005) Gründe für den Geburtenrückgang. In: Institut der deutschen Wirtschaft Köln (ed) Perspektive 2050. Ökonomik des demographischen Wandels. Cologne, pp 35 ff.

Dorbritz J (2005) Kinderlosigkeit in Deutschland und Europa – Daten, Trends und Einstellungen. Zeitschrift für Bevölkerungswissenschaft 30

Frenkel M, Hemmer H-R (1999) Grundlagen der Wachstumstheorie. Munich

Giersch H (1999) Marktökonomik für die offene Gesellschaft. Walter-Adolf-Jöhr-Vorlesung, Universität St. Gallen (translated into English)

Goldin C (2006) The quiet revolution that transformed women's employment, education, and family. In: American Economic Association Papers and Proceedings 96, pp 1 ff.

Grömling M (2005) Wirtschaftswachstum. In: Institut der deutschen Wirtschaft Köln (ed) Perspektive 2050. Ökonomik des demographischen Wandels. Cologne, pp 67 ff.

Grömling M, Lichtblau K (2006) Deutschland vor einem neuen Industriezeitalter? Cologne, pp 69 ff.

Hemmer H-R (1999) Die endogene Wachstumstheorie als Reaktion auf die Erklärungsdefizite der traditionellen neoklassischen Wachstumstheorie – ein Überblick. In: Eisenhans H, Schubert R (eds) Neue Wachstums- und Außenhandelstheorie: Implikationen für die Entwicklungstheorie und -politik. Berlin, pp 11 ff.

Hondrich KO (2006) Der demographische Wandel in ökonomischer und sozialpsychologischer Sicht. In: Orientierungen zur Wirtschafts- und Gesellschaftspolitik 109(3/2006), p 34 (translated into English)

Horn C, Scarano N (eds) (2002) Philosophie der Gerechtigkeit. Texte von der Antike bis zur Gegenwart. Frankfurt am Main

Hülskamp N (2006) Ursachen niedriger Fertilität in hoch entwickelten Staaten. Soziologische, ökonomische und politische Einflussfaktoren. Cologne

Hüther M, Straubhaar T (2007) Plädoyer für ein Leitbild für Deutschland. Roman-Herzog-Institut, Munich

Institut der deutschen Wirtschaft Köln (ed) (2005) Vision Deutschland. Der Wohlstand hat Zukunft. Köln

Institut der deutschen Wirtschaft Köln (ed) (2007) Föderalismus in Deutschland. Ökonomische Analyse und Reformbedarf. Cologne

James H (2005) Familienunternehmen in Europa. Haniel, Wendel und Falck, Munich, p 8 (translated into English)

Klein H (2005) Direkte Kosten mangelnder Ausbildungsreife. In: IW-Trends 32(4/2005), pp 61 ff.

Krey K, Meier B (2005) Innovationsfähigkeit. In: Institut der deutschen Wirtschaft Köln (ed) Perspektive 2050. Ökonomik des demographischen Wandels. Cologne, pp 156 ff.

Landshut S (1973) Historische Analyse des Begriffs des "Ökonomischen". In: Wehler H-U (ed) Geschichte und Ökonomie. Cologne, pp 40 ff.

Lumer C (2006) Principles of generational justice. In: Tremmel JC (ed) Handbook of intergenerational justice. Edward Elgar, Cheltenham, UK, pp 43 ff.

Malthus TR (1798) Das Bevölkerungsgesetz. London

OECD (2003) The sources of economic growth in OECD Countries. OECD, Paris

PISA-Konsortium Deutschland (ed) (2005) PISA 2003. Der Bildungsstand der Jugendlichen in Deutschland – Ergebnisse des zweiten internationalen Vergleichs. Münster, p 102

Rawls J (1999) A theory of justice, revised edn. Oxford University Press, Oxford, NY

Rawls J (2001) Justice as fairness. A restatement. Harvard University Press, Cambridge, MA

Sachverständigenrat (2001) Jahresgutachten 2001/02, Ziffern 244 ff.
Schäfer H (2005) Arbeitsmärkte. In: Institut der deutschen Wirtschaft Köln (ed) Perspektive 2050. Ökonomik des demographischen Wandels. Cologne, pp 98 ff.
Sinn H-W (2003) Das demographische Defizit. Die Fakten, die Folgen, die Ursachen und die Politikimplikationen. In: Leipert C (ed) Demographie und Wohlstand. Opladen, p 67 f.
Statistisches Bundesamt (2006) Bevölkerung Deutschlands bis 2050. 11. koordinierte Bevölkerungsvorausberechnung. Wiesbaden

Chapter 4
Demographic Development: Not Really a Problem for Coming Generations

Thomas Straubhaar

4.1 Introduction

Michael Hüther is pessimistic in his contribution (Chap. 3, this volume): A shrinking population leads to a loss in welfare and prospects. It is incompatible with the pursuit of intergenerational justice . He may be, but not necessarily, correct.

A shrinking population does not lead inevitably, unavoidably, and irreversibly to a prosperity loss. Some evidence can be found for this optimistic view in economic history, but economic theory also gives enough arguments for a positive assessment. The demographic monster of shrinking and aging populations is no new threat; rather, it frightens the European population with remarkable regularity.

So it was, for instance, at the time immediately before and after the First World War when the cultural and historical philosopher Oswald Spengler foresaw problems of this scenario in his two-volume seminal work "The downfall of the Western World" (Spengler 1918, 1922). In the 1930s, declining populations received a special focus once again. In this case, the stagnating population allegedly led to the fall in demand seen as the essential cause of the Great Depression. In a 1937 article in the Eugenics Review, Keynes examined more closely the economic effects of decreasing populations. According to John Maynard Keynes (Keynes 1937) and Alvin Hansen (Hansen 1939), a shrinking population leads to a long-term reduction in growth, or even a "secular stagnation".

In the time after the war, marked by rapid population and economic growth, the shrinking population problem was no longer current, and thus found hardly any interest. Relevant publications such as the St. Gallen dissertation by Franz Xaver Kaufmann (Kaufmann 1960) remained the exception. Only since the middle of the 1960s, when the birth rate started to clearly decline in

Joerg Chet Tremmel (Ed.) *Demographic Change and Intergenerational Justice*
DOI 10.1007/978-3-540-77084-8

the industrial states, did one again find interest on the topic of a shrinking, and thus aging society.

Today, leading intellectuals of all persuasions are writing about the "Malthusian Conspiracy" (Schirrmacher 2004), the "new demographic era" (Birg 2001), or the "euthanasia civilization" (Schirrmacher 2004, p. 63). The pessimistic perspective is dominating once again. But why, in fact? Neither the cultural pessimism of Oswald Spengler nor the stagnation theory of Keynes have proved to be empirically valid. Would not then a somewhat optimistic view of the consequences of a shrinking population be more appropriate to the reality?

4.2 Demographic Change and Economic Consequences

4.2.1 A Few Theoretical Preliminary Remarks ...

In neoclassical growth models, a shrinking population – with constant age, and society-specific labor force participation rates – is associated with increasing capital intensity, and thus increasing net per-capita income – because less capital is spent on replacement investments, the capital stock pro worker increases, thereby raising work productivity, and with it per-capita income. Furthermore, a shrinking population reduces the number of "hungry mouths". Thus, per-capita income is increased because productive income is distributed between fewer people. For this reason, according to neoclassical standard models of economic theory, a shrinking population leads to a shrinking economy of fewer, but ever richer individuals. The economic shrinking process can moreover be slowed, stopped, or even overcome by sufficiently strong technological progress. The effects of a shrinking population are, in this perspective, macroeconomically positive.

4.2.1.1 Keynes' Expectation of a Secular Stagnation ...

Keynes was interested by the question of whether the demand for goods rises or falls as a consequence of a declining number of consumers. The answer depends on the extent to which the additional per-capita income is used or saved. Keynes formulated the hypothesis that a shrinking population would lead to a global lack in demand. His rationale was that propensity to save would rise, and propensity to invest would sink.

Keynes bases his pessimistic theory of lack of demand on the assumption that savings and investment are relatively inelastic to interest rates. This assumption contradicts economic logic: it is hardly reasonable that financial security and investment motives should be so strong that savings will not sink with a negative real interest rate. From an economic perspective, there is also hardly any reason why, with sufficiently strongly sinking real interest rates, investment incentives and thus investment should not increase.

It can be held, on the contrary, that the pessimistic evaluation of sinking economic demand as a consequence of a shrinking population applies only for that part of investment that is directly determined by demographic factors. A further question remains as to what extent deficits of demographically determined investment possibilities will be (over)compensated by other effects. The necessary amount and quality of living space per person is not a fixed number, and an increase in average conditions of living quality leads to a decrease in average amortization. The investment rate does not necessarily sink when a larger part of the population lives in "new" apartments. In other words, the shorter the payback period, the more quickly a shrinking society will successfully adjust. Likewise, a raised amount of living space per person can compensate for a demographically determined drop in apartment demand.

4.2.1.2 ... What Speaks Against It?

Insofar as the last central assumption of the Keynesian demand deficit hypothesis applies, namely, in the drop in propensity to consume, or the increase in the propensity to save in a shrinking society, this assumption depends especially on two factors: the influence of age structure on the average individual propensity to consume, and the influence of age structure on the composition of the average consumption basket. In the light of empirical evidence, it can be assumed that the availability of aggregate income and its distribution has a stronger influence on the average propensity to consume and the composition of the demand for consumer goods than do demographic factors. Consumer goods with a demand elasticity smaller than 1 will lose weight in favor of income elastic products and newer products. One can assume that within a shrinking population, demand for food, fossil fuels, furnishings, and services will lose weight in favor of clothes and shoes, transportation services, living space, and durable (luxury) goods.

In the Keynesian perspective, individual behavior stands at the center. For most considerations, however, a better suited basis would be the economic units of the "family" or "household", and their size and age structure. A shrinking population does not necessarily lead to a direct reduction in the number of economic units (i.e., households). Rather, these changes can be absorbed by smaller family or household size. Accordingly, consumer or savings behavior will be determined through households, not through individuals; the Keynesian individual considerations in this case tend to skew results.

In the application of the hypothesis of demographically determined drops in consumption, households or families with fewer children must have a higher savings rate. This result cannot, however, be empirically determined. Aggregate consumer demand is influenced neither through changes of household size nor by their age structure, and household size and age groups determine aggregate consumption far less strongly than does disposable income.

Furthermore, household consumer behavior within a shrinking society would not deviate that much from that in a growing society, due to the indivisibility of certain goods. Smaller or older families would also own a car, TV, or other durable consumer goods, the possession and use of which is largely independent of the number of users (family members). Thus, the Keynesian conception of the economic effects of a shrinking society is weakened even by these aforementioned criticisms. The expectation of a demand deficit is based to a large extent on speculative elements, which do not withstand a deeper economic analysis.

4.2.1.3 More Consumption or More Savings?

People in retirement no longer earn their own income, and to cover their living needs they must draw on the savings and capital stock that they have accumulated over the course of their active employment (funded principle), or be supported by current contributions of the members of the following generation who are still in the midst of their working lives (pay-as-you-go principle). In either scenario on the macro-level, more will be consumed, and less saved. The negative effect of a relatively smaller amount of savings can be partially avoided when real interest rates rise as a result of a decline in savings, creating new incentives for private savings. This increase in real interest rates will for its part negatively influence investment activity, however, and thus affect long-term growth.

To account for the rising number of retirees within a pay-as-you-go pension system, the net per-capita income has to be adjusted with a rising tax burden. But the higher the tax burden becomes, the smaller the net per-capita income, and the larger the incentives to exit from the legal economic system. Rising social contributions to finance the retirement system create incentives to engage in the informal economy. Thus, labor supply sinks further, further raising the gross pay in the (still) formal sectors, but at the same time raising the tax burden.

To fulfill the commitments of the state pension payments, the government has to go into debt, or has to raise tax rates. In doing so, it either raises the burden on the work force (thereby once again narrowing net income), or increases interest rates. Investment correspondingly diminishes, and thus negatively affects macroeconomic growth.

4.2.1.4 Higher or Lower Interest Rates?

Similarly decisive is the interest rate reaction. Because retirees are dissaving, the macro-level potential for accumulation of savings in a shrinking and aging society will decline. If the working generation also saves less (and can also save less due to rising taxes), one can expect that the equilibrium interest rate will rise. Through this rise, the positive effects of shrinking labor force participation on capital intensity would be neutralized. Rising interest rates would also, correspondingly with declining number of workers, lead to shrinking capital demands, and thereby to a more or less constant capital intensity.

Whether interest rates would rise as a result of a shrinking population depends on the capital supply. One must remember that aging populations are the result of falling birth rates. In this case, working parents have more resources free, because they have to care for less children. These newly freed resources can now join the capital market, thus raising capital supply and sinking interest rates.

Ultimately, parents have more resources available with fewer children, so that they can spend more per child to, for example, invest in education. This investment raises human capital and improves future quality of work, and with it productivity, thus leading to economic growth potential.

Quintessentially, the analysis of a correlation between a shrinking population and economic development shows that theoretically no clear-cut pronouncements and no preliminary final judgments can be made. The growth effects of a shrinking population can also not be clearly predicted. They depend particularly on individual savings reactions, technological progress, flexibility and openness of international capital markets, and the influence of regulatory policies on the ability of the economy to quickly and flexibly react to demographic changes.

4.2.2 … and Their Empirical Relevance

Without a doubt, a number of problems will be caused by the current historically unprecedented demographic change, because at least in Germany, the current framework for the realization and improvement of living standards is based on the assumption of a young and growing society. The most apparent problem emerges with the pension system, which in Germany functions on the pay-as-you-go principle. Contrary to the funded system, workers do not finance their own retirement during their working life, but instead finance the current retirees through direct contributions. When birth rates fall, there are ever fewer workers paying into the system. At the same time, costs are rising because of longer periods of retirement caused by rising life expectancy. This leads directly to higher retirement contributions, and thus less net pay for the actively employed.

In the future, the federal subsidy will surely increase, as over the time in which retirement expenses have accumulated, the deficit of payments has mostly been turned into national debt. This debt leads unavoidably to a lack of funds to, for example, invest, thus impairing growth and thereby also net income. As a result, to resolve this imbalance, one solution would be to raise worker contributions considerably. If we refuse this option, without other changes to the system the government would no longer be in the position to be able to finance the system.

4.2.2.1 Changes in the Labor Market

The job market is changing fundamentally. Through low birth rates, the number of workers is reduced. Because of technological progress and increasing international competition, qualification requirements are also increasing, raising demand for highly skilled workers, but at the same time decreasing demand for low-skilled work. When in the future the average age of workers increases, and thus their education lies ever further behind them, this tendency will lead to an unfulfilled demand for highly qualified workers, and an oversupply of the low-skilled. Thus, chances for growth remain unused, necessarily lowering the gross domestic product (GDP), and consequently per-capita income. A further point is a possible hampering of innovation ability: older societies are in general less innovative. The reason for this is that every innovation "devalues" existing human capital, and therefore narrows its return. For this reason, individual incentives toward mobility, flexibility, and structural change will be less in an aging society. The effects on economic growth will be correspondingly negative.

4.2.2.2 Changes in Settlement Patterns

In addition, demographic change develops differently in different regions, leading to significant changes in settlement patterns. At present, we are observing migration from rural to urban areas, and particularly from the former East German states to the West. Because of low birth rates, these population outflows cannot be compensated for. The regional differences will be strengthened by several factors, including the fact that especially young people are moving, whose children will then be born in urban areas. Also, more women than men are moving within Germany. This shows that the total birth rate will be lower in rural areas than in urban ones. This development leads to rural populations becoming increasingly more aged, and these areas more unpopulated. According to calculations of the Federal Statistics Office, the states of Sachsen-Anhalt and Brandenburg are the most strongly affected, and will lose up to 30% of their population by 2050. In the same time period, however, Bavaria can expect growth of almost 1%, and Hamburg growth of 3.3%. Because of differing demographic developments, costs of infrastructure – which are connected with the principle of equal treatment of all regions of Germany – will increase disproportionately more per person in rural areas than in more densely populated ones.

Two alternatives now confront us in association with demographic change:

1. Society accepts the changes and sinking living standards that come with imbalanced job market demand (and infrastructure investments).
2. Society desires to keep its current living standards, and thus tries not to passively accept the change, but rather to shape it.

Within the second option, there are in turn two possibilities: (1) to take measures to try to recreate a young and growing society, or (2) to fit the general conditions of realization and improvement of living standards to the changed demographic conditions. It is currently questionable which of these options will lead to success with the least costs.

4.3 Prospects

The fundamental challenge of current demographic development is not necessarily low birth rates, but rather the associated societal aging process. When we shift this issue to the side for a moment, the mood of catastrophe loses much of its apparent explosiveness, and we can even see positive effects. A decrease in population from today's 82.5 million to 75 million is less than a 10% reduction. This seems a lot when one sees it as roughly equivalent to the population of the state of Niedersachsen, but little when one remembers that Germany's population at the time of the "economic miracle" was no more than this amount. Moreover, even with a population of only 75 million, Germany's population density would be 210 people/km^2, a third more than that of China, the land of future prospects. An interesting point, even, of course, if population density does not play a major role in demographic challenges.

4.3.1 More Goods for Less People

Similarly, competition decreases with a population decline, because existing capacities can be divided between less people. For example, the demands for parking, roads, hospitals, places at university, swimming pools, recreational facilities, and weekend destinations would all be less, and in general there would be more for each person. This applies also for the factor of time: with declining birth rates, the fewer children born would receive more support and attention, as parents would have more time per child. Parents could also better concentrate their budgets for their children's upbringing and education, at least allowing for the possibility that children could be better educated in the future, which would enhance long-term economic growth potential.

Likewise, with a population decline there would be more machines, equipment, facilities, and resources per worker, thus raising wages. Exactly for this reason, per-capita growth would rise, not fall, for the remaining people in a shrinking population. Ever fewer people would be ever more well off. Are there actually grounds for worry? When yes, for whom?

Those who complain of a shrinking population must have a very specific world view in mind, one that is dominated by nationalistic thinking with closed economies. This perspective leads to a narrow view in which population size is correlated with power and influence in world politics. Perhaps more or less subliminal, or even nationalistic reasons play a roll in this formulation. It often seems as though arguments stemming from mercantilism and the long-known perspective of Oswald Spengler are warping current views of the evaluation of future demographic processes.

4.3.2 *Growing Populations in Other World Areas*

In the era of globalization, national population developments lose their ability to scare. Germany will not collapse simply because it will lose 10%, or more, of its population in the next 40 to 50 years. In an economy in which labor is highly diversified, as long as there still are strongly growing populations in Asia, Africa, and Latin America – which will be the case for a long time – German nationals and foreigners alike could be replaced by workers in those countries if necessary. This suggests, however, the undesired scenario of (even) more emigration for many Germans. Instead of selling goods and services in Germany, these products could also be exported to China. Savings could be invested in quickly growing areas of the world, rather than in Germany. Rather than investment in the Ruhr industrial area, or in East Germany, private capital can find high returns in Southeast Asia. At this point, it would be clear that the allegations that outsourcing of production abroad is unpatriotic are misleading. The final point is that the more open Germany is, and the stronger it is integrated in the global economy, the less the economic consequences of a declining German population will be.

4.3.3 *Aging, Not Shrinking Is the Problem*

Thus, the only remaining challenge of demographic change is the aging of society. At first glance, these challenges for the economy and society are dramatic. Hardly any area of a modern service economy will be unaffected. Especially the threats of effects of an aging population on the retirement system, and their repercussions on the state budget seem to merit grounds for concern. The rising costs needed to finance the system, in addition to the already dramatic budget deficits in some states, could indeed have negative consequences on intermediate-term stability and long-term growth. For example, OECD simulations show that in the next decades, state expenditures associated with age will correspond to a percentage of GDP 7% higher than that of today.

The bottom line of demographic analysis shows that a dramatic aging of the German population is unavoidable. We will have to live with ever more older Germans, and correspondingly ever fewer numbers of German workers. At first glance, there are apparent problems that can be dramatically illustrated through age ratios. The following will show that contrary to the commonly asserted opinion, demographic development by no means necessarily leads to economic problems when the right measures are implemented in time.

4.4 Political Recommendations

Just as the causes of demographic change cannot be explained by a single key event, the solutions to these challenges cannot all be solved by one set of measures. Rather, a whole number of economic and sociopolitical measures are needed, which, because of their dependence and interdependence, also need to be seen in their entirety. Only a few measures will be enumerated here: those that with well-timed political implementation would be capable of producing noticeable results in making demographic development sustainable in the next years.

4.5 Family Policy

One of the possible options to counter demographic change is to try to halt current developments and reestablish a young and growing society, or at least take steps in this direction. There are only three factors that influence demography: fertility, mortality, and migration. We can immediately exclude one of these: life expectancy cannot be changed, and its rise is a welcome achievement of modern society. Thus, there are only two variables remaining.

In Germany, the birth rate per woman is ca. 1.3; yet, to keep population numbers stable, this number must be 2.1. In 1870 the number was still around 5, and has since then steadily declined. In between, a high of 2.7 was reached in the 1970s. Because children are no longer seen as a source of old age care, but rather in many ways as a "cost factor", at the most, the framework of family policy can be designed so as to minimize the costs of having children. Such measures would include financial support for parents, or (as the case may be) mothers, as well as the development of childcare centers, but also improvement of professional reentry in relationship to time needed to care for the new child. With a realistic assessment, however, these measures could raise the birth rate only gradually.

4.6 Migration

It would seem an easy option to solve the problems of a shrinking and aging population by replacing lacking children with immigration. This would especially seem sensible as birth rates and also youth unemployment are very high in many less developed countries.

The biggest wave of immigration was in the 1990s, with ca. 800,000 new immigrants on record per year. Since then, this number has constantly declined, and at present it is below 100,000 per year. Today, the proportion of people with a migration history living in German is more than 15% (Statistisches Bundesamt, Federal Bureau of Statistics, 2006a).

According to the Federal Bureau of Statistics, with 300,000 immigrants per year the German population could be 82 million by 2050, thus staying roughly constant (Statistisches Bundesamt, Federal Bureau of Statistics, 2003). In this scenario, a total of 13.9 million people would immigrate between 2005 and 2050. But with a yearly immigration of 100,000, the total immigration in this period would amount to 5.3 million, resulting in a population decline of 67 million. The difference between these two projections shows that many fundamental effects are unaccounted for. In effect, a massive amount of immigration is needed to keep population levels steady. Moreover, these immigrants would also grow older, and the age structure of this group would be changed by, for instance, the subsequent immigration of (older) family members. In addition, it has been shown that the birth patterns of immigrants adjust to correlate with those of Germans. In the end, there is an insignificant difference in the age ratio (AR) between the two scenarios: 0.51 with 300,000 immigrants per year, and 0.59 with 100,000 (based on an average retirement age of 65).

4.6.1 Immigration Is a Help but Not a Solution

Thus, we see that the economic effects of immigration are generally overestimated. Immigration can definitely have a strong influence on overall population size, but with relatively low immigration rates there are only small impacts on age structure and the societal aging process. The demographic effects of immigration are therefore overestimated. Immigration can help to moderate the effect of a rise in AR, but when the objective is to create a sustainable and long-lasting drop in AR, it can help only when there are constantly very high numbers of new immigrants. UN estimates place this number at 3.6 million per year between 2000 and 2050 to maintain the current level of the AR.

Immigration additionally, of course, has its own costs. These immigrants will, for example, also sooner or later make demands on the pension system. And this process can only really be successful when immigrants are effectively integrated into society. The fact that immigration is never without problems can be seen presently in the results of the PISA study, which uncovered the difficulties of children of immigrants in the German school system. The study especially showed that children whose first language was not German had worse academic performance. Furthermore, the relationship between children's academic performance and the social status of their parents is nowhere stronger than in Germany.

Even when migration cannot stop the effects of demographic change, it does go a long way in moderating its consequences. The targeted recruitment of particularly qualified foreigners is a cost-effective way of satisfying the short-term needs of the labor market, as the education system cannot normally adjust itself to current market demands quickly enough. Despite current high unemployment, in specific fields there exists a high demand for specially qualified workers of whom there are presently not enough in Germany. In the future, the demand will rise further in the IT field as a result of technological development, but a similar rise will also come, for example, in elderly care. To design immigration sensibly, it is necessary to have immigration policies that determine how many people are immigrating, how long they are staying, and what Germany's selection mechanisms for new immigrants are. Many countries such as Canada and Australia have already developed very successful models.

In this context, immigration is not seen as a measure to prevent the aging of society, but rather as a short-term and cost-effective instrument to fulfill short-term needs in the labor market. However, one must not overlook that immigration is an emotionally wrought subject, and is thus often used as a political mechanism. Despite many provisos, intelligently designed immigration can lead to economic growth and a raise of prosperity in Germany (see, for example, Straubhaar and Boswell 2005).

4.7 Increasing Duration of Working Life

Within the analysis of the consequences of demographic change, it is important to keep in mind that the value of the AR is not unchangeable – it can be influenced. The consequences of the aging process mentioned above assume that the remaining conditions are constant. If a rising AR is the cause of economic problems, then the first economic measures to be taken are obvious, because they arise directly from the calculation of the AR. Because the AR is an expression of the relationship between the retired and working populations, either the numerator (the number of retired) or the denominator (the number of workers) can be altered in order to decrease the AR once again.

The first solution could therefore simply be that the length of working life must be increased. This would be effective in two ways: on one hand, the number of retirees (the numerator) would rise more slowly, on the other the number of workers (the denominator) would stay higher, and thus lower the AR. It is then simply a mathematic question of which retirement age could freeze future AR at today's level. This step is not the last possible option within a knowledge-based economy. Especially as youth need ever more time for their education and come to the job market later, and because workers direct themselves ever more toward lifelong learning and are thus temporarily absent from the labor market, it arises that over the course of life, acquired human capital must also be used for a longer period of time than at present. We must also take into account here that the increase of working time raises the yields of education, and thus the incentives for advanced and continuing education. The other political economic and societal question remains, of course, whether this raise in the retirement age is desired.

4.7.1 Work Longer!

When the current pension system was introduced in 1957, the average life expectancy was 72 for women, and 67 for men. Since then, two contradictory trends have developed: actual retirement age has progressively sunk while life expectancy has continually risen. Today, average life expectancy is 81 for women and 75 for men, and will rise to 86/81, respectively by 2050. While at the time of introduction of the system, life expectancy and retirement age were not far apart, today 15–20 years of retirement, especially for women, are the normal case. In response to the question of whether it is appropriate to raise retirement age in correlation with rising life expectancy, the following formula has been suggested: "a 1-year rise in life expectancy = a 3-month rise of the retirement age", so that today's retirement age would be 67. The Federal Bank estimated in 2004 that by raising the retirement age by 2 years by 2015, the labor force potential would increase by 2 million, an increase of 4.5% relative to today (Deutsche Bundesbank (German Federal Bank) 2004).

4.8 Increase of Labor Force Participation

It is important to examine the labor force participation rate (LFPR) in addition to the AR to be able to see the extent to which the working age population is active in the labor force. The LFPR is for this reason decisive, because a rising AR is primarily a mathematical issue. As long as the LFPR raises in correlation to AR, the active part of the population will rise, effectively countering the effect of a rising AR. Simply stated, by putting our unused "hidden reserves" to best use, we can at least partially compensate for the aging of society.

4.8.1 Women at Work!

We find "hidden reserves" especially with women. The number of women active in the labor force has risen with the change from an industrial to a service economy. This number is, however, still significantly lower than for men. The LFPR for women aged 15–65 was 66.8% in 2005, while this number was 80.4% for men. The average weekly working time is also much lower for women than for men, because women more commonly work part time. During 2004, only 6.3% of men worked part time, while this number was 37% for women. In an international comparison, these rates of German women's participation lay far behind: the Scandinavian countries lead in this field.

In the framework of traditional gender rolls, especially women become less active after the birth of a child. The differing labor force participation rates between 20–45 for women, and thus the "family phase", are especially pronounced. No corresponding change can be observed with men in Germany, which is not the case, for example, in Scandinavia. It would be of long-term advantage to improve this socioeconomic condition, so that women can be more active in the labor force. We should thus pursue all means to more evenly distribute labor force participation, especially because primarily women have benefited from the expansion in education of the last decades. No former generation of women is so well educated as that of today, and in the last 30 years the professional qualifications of women have progressed ever further. In this time, the proportion of women with professional training has risen from 40 to 60%, and the proportion with vocational education has gone from basically nothing to over 10%. Only 30% of women do not pursue professional training – half as many as 30 years ago. Women have already surpassed men in levels of education and degrees obtained, and they have a clear majority in pre-college high schools and vocational high schools (Statistisches Bundesamt (Federal Bureau of Statistics) 2006b) (as opposed to applied sciences high schools). Thus, not using this raised human capital will become ever more costly, not only for individual women, but for society as a whole.

4.8.2 Old, Not Stupid!

Another "hidden reserve" is older Germans. Through the trends of early retirement and partial retirement, the labor force participation rate for older Germans has continually decreased in the last years. At the same time, the professional situation of older workers has worsened, as one OECD study (OECD 2005) documented: older people have higher rates of unemployment, are overrepresented in shrinking fields, and have on average a lower level of education than the younger generations. The LFPR in 2004 was 41% for those aged 55–64, clearly under the OECD average, and also below the stated Lisbon strategy level of 50% by 2010.

To integrate older people into the labor force, it is necessary to correct some former policies. The former procedure of classifying those over 50 as hard to place in the labor market, and thus supporting their early exit, has only strengthened existing problems. Rather, it is necessary to enable older workers to use their social competencies, as well as professional and life experience on the job. This strategy includes making possible especially work with shorter and more flexible hours, part-time work, job sharing, and other forms of individually tailored work arrangements. Age-specific continuing education to raise productivity, and improve mobility of older workers are also called for. There is often, however, a lack of initiative. Demand for continuing education by older workers is particularly low. However, contrary to commonly accepted bias, the knowledge and abilities of those over 50 are not devalued more quickly by the fast pace of technological progress. It is exactly the structural change from an industrial to a service era that offers older people an especially good chance to integrate into the job market. In the future, social competence, ability to communicate and work in a team, experience, patience, creativity, and curiosity will become ever more important, and these are the factors that as a rule do not decline with age.

At first glance, an increase in labor participation for older people seems like a dismantling of modern societal accomplishments. However, the more the burden of demographic change grows on OECD economies, the less they will be able to support the retirement of people who still want to, and are capable of work.

A further "hidden reserve" are the unemployed. They are of course included in the AR, but in terms of LFPR and of demands on the social system, they represent a double burden for the state, both in terms of costs and in lacking contributions. The effect of high unemployment on the public budget is even higher for an aging society, especially when its cause is not economic, but rather structural.

4.9 Reform of Labor Force Behavior

In addition to the aforementioned sociopolitical measures, possibilities exist for other economic solutions. Their aim would be to compensate for the economic consequences of societal aging by generating more income for coming generations through the effects of growth, making the rising tax burden more "bearable". For this reason, the increase of labor force participation and the duration of the working life must be part of a comprehensive redesign of labor force behavior. The fundamental idea is that people in Germany should not only begin their professional life earlier and end it later, but that they should also be more productive over their working life, meaning that they should improve their skills and knowledge in a permanent process.

4.9.1 Lifelong Learning

The macroeconomic problems of an aging society are reduced for workers when work productivity rises as a consequence of technological progress and/or a larger macroeconomic capital stock, thus also raising real wages. The demographically influenced rising tax burden could then be countered by a rise in productivity per worker. Net wages do not have to fall – they could feasibly even rise. However, retirees would not need to be fully accounted for in terms of real pay development. The question of the extent to which an aging society is in fact receptive to innovation and technological progress should only be mentioned here, because aging societies are naturally less innovative because innovation devalues their human capital.

The future course of productivity development will, however, be essentially determined through human capital development. With the internationalization of markets, work-intensive production is now being shifted to low-paying countries. Activities that require highly qualified workers will, however, with all probability stay based in OECD countries. Thus, between 1975–2000, work for the highly qualified rose 180%. For this reason, the qualification of workers is a factor with much meaning in a modern economy.

It will be decisive to see whether giving parents, workers, or employers incentives to invest in human capital will be effective. Through a constant process of lifelong learning, the know-how, competencies, and abilities of the actively working generation, and especially youth newly entering the job market, can be supported and increased, thereby promoting worker productivity. A decrease in quantity can be compensated or even overcompensated for by a rise in quality. I shall only mention in passing that an education system with its own strong sources of funding has the best possibilities for maximizing the returns on its educational investments.

4.10 Reform of the Pension System

The biggest challenge that results from demographic change, however, is an extensive reform of the pension system: the existing contribution system, for the reasons mentioned above, does not work for an aging society. While in the past the advantages of the funded system were relatively one-sidedly emphasized, much new research suggests caution (Europäische Zentralbank (European Central Bank) 2000), and the effects and the mutual repercussions of an aging population on the macro-level economy cannot easily be reduced to a simple choice between a contributory and a funded system. If, for example, an aging population dissaves because more money is needed to support more retirees, the real interest rate would rise to create new incentives for private savings. This real interest rate increase would, however, negatively influence investment and long-term growth.

In this case, private savings would become central to the debate. The influence that mandated private savings have on voluntary measures is, however, not without controversy, and not only because private saving depends on many factors. Here, especially growth and income development cannot be isolated from the effects of state-mandated savings. It can at least be said that neither completely replacing private savings with a state system is plausible nor can any positive effects of this change be supported by empirical data. Similarly, one must also agree that the outcome of a funded system is dependent on the age structure of the population.

4.10.1 Many, Instead of Single Pillars

In short, a "mixed system" with elements from both the contributory and funded systems could be a particularly positive solution for today's problems.

The "many-pillared model" of Switzerland could, for example, serve as model of a system that is not affected by age structure.

The question of the relative advantages of a pay-as-you-go or funded system is also closely connected with whether the people in an aging society will save more or less than today. When adults have fewer children, do they have more or less incentive to forgo current consumption in favor of the future? Here, there are a multitude of arguments supporting either side, arguments that are also interconnected with the needs of employment markets, and the development of real wages. Thus, one cannot find exact answers: the effects of an aging population on growth are not clear-cut, and cannot therefore be diagnosed in advance. They depend too strongly on reciprocal effects, individual reactions in private savings, the rate of technological progress, and the degree of openness of national capital and labor markets.

4.10.2 Make Your Choice!

Should we keep the pay-as-you-go system, which would mean that today's working population, and especially their followers would be more heavily burdened by higher social contributions to finance the rising number of retirees, it would be conceivable to correlate either retirement benefits positively, or retirement contributions negatively with the number of children. Seen in this view, in determining retirement benefits it would be a positive step to take into account the time spent in parental leave as part of the working life. An option that would be even more economically efficient would be to give the current working generation a choice between contributing to an obligatory pay-as-you-go pension system either in the normal fashion (contributions going directly to retirees when contributed) if they have children, or in a quasi-funded system where they must contribute for their own retirement when they chose not to have children. To provide for consumption in old age, workers could apply unconsumed resources:

- to enable the consumption of their own children by forgoing current consumption (an explicit generational contract),
- or to finance the education of their children, thus accumulating human capital in place of current consumption, contributing to general increases in productivity, and financing costs of living in old age through the transformation of human capital into consumer goods,
- or, in the case that they do not have children, by investing in real capital to raise growth potential, and to finance old age consumption through this accumulated capital stock.

Thus, having children, private investment, or a reduced demand on retirement payments would be the possibilities to counter the demographically related finance problems of the pension system.

4.11 Summary

Seen all together, the demographic aging process does not require extreme economic measures. At least, it does not require any large adjustments topping those that are already necessary in the structural change to a globalized world with a high division of labor.

So, what remains of the demographic monster? Not much! These apparitions are threatening only when one believes in these without really considering their real consequences. After all, it is not shrinking, but aging that presents the demographic challenge. To minimize the negative effects of an aging population on net income and living standards, we need optimally functioning product, capital, and employment markets, as well as a regulatory framework that can quickly and flexibly adjust to the altered age structure. Open and free markets are essential. It is fundamentally true that in an open economy, macroeconomic effects will be compensated for through transactions in the international product, capital, and employment markets, thus having little effect on the domestic growth path. Additionally, fundamental changes are needed in the job market: more people must perform more and better work. To counter the rising numbers of retirees, we must mobilize our reserves, especially including the major groups of women and older people who are underrepresented in the labor force. And to do this, we must make family and career compatible, as well as stop the early retirement trend. By the same token, the qualifications of the work force play a particularly important role, and the fewer the workers, the more productive they must be. Thus, we need a complete reform of employment behavior. The classic paradigm of a one-time education followed by the working life until retirement needs to be replaced by the concepts of lifelong learning and flexibility toward the quickly changing needs of the market. In this vein, the retirement age should be reviewed, and as the case may be either made more flexible, or changed to adjust to increased and increasing life expectancy. Raising the retirement age, for instance, in step with rising life expectancy, would unburden the system doubly: by lengthening productive work time, and by shortening the length of retirement.

References

Birg H (2001) Die demographische Zeitenwende der Bevölkerungsrückgang in Deutschland und Europa (The new demographic era population decline in Germany and Europe). C.H. Beck, Berlin

Deutsche Bundesbank (German Federal Bank) (2004) Monatsbericht Dezember 2004 (Monthly Report December 2004)

Europäische Zentralbank (European Central Bank) (2000) Die Finanzpolitik im Euro-Währungsgebiet unter den Bedingungen einer alternden Bevölkerung (Financial policy in the European Union under conditions of an aging population). EZB-Monatsbericht (ECB-Monthly Report) July 2000

Hansen AH (1939) Economic progress and declining population growth. Am Econ Rev 29(1):1–15

Kaufmann F-X (1960) Die Überalterung – Ursachen, Verlauf, wirtschaftliche und soziale Auswirkungen des demographischen Alterungsprozesses. Polygraphischer Verlag, Zürich/ St. Gallen

Keynes JM (1937) Some economic consequences of a declining population. Eugenics Rev 29:13–17

OECD (2005) Ageing and employment policies – Germany. OECD, Paris

Schirrmacher F (2004) Das Methusalem-Komplott (The Malthusain conspiracy). Karl Blessing, München

Spengler O (1918) Der Untergang des Abendlandes – Umrisse einer Morphologie der Weltgeschichte, Band 1. Gestalt und Wirklichkeit. Braumüller, Wien

Spengler O (1922) Der Untergang des Abendlandes – Umrisse einer Morphologie der Weltgeschichte, Band 2. Welthistorische Perspektiven (The downfall of the Western World – contours of a morphology of world history, vol 2. World historical perspectives). C.H. Beck, München

Statistisches Bundesamt (Federal Bureau of Statistics) (2003) Bevölkerung Deutschlands bis 2050, 10. koordinierte Bevölkerungsvorausberechnung (Germany's population until 2050, 10th Coordinated Population Report)

Statistisches Bundesamt (Federal Bureau of Statistics) (2006a) Leben in Deutschland, Haushalte, Familien und Gesundheit – Ergebnisse des Mikrozensus 2005 (Living in Germany, household budgets, families and health – results of the Micro-census 2005)

Statistisches Bundesamt (Federal Bureau of Statistics) (2006b) Frauen in Deutschland 2006 (Women in Germany 2006)

Straubhaar T, Boswell C (2005) Braucht Deutschland die Zuwanderung von Arbeitskräften aus dem Ausland? Focus Migration Kurzdossier Nr 2 (Does Germany need foreign workers? Migration Focus Rep no 2)

Chapter 5
Macroeconomics and Age Structure in a Welfare State – Sweden 1946–2005

Thomas Lindh and Bo Malmberg

5.1 Demography and Welfare State Macroeconomics

During the last years, it has been increasingly acknowledged that shifts in the population's age structure can have important effects on key determinants of economic development, such as fertility, savings, and human capital investment. In general, these models have focused on the very long run where stable equilibria are established. Similarly, most macroeconomic models assume a stable macro-demographic situation characterized by constant life expectancy, and constant or zero population growth. Demographic transition theory, however, implies that the transition from one stable combination of life expectancy and fertility to another is a process that takes several decades, or even centuries. Moreover, in most countries both life expectancies and fertility rates are continuously changing, not to speak of migration flows. Thus, the macroeconomic data we observe are from economies in demographic disequilibrium, with huge variation in the age distribution of the population. This variation in the age distribution defines a largely predetermined variation in economic fundamentals that should be taken into account in order to correctly understand actual economic development.

This line of thought has a long and distinguished history in economics.[1] Nevertheless, demographic variation is to a surprisingly large extent ignored in modern macroeconomic literature. Overlapping generations (OLG) models have, of course, been extensively explored, but are mostly analytically intrac-

[1] Easterlin (1968) and Kelley (1969) propose age variation as a fundamental factor behind long swings in the economy, and Perlman (1975) traces the basic ideas back to the 17th century through famous names such as Malthus, Wicksell, Keynes, and Myrdal.

Joerg Chet Tremmel (Ed.) *Demographic Change and Intergenerational Justice*
DOI 10.1007/978-3-540-77084-8

table during the transition to a stable population.[2] This makes it difficult, if not impossible, to test OLG models, with their very diverse predictions, against observable data. In the last decades, however, a growing empirical literature has emerged showing that there are pervasive and quite strong age structure correlations with a wide range of macroeconomic variables. These results are still viewed with some suspicion in the mainstream literature. The growing awareness of the rapidly aging population in developed economies has nevertheless led to an increasing appreciation of the importance of demographic variation for applied economics.

There is, however, far from any consensus about the mechanisms by which this aging will affect the economy. The only widely accepted mechanism that has made it into the textbooks is life cycle saving, but even in this case controversy is rife concerning the rather mixed empirical evidence. Part of the confusion is no doubt due to the difficulty in linking relations between aggregate macroeconomic variables to our knowledge about individual microeconomic behavior. Although the phrase "microeconomic foundations" has been a recurring mantra in macroeconomic debate for a very long time now, very little progress has been made. It simply seems to be infeasible to sum up individual behavior to obtain a valid predictor of macroeconomic aggregates. The equilibration of the macroeconomic system creates feedbacks that we are unable to analyze with any precision. At least, that is the case outside long-run steady-state equilibrium, and our observations certainly do not derive from any such long-run equilibrium.

To widen the perspective, and accumulate more information on this interaction between macroeconomic aggregates and population structure, we estimate how demographic change relates to macroeconomic variables using Swedish postwar time series data. Our aim is threefold: firstly, to quantify how much of postwar development may be attributed to changes in the age structure. Secondly, by comparing how growth, savings, investment, inflation, and budget deficits relate to age structure, we can make an educated guess as to what the main macroeconomic mechanisms are that are affected by age structure changes. Thirdly, our estimates yield a basis for predicting the future trends of macroeconomic variables by using demographic projections[3].

Swedish data are well suited to this endeavor, for two main reasons. First, welfare states of the Nordic type manage a major part of life cycle redistribution through the public sector, thus substituting for individual household deci-

---

[2] Following the seminal contributions by Allais (1947) and Samuelson (1958), this type of models, which explicitly takes account of change over the life cycle, has been one of the main analytic tools of macroeconomics.

[3] Lindh (2004) demonstrates the usefulness of demographically based forecasts in Swedish time series. Lindh and Malmberg (2004) apply this method to global income forecasting, and de la Croix et al. (2006) show that the approach is capable of backtracking Swedish GDP to the 19th century.

sions. Variations in the age distribution are therefore very likely to show up in the budget deficits, or in some other part of the National Accounts, rather than being hidden in household production and private transfers for which we do not have much data. Second, Sweden has more variation in the age distribution than most other countries, due to three distinct, but rather short baby-boom episodes in the 1940s, the 1960s, and at the end of the 1980s extending into the early 1990s. This considerably aids the econometric identification of macroeconomic effects. Due to comprehensive population registers, the demographic data are also of a very high quality.

We argue from our empirical findings below that there seem to be three important transmission effects where age structure is important for macroeconomic variables. Although life cycle savings is commonly believed to be a main mechanism for age structure effects on national savings, we would instead emphasize the budget deficit, which may be in part peculiar to the Swedish welfare state institutions. The second important transmission channel is age effects on production; the gross domestic product (GDP) tends to grow faster when the active part of the population increases. This relation interacts with the public budget variation to create a feedback reinforcing both effects. From our empirical results, it also seems to be necessary to take account of a third age effect, viz. on housing demand where increases in the very old population has a strongly negative effect on residential investment. This, or some other mechanism that works similarly, is necessary in order to explain why variables like inflation and the current account are correlated with the young and old retired population, respectively. Undoubtedly, there are a multitude of other hypothetically plausible channels for age structure effects, but these three appear as a parsimonious minimum necessary for the explanation of the correlation pattern of the Swedish postwar experience.

An obvious objection to our proposed explanation would be that the budget deficit is a policy variable that should not be endogenously determined by age structure. We argue, however, that the structure of a welfare state with a large public sector that manages a substantial part of the intergenerational transfer system almost unavoidably leads to this, unless we impose budget constraints that hurt, and favor different birth cohorts in unjust ways. Such policies will turn out to be hard to defend for politicians and economists alike. To politicians it is self-defeating, because the electorate is not likely to put them in power if they experience such injustice. To economists it is dishonest, because there is no sound theoretical reason for imposing such constraints on the budget, especially when it comes to public support for young adults and families investing in the future human capital base of the economy.

The great variety of different age effects must necessarily interact in the equilibration of the economy, but practical obstacles like collinearity and insufficient variation make it very hard to estimate and identify a full simultaneous equation model. We take a simplified approach here by estimating reduced-form parameters of age structure effects on saving[4], growth[5], investment and the current account[6], the budget deficit[7], and inflation[8], and find cohort-size variations responsible for most, but not all of the medium-run trends in these macroeconomic variables. In fact, the deviations turn out to be most interesting, since they are indicative of failed macroeconomic policies. The long swings our model uncovers cut through the short-range business cycle fluctuations. The swings are almost regular, and more or less cyclical in a pattern that closely resembles the reference cycle patterns that have been found to be a stable dynamic feature in Sweden over the last 200 years.[9]

5.2 Macroeconomic Mechanisms for Age Effects

The variation in the age distribution reflects in the macroeconomic development of the economy, because economic behavior and resources of individuals vary in a fairly regular way over the life cycle. From total dependency in childhood we learn the skills to master our environment in order to support ourselves, and eventually also a family. The surplus produced in our mature years also benefits the elderly who have again become dependent on others. Each of these phases is characterized by accompanying changes in economic behavior and resources. As the age structure of the population changes the supply and demand conditions in almost all the markets of the economy, it ultimately also shifts the economic equilibrium. With this shift in the equilibrium following shifts in the relative prices and outputs of the economy, the final outcome can

[4] Leff (1969) is a pioneer work that has been followed by a host of studies. Some important studies are Fry and Mason (1982) and Mason (1987), who show that controlling for growth rates stabilizes the relation. Recent studies by, for example, Kelley and Schmidt (1996) use modern time series techniques to confirm robust relations between dependency rates and savings. Bloom et al. (2003a) give more perspectives on the issue.

[5] GDP growth effects have been found by McMillan and Baesel (1990) on US time series, Malmberg (1994) on Swedish time series, Bloom and Sachs (1998) and Bloom and Williamson (1998) on world samples, and Lindh (1999) and Lindh and Malmberg (1999) on OECD samples. Bloom et al. (2003b) make a comprehensive evaluation, and Kelley and Schmidt (2005) sum up the recent evidence.

[6] Separate age effects on investment are much less investigated. Higgins and Williamson (1997), Higgins (1998), and Lindh and Malmberg (2007) study these and the implied effects on the current account. The latter effect is also the theme in Herbertsson and Zoega (1999).

[7] Lindh (2003) makes the case for Sweden; Herbertsson and Zoega (1999) show that this correlation holds also in much more general, global samples.

[8] Age effects on inflation are shown in Lindh and Malmberg (1998, 2000) on an OECD sample. McMillan and Baesel (1990) show it on time series from the USA.

[9] We are grateful to Lennart Schön for bringing this to our attention. Schön (2000) is a comprehensive discussion in Swedish, and a brief account in English is given in Schön (1991).

be traced in aggregate variables like GDP, inflation, current accounts, and budget deficits.

Macroeconomic effects from this age structure variation can arise in two ways. To start with, there is a direct, pure summation effect. For instance, an increase in the number of middle-aged net savers translates directly into a higher savings rate ceteris paribus. Market adjustments and interaction with other behavioral changes imply, however, that the observed outcome of a shift in the age distribution may reinforce, dampen, or even reverse the direct effect contingent on the whole age distribution. Take savings, for example: a contemporaneous increase of children in the population would depress the growth rate, and tend to increase budget deficits, causing the national saving rate to fall in spite of the increase of net savers. Such an increase in children could even be caused by young people expecting their wealthy parents to contribute with gifts or inheritances (or with taxes, in the case of Sweden) to their future economic resources. The exact balance will depend in complex ways on economic policy, institutions, and other factors, as well as the relative sizes of different age groups. It is, and will remain, an empirical question exactly how this balance will play out in any given context. While we have found most of the patterns demonstrated here to be general, and approximately valid for most developed economies, there are differences in the details regarding how different countries transmit the pressures generated from the age distribution to macroeconomic outcomes.

The analysis of simple direct age effects is different from the analysis of compounded indirect age effects. The former can be calculated from invariant age-specific behavior at the micro-level – given, of course, that such invariants can be found. The latter are harder to analyze, since they involve macroeconomic feedbacks and equilibrium shifts. However, regression analysis of how macroeconomic variables depend on age structure will provide estimates of the total effects of age structure changes, and – to the extent that these correlations remain stable – we can use these to predict macroeconomic responses to foreseeable changes in the age distribution. Although such reduced-form regressions do not yield direct information about economic mechanisms, they do give clues to what may, or may not be important to have a closer look at.

Our main purpose here is to search for those clues in the Swedish context. Therefore, we eschew overly technical details in the following, in order to focus on discussing the main traits of our findings. We use an inductive approach where we not only consider the statistical evidence per se, but relate it to the policy issues that have been dominating the postwar experience. Our conclusions draw heavily on our previous work, in conjunction with the empirical evidence presented below.

Any estimated age effects from a reduced form model are likely to result from equilibrium interactions between several different mechanisms. However uncomfortable, we are led to the conclusion that simple partial models of the type represented by the life cycle hypothesis for saving are insufficient explanations for the age group correlation with macroeconomic development observed here.

A number of indirect mechanisms are interacting to generate this development, and some of these are important enough so that they must be taken into consideration. For example, age structure will affect saving not only through direct household saving mechanisms, but also through effects on inflation and growth rates. In the case of national savings, there will be interaction between private and public saving (i.e., the budget surplus/deficit) and household savings. There is also a direct dependence on the current account through relative price effects from imports and exports, as well as capital flows. It is impossible to a priori predict whether this will reinforce the direct effects, or dampen or even reverse the simple direct effects. Also other variables depend on age structure, such as asset prices[10], mobility of labor markets, relative wages, and housing markets[11]. All these channels interact through more or less inert adjustment mechanisms with the variables already mentioned.

The correlation patterns we observe are, of course, a consequence of how the macroeconomic system reacts to these age structure changes. Since we know that quite substantial changes have taken place in the Swedish welfare system over the postwar period, this would be very hard to model in any structural detail. More old-fashioned macroeconomic models in the Keynesian tradition can be constructed that are able to replicate the correlations that we find.[12] Here, we give a more impressionistic account of the main mechanisms at play.

Starting with GDP and the growth of GDP, it is a safe assumption that domestic production capacity will depend on the population. Obviously, the relation between the actively producing population and the rest of the population will be crucial for GDP growth. The more detailed age structure is also likely to be of importance. Older workers are more experienced, and less occupied with household production outside of the GDP. In general, they have higher income for given education levels, and consequently pay more taxes, and they make less demands on public consumption and transfers. Moreover, they are often net savers, and in particular have shifted from saving that consists mostly of amortization of loans, especially housing loans, to saving in financial assets. Thus, population structure is important not only in terms of labor input, but also as suppliers of capital, tax payers, and in determining the demand structure of the economy.

Favorable conditions for capital formation of domestic savings are created when there is no, or only small budget deficits to finance by government borrowing. The opposite, of course, holds as the share of dependents increases. Less crowding-out of investment resources from the public sector, and abundant supplies of domestic saving will tend to lower the price of investment.

---

[10] Bakshi and Chen (1994) is an early example, Poterba (2001) a more skeptical study. Maddaloni et al. (2006) is a recent assessment.

[11] Following Mankiw and Weil (1989), there is a large literature on demographic housing demand and the connection to house prices, but there is also a direct connection to residential investment (Lindh and Malmberg 2006).

[12] In Lindh and Malmberg (2003), we do this explicitly.

Sweden is a small, open economy where the current account is important for the money supply, and it is expected that direct effects of the age structure on saving and investment generate current account effects. Shifting preferences for imports, and non-tradable goods and services relative to the supply prices of exports that are determined on the world market will affect the trade balance. Capital flows will also change, to the extent that savings and investments are differentially affected by changing age structures. A positive current account implies we are lending to foreign countries, as our own investment demand at current prices is less than the supply of savings. To complete those transactions, Swedish currency is deposited in foreign banks, or to the same effect, diminishing the reserves of foreign currency in Sweden, and effectively diminishing the money supply available for domestic transactions. In that case, inflationary pressures are dampened, and in the reverse case with deficits in the current account, inflationary pressures will result. The Central Bank can neutralize these pressures by, for example, restricting or extending credit. Such actions always have a cost, however, and thus must be balanced against other policies in the economy.

Disposable income for the households will, in Sweden, to a high degree depend on the budget balance, since government consumption and transfers will directly influence the consumption-saving trade-off for the households. Taxes are, of course, the actual deduction from income, but the households also have non-accounted claims on services and transfers from the public sector, which will influence their choices and actions.

Different components of investment will depend in different ways on the age structure. The component that most people think about when investment is discussed is private business investment, which is the actual productive capital formation in the economy. This will benefit from a large middle-aged population that provides domestic financial savings. The other large component of investment is, however, residential investment, which is positively influenced by a large young adult part of the population who is moving out from the parental home and needs housing, and will react negatively to a large old population that, through death or institutionalization, generates an increased rate of vacancies in the housing stock (Lindh and Malmberg 2006). The other components are smaller, and more ambiguous with respect to the age structure; so, we ignore these here.

Thus, we have six variables of interest for which we expect to find more or less obvious age effects.

1. *GDP growth*, positively influenced by the active share of the population.
2. *Government budget balances*, which should benefit from large middle-aged shares.
3. *National savings*, positively influenced by the middle aged either by life cycle saving, or by number 2 (government budget balances).
4. *Gross investment*, with potentially ambiguous age effects depending on which components are dominant.
5. *Current account balances*, generated by the differences of numbers 3 and 4.
6. *Inflation*, which will tend to follow the reverse current account pattern.

All of these mechanisms will interact with each other (as well as other variables) to create our actual observations.

In practice, there is no independent measure of national savings. The variable is measured as the residual we obtain by adding the current account to investment. If the current account is negative, then savings are consequently not sufficient to finance investment, or we are lending money to the rest of the world. That leaves us with five independently measured variables by which to estimate the age effects.

5.3 Estimation Methods

We estimate single-equation parameters by regressing the dependent variables on population age shares. One of the difficulties with regression analysis in this context is that age shares in the population change relatively slowly; so, to achieve sufficient variation, we need fairly long time series to obtain reliable results. In Fig. 5.1 we can see that the Swedish age structure does exhibit a fair degree of variation, albeit slow. Many other countries, in particular developing countries, have much less time series variation. This higher degree of variation makes it easier to identify stable and robust cohort-size effects in Swedish time series data.

A basic problem with regression models with age variables is that we cannot use the whole distribution as an independent regression variable, as we would ideally like to do. Not all 1-year age groups, or even 5-year age groups can be included in the regression, since multicollinearity would prevent identification of individual coefficients. Often, age effects are therefore represented by a single aggregate measure – for example, population mean age, old age dependency rate, youth dependency rate, or total dependency rate (old age plus youth dependency rate). A weakness with this approach is that some important variations in economic behavior and economic resources that occur during the course of an agent's normal life are ignored.

Another approach, pioneered by Fair and Dominguez (1991), is to use a polynomial restriction to represent the age distribution effects as a smooth function of age. The age profile of the demographic effects must then be restricted to a low-order polynomial, mostly a quadratic function by which construction estimates either a U-shaped profile, or an inverted U shape or hump. Some rather abrupt changes in behavior and resources that take place at retirement, and at the end of education are hard to fit in with this restriction.

A middle way is to include population shares for a set of aggregated age groups that approximate the most important phases of an individual's economic life cycle. This age share approach allows a fuller representation of the age structure, and still offers a more direct and flexible way of estimating age effects than does the polynomial approach. Although we prefer this approach, it should be noted that it is a compromise that may be sensitive to collinearity,

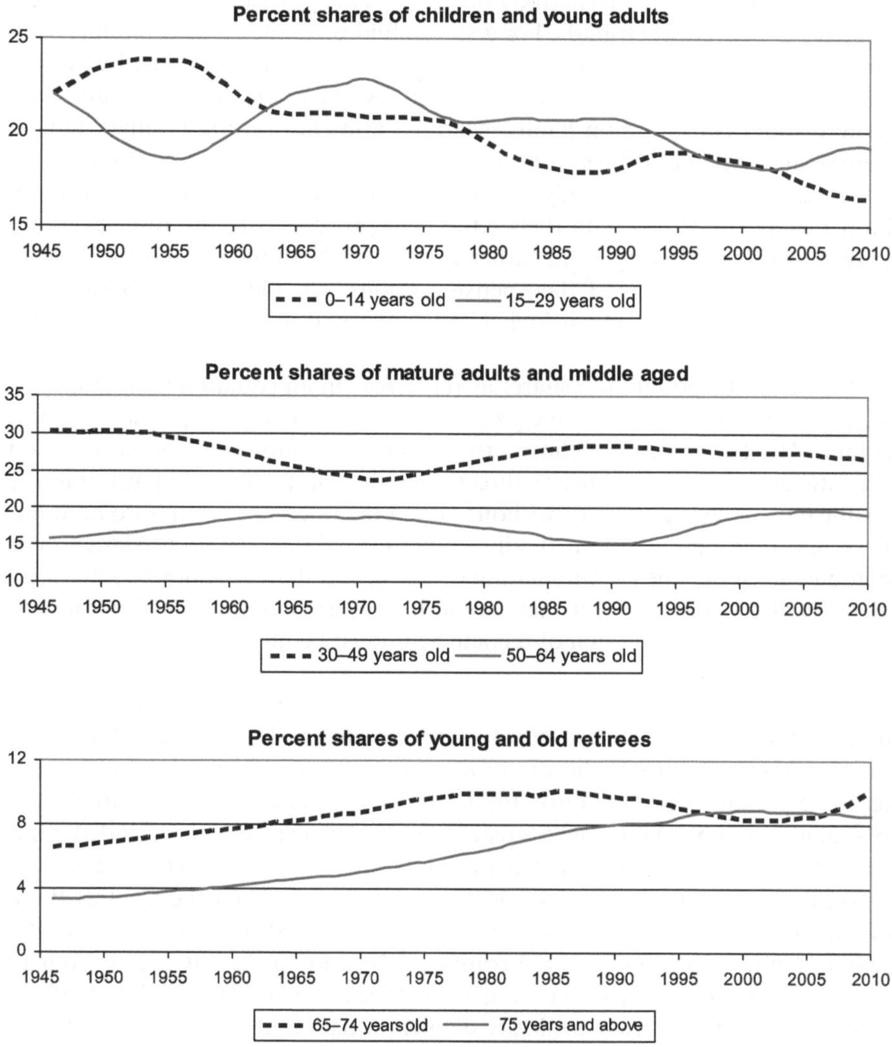

Fig. 5.1 Development of age group shares in Sweden 1946–2005, and the Statistics Sweden projection to 2010

and the exact delimitations of age groups that may not work equally well in all contexts.[13]

We have found a subdivision into five or six age groups to work well in most cases: children 0–14 years old, young adults 15–29 years old, mature adults 30–49 years old, middle aged 50–64, young retirees 65–74, and old retirees

[13] Bloom and Canning (2001) have investigated the properties of different alternatives.

above 75 years of age, alternatively only 65+. This general division can be motivated on theoretical grounds. For a start, children do not take economic decisions themselves, and are dependent on adults. Young adults often live single, or still with parents. They are also to a high extent still in education, and have quite distinct consumption habits. Mature adults are raising families, buying homes, and starting in earnest to accumulate wealth. The middle-aged people are generally past their family years, they have high incomes, and are more immediately concerned with their retirement prospects. Young retirees are no longer working, although still rather active and healthy, and have started to dissave, at least in terms of their pension claims. The oldest have considerably more health problems, much higher mortality, and are more concerned with passing on their savings.

To use all the population shares as regressors in an equation with intercept, we would have to abandon some group to use as reference group, due to perfect collinearity. Here, we have chosen to use all age groups, and rather abandon the intercept. It is then easier to directly see the whole life cycle pattern in the coefficients of the age groups without taking the reference group into account. It should then be noted that the interpretation of the coefficient signs is ambiguous, since the linear combination of age group shares cannot be separately identified from any constant that should have been present. One therefore has to keep in mind that the sign of a coefficient must be interpreted relative to the other coefficients.

Here our focus is, however, not on the econometric specification of the age models.[14] We therefore present only simple ordinary least squares (OLS) estimates where age group shares are used as regressors. Nevertheless, the patterns we present below are fairly robust and stable. The data we use are mostly National Accounts data from Statistics Sweden, which we have extended a few years back by using historical statistics from a diversity of sources. The current account series is complemented for the 1990s by data from the Central Bank of Sweden combined with some from the National Institute for Economic Research. National saving rates are computed by adding the current account to the gross investment series. The Consumer Price Index (CPI) series is the official series from Statistics Sweden. More details on data and sources can be found in the Appendix. It should be noted here, however, that because of changing definitions and methods used in compiling the official series, linking has been necessary not only to the historical sources in the beginning of the time series, but also between different periods thereafter.

The dependent variables of national savings, gross investment, the current account, and (the) consolidated government saving are normalized as rates of GDP. Inflation and GDP growth are the logarithmic growth rates of the CPI index and the real GDP estimates, respectively.

[14] We refer readers to our other papers in the references, where extensive testing and specification searches are reported.

5.4 Estimated Age Patterns

The estimation results are collected into Table 5.1 below. In three cases, statistical tests confirm that we should use the 65+ age group share, rather than subdividing it into young and old retirees. This holds for the saving rate, the financial saving of the government, and the growth rate. In the other cases, this restriction is rejected. The absolute *t*-statistics indicate that not all coefficients

Table 5.1 Regression coefficients, Swedish macroeconomic variables 1946–2005 (1950–2005 for government financial saving)[a]

Dep. variable	Savings (rate)	Investment (rate)	Current (account/ GDP)	Govern. fin. (saving/ GDP)	GDP (growth)	Inflation (rate)
Share 0–14	–0.04	–0.31	0.34	*–1.29*	*–0.92*	–0.12
	(0.13)	(0.70)	(1.15)	(2.20)	(3.41)	(0.20)
Share 15–29	0.08	0.19	–0.07	0.52	*0.40*	–0.34
	(0.43)	(0.80)	(0.41)	(1.49)	(2.63)	(1.05)
Share 30–49	*0.41*	*0.60*	–0.24	0.26	*0.54*	–0.03
	(2.29)	(2.45)	(1.44)	(0.81)	(3.85)	(0.10)
Share 50–64	*1.58*	*1.00*	*0.52*	*1.55*	*0.62*	–0.14
	(6.21)	(3.27)	(2.46)	(4.38)	(3.11)	(0.35)
Share 65–74		0.82	*–2.03*			*3.19*
		(1.66)	(6.02)			(4.79)
Share 75+		*–2.60*	*1.64*			*–1.63*
		(4.92)	(4.54)			(2.28)
Share 65+	*–1.09*			*–1.23*	*–0.83*	
	(5.39)			(3.22)	(5.23)	
Adj. $\overline{R}^2$	0.73	0.81	0.72	0.36	0.36	0.42
F(1,54)	0.06	12.86	31.66	0.45	0.27	14.00
(*p* value)	(0.81)	(0.00)	(0.00)	(0.50)	(0.61)	(0.00)

[a]Absolute values of *t*-statistics are reported in parentheses below the coefficients. Italics means that the coefficient is statistically different from zero at the 5% level. The F test is for the null hypothesis that 65–74 and 75+ take the same coefficient.

are significantly different from zero, but the regressions are significant without exception at the 1% level, and since we have both negative and positive coefficients, there are statistically significant differences between the effects of the age groups. Note that since the current account, savings, and investment are linearly related, only two of these three equations are independent. For completeness, we present all three.

Some statistical problems can be detected – for example, high autocorrelation of the residuals for investment, saving, and the budget balance. Since both we and others have tested most of these equations extensively in previous work, and performed out-of-sample forecasting with good results, we refer to that work for proof of the stability. Note, however, that the reported standard errors may be somewhat biased, but since correction for this does not change the conclusions in any substantial way, we report only the straight OLS estimates.

In Fig. 5.2, smoothed curves connecting the estimates of age coefficients give a visual impression of the age patterns. (The smoothing gives a somewhat misleading impression of a difference for the cases where coefficients are restricted to be the same for 65–74 and 75+.) The difference between the somewhat

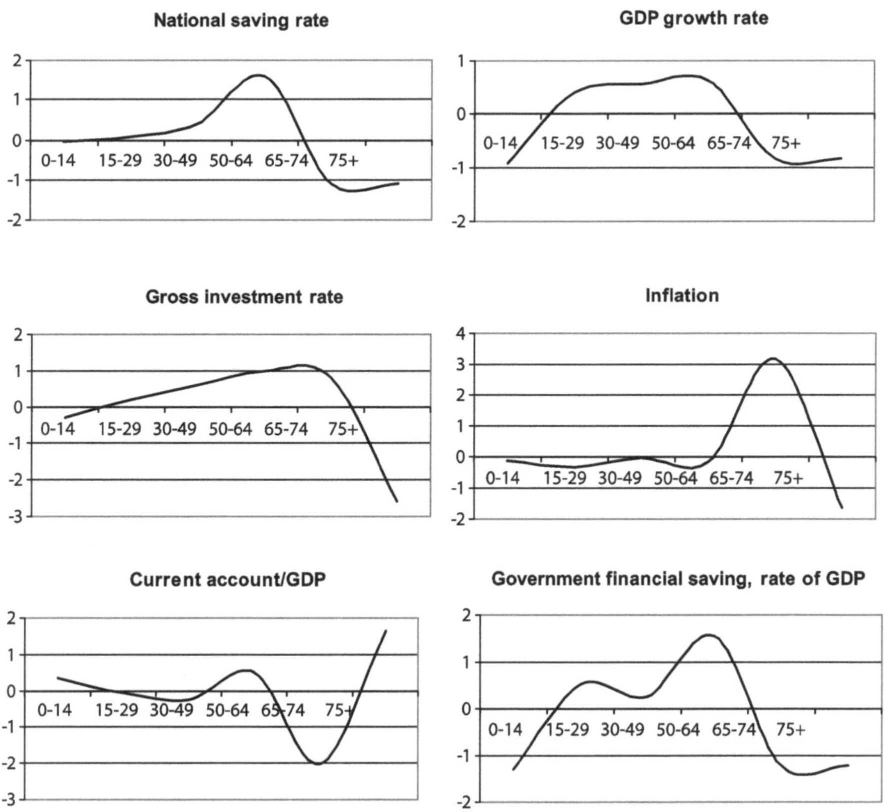

Fig. 5.2 Estimated age effects for six age group shares, connected by a smoothed curve

broader hump shape of the investment pattern, and the more pointed hump of savings has its counterpart in the current account pattern. The main difference is that while all retirees have a significant negative effect on savings, only the 75+ group has a significant (and greater) negative effect on investment.

Young and mature adults have negative, but insignificant point estimates, indicating that they may cause current account deficits by having more positive effects on investment than on saving, while the opposite holds for the middle aged. However, the dominant and highly significant effects are the negative from young retirees, and the positive from old retirees. The somewhat surprising positive effect from young retirees on investment, and the strongly negative effect from old retirees cause this. Thus, our conjecture above that decreasing residential investment with the 75+ group is a key factor for positive current account effects is supported. The negative effect from young retirees is due to savings, however, as is the positive middle-age effect.

Note that national saving is a residual that should not be equated to household savings. Retained profits, as well as public budget balances are large and important components in national savings, but on the other hand, capital gains (mostly) and pension claims are not included in the national savings measure. Both tax revenue and expenses for the public sector are strongly affected by the age distribution, as seen in the age coefficients for financial savings of the consolidated government sector, with young and old dependents negatively correlated to the budget deficit, while working tax-paying groups have a positive effect.

The pattern of age effects on the financial saving of the consolidated public sector shows that the middle aged have significantly positive effects, and young active adults have almost significantly positive effects. The weak and insignificant effect from mature adults is probably due to increasing public expenditure on family support.

Growth increases with a high share of the population in working ages, while higher dependency rates lead to lower growth, and the more experienced the working population, the higher is the growth effect. Except for mature adults, this pattern corresponds to that of the budget balance, showing that these dependent variables tend to covary. Even the coefficient of variation ($\overline{R}^2$) is almost the same.

Young retirees appear as the group mainly connected to increased inflationary pressures, while old retirees exercise a deflationary influence. The age effects on inflation are more or less a mirror image of the age effects on the current account. This provides support for our conjecture above that age-related inflationary pressures are connected to the shift in foreign balances as a mediator of that pressure. Causally, it could work either way. High inflation may cause a deterioration of the terms of trade. This in turn would lead to decreasing current accounts through a price effect, but a deteriorating trade balance may also increase inflationary pressures through a quantity effect.

The patterns for the six variables here show intuitively consistent patterns, although they are estimated independently. We would have been surprised if inflation was boosted by the middle aged, since high inflation then would have coincided with high growth and budget surpluses. The particularly high growth effect from the middle aged tallies well with the maximum in the savings rate, and so forth. By itself, this is an argument against nonsense correlations and spurious regressions, since it would then be a remarkable stroke of luck to obtain this consistency.[15]

5.5 Discussion of the Estimates

Our estimates imply that the effects on output and the budget surplus are similar. Thus, the income increase from higher growth rates tends to make revenue increases dominate over higher expenditure for education of the young, and the lower relative tax revenues they generate. The more distinct hump for the middle aged is expected, but is enhanced further by the income increase. That mature adults aged 30–49 have less of a positive influence on the government budget than on growth indicates that family support is not outweighed to the same extent of the increase in income that they generate.

A deficit in the current account arises when domestic saving is insufficient to finance domestic investment. Total domestic demand (private and public consumption and investment) is therefore necessarily greater than total domestic supply. Domestic prices therefore tend to rise. In a fixed exchange rate regime, domestic inflation then spills directly into a current account deficit as foreign goods become relatively cheaper and substitute for domestic goods, thus creating a reinforcing feedback. At floating exchange rates, this substitution is partly offset by a depreciation of the currency, but this has the same effect on the current account, since exports become cheaper, imports more expensive.

Investment combines the negative of the current account effect, and a negative fraction of the budget deficit effect. This yields the broad hump shape, the most important element being that the negative current account effect from young retirees means a positive effect on investment, while the positive active age effects compensate a slightly negative effect from the middle aged.

Since variation in savings is determined mainly by the budget deficit in Sweden (see further below), it effectively puts most of the action in the middle-aged group. Comparing the patterns in Fig. 5.2, the clear difference is that public saving has a positive relation to young adults, whereas national savings do not. Thus, we may not need to rely on life cycle household saving, which is controversial. This mechanism could be added, and perhaps should be added, to

[15] Since we get essentially the same pattern using data only up to 1998 in Lindh and Malmberg (2003), we deem it essentially impossible to obtain such consistency by sheer (good or bad) luck.

obtain a pattern more like the actual saving effect. It would, however, not be a crucial factor.

In Sweden, there is an almost perfect negative correlation between private and public financial savings. Even if we do not have complete crowding-out of private savings from public savings, it can safely be assumed that there is a substantial crowding-out effect. Comparing the profiles of government financial saving and the national saving rate, the positive effect from the 15–29 age groups on the budget balance can partly be explained by the positive growth effect from young adults. This increases revenue, but since a large part of that age group is still in education, a corresponding negative influence on the budget could have been expected that seems to be missing. On the other hand, most young people will depress aggregate household savings by being net borrowers, in some cases to finance adult education, but also to buy their own housing, and even in many cases to keep consumption in general above their current income level. Thus, the national savings effect from this group more or less vanishes, because their negative household savings effect is counteracted by their positive budget effects.

Age effects on the government budget can be decomposed into revenue effects and expenditure effects. This links output effects to the budget effects. As the share of dependents increases relative to the economically active population, revenue decreases and expenditure increases. The budget deficit will therefore be negatively correlated to the share of dependents, and react positively to increases in the middle-aged population.

Residential investment plays a crucial role for differentiating between age effects from the two oldest groups. The strong negative investment effect from the 75+ group drives the positive effect on the current account, as well as their dampening effect on inflation. The effect comes from the vacancies created in the housing stock, as this age group dies or moves to nursing homes (see Lindh and Malmberg 2006). This increases the housing supply, and for a given level of housing demand, reduces the demand for construction of new residential buildings and private homes. To some extent, this may be further reinforced by a decrease in housing demand also from those elderly who are still alive and living outside of institutions.

The attraction of the explanation given above is that it requires only a few adjustments – all of which are intuitively rather straightforward – to fit a standard macroeconomic framework. These small adjustments still have far-reaching implications. For one, it implies that macroeconomic balances are quite sensitive to the balance between age groups in the population. Because individuals will become 1 year older for each year that passes, this introduces long swings in the macroeconomic variables, with an approximate period varying from 20 years (for example, growth rates) to 40 years (for example, national savings) in the case of Sweden. Without controlling for other factors, it is somewhat speculative to determine the magnitude of the age-related part of those swings, but the implied variation in growth rates is on the order of two percentage points, which is enormous. An unfavorable demographic situation lowers the growth rate of GDP by 50% or more! The effects on national savings and investment rates are of a similar order, and on inflation rates are even much greater. There are, however, other external events that are also of importance. A general slowdown in growth rates of our main trading partners, oil crises, etc. undoubtedly also play a role in determining these magnitudes. But if we compare to other estimates of, for example, the demographic impact on GDP growth from global studies, the quantitative effects are not much smaller.[16] We should nevertheless for several reasons be cautious in attributing everything to age structure. We also need to consider the role of increasingly higher education for the younger cohorts, the entry of females on equal terms into the labor market, etc. There is no doubt, however, that age structure variation is associated with a degree of macroeconomic variation that cannot be ignored. Even if the effects may be somewhat exaggerated in our estimates, they are in no sense negligible.[17]

At the very least, any macroeconomic model that does not condition on the age structure will be quite useless, and in the worst case utterly misleading. From a more constructive point of view, conditioning macroeconomic forecasts on age structure may be extremely helpful in improving their rather poor predictive performance on longer horizons. With regard to economic policy, this is already an important contribution to develop further. But here our focus is on more direct implications for economic policy.

Age structure dependence in macroeconomic variables has important implications concerning timing and design of policies. Take, for example, the inflationary pressures implied by a baby-boom cohort going into retirement. Obviously, central banks need to consider how this will change the conditions for managing monetary policy.[18] In order to more clearly distinguish and illuminate policy implications, it is helpful to more closely investigate the actual events in the postwar Swedish experience (Fig. 5.3).

---

[16] Kelley and Schmidt (2005) estimate that at least 34% of European growth in the postwar period can be attributed to demographic factors, and Bloom and Williamson (1998) that 49% of the Asian growth experience is due to demography. Actually, already Krueger (1968) did a shift-share analysis indicating that over half of the income differences in the world were due to demography and human capital endowments.

[17] In our own studies on country panels, effects on the macroeconomic variables are generally more subdued, but still very substantial. Evidence is available in the articles we have cited above.

[18] Miles (2002) shows that the effectiveness of monetary policies depends crucially on how different age groups manage their savings. It is well known from microeconomic studies that risk aversion and portfolio choice vary with age, and consequently monetary policies need to be designed with this in mind.

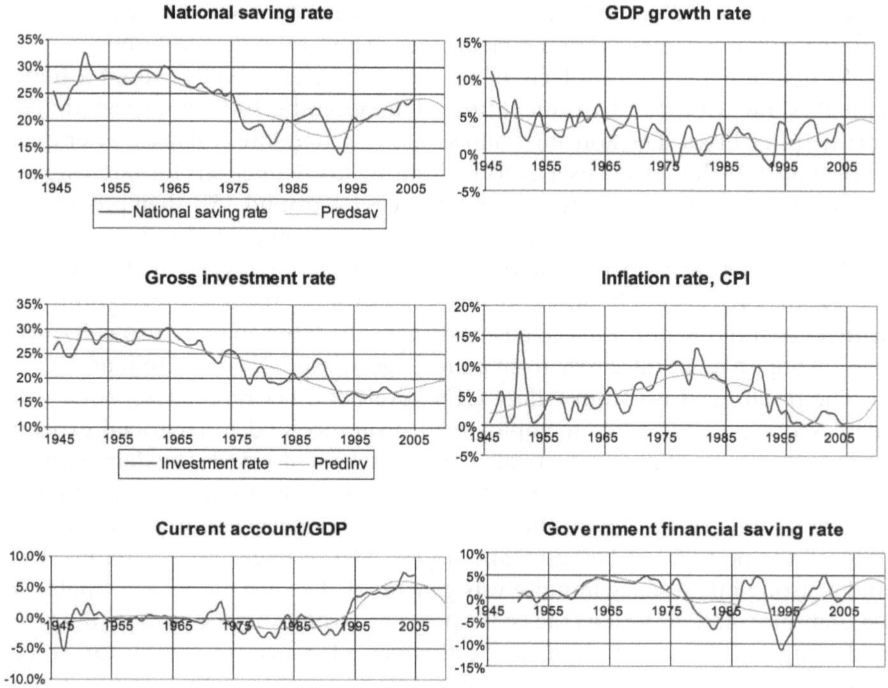

Fig. 5.3 The age model explained part of Swedish postwar development and forecasts

5.6 The Importance of Age Structure for Swedish Economic Development

In Fig. 5.3, the six panels show the actual development of our six macro-variables during the postwar period, and compare it to the much smoother development predicted from our estimated age models. The forecast made on demographic projections up to 2010 shows that, in all cases except investment, the age-predicted positive trends that Sweden has experienced for the last 10 years are about to turn negative again. Inflationary pressures are increasing, the current account will be deteriorating as will the budget balance, and growth rates will be turning down again. Given this rather gloomy perspective, what are the policy lessons from the postwar period? To answer this, we need to first give a brief account of what actually happened during the period, and how this relates to the age structure changes.

From Fig. 5.3, it is obvious that actual outcomes follow the age-predicted development much more closely before 1980 than afterward. This would be anticipated, since the period from the end of the 1970s to the mid-1990s is well known for a number of less well-advised policy experiments. An age model should not be able to predict events like the devaluation policies pursued by both right and left governments at the end of the 1970s up to 1982, nor would we expect age structure to be behind the overheated economy in the late 1980s, and the collapse in 1992 after a concurrence of several policy failures.

At first, a deregulation of credit markets in the mid-1980s caused a boom in real estate, with loan-to-value ratios often exceeding 100% in expectation of further price hikes. The housing finance markets therefore collapsed after a tax reform in 1991 that raised user costs by limiting tax deductions for interest payment. The estimated fall in private home prices by around 25% then provoked a financial system crisis. As attempts to keep the exchange rate fixed at an excessively low level failed in 1992, and floating exchange rates quickly depreciated, the Swedish Krona fell by some 50–60%, aggravating the crisis. In conjunction with a general downturn in the business cycle, the labor market also collapsed, and unemployment rates rose from an average around 2% to more than 10%.

The resulting stress from falling GDP levels and tax revenue, together with increased expenditure for unemployment insurance and other social expenditure, gave rise to budget deficits of more than 10% of GDP. The demographic situation at the beginning of the 1990s also was unfavorable, with few middle aged and numerous children when Sweden was the oldest country in the world, 18% of the population being 65 and above. The recovery was therefore slow, and a strong inflationary impulse was generated. The age model was unable to predict this trend, as well as the corresponding strong variations in saving rates and budget deficits that characterize this period. Since we would not expect demography to have any influence on political mistakes in the timing of economic reforms, this is actually reassuring.

That the age models are unable to predict those episodes is a strong argument against any suspicion of spurious regression. The probability that six spurious regressions would be internally consistent, and still indicate these periods as deviations from the normal must be very remote. We can also note that the Korean War inflation impulse at the beginning of the 1950s could not be predicted by age structure, although the ensuing rise in the level of inflation in the 1970s is predicted as a consequence of the retirement of the large cohorts born at the beginning of the century. Most of the productivity slowdown taking place in the 1970s is explained by the large cohorts from the 1910s retiring at the same time, so that the sparse cohorts from the 1930s dominated the mature adult part of the working age distribution. In most respects, it was a rather disadvantageous age structure that pushed inflation upward, and the current account and growth downward. This process created what is known as a stagflation episode, which at the time caught most economists by surprise. The deterioration of government financial saving led to a budgetary crisis, as public expenditure expanded heavily and the economy was hit by further oil price hikes.

Going back to Fig. 5.1 in conjunction with Fig. 5.3, we see that a very similar demographic situation looms ahead in Sweden now. Nearly the same coincidence of a large retiring cohort with another large cohort entering the labor market was under way at the end of the 1960s. Consequently, our age models also predict the beginning of a new stagflation episode. Policies 30 years ago were built on Keynesian ideas emphasizing expansive fiscal policies to bridge over what was thought to be simply another business cycle downturn. This policy essentially only increased inflation, and led to deterioration of the current account, while at the same time the government budget deficit increased. To restore competitiveness in the international market, devaluation policies were applied that in the mid-1980s looked rather successful, with restored internal and external balances, higher growth rates and investment rates, and inflation on the way down again.

At the end of the 1980s, the sustainability of this policy regime became questionable, as inflation started to build up again and a number of market-oriented reforms were initiated, which accelerated as the government shifted from left to right again in 1990. At that time, the crisis had already started, and untenable exchange rate policies only made it worse, resulting in negative growth rates, widespread unemployment, and a minor catastrophe for the government budget.

The Swedish age structure then remained disadvantageous up to the middle of the 1990s when a turning point was reached. The age structure had its peak inflationary pressure around 1980, which turned into a deflationary pressure during the 1990s. At the turn of the century, demographic conditions for growth are again as good as they were during the 1960s. The age influence on inflation makes it easier to get inflation under control again.

National savings have been affected by a long-run negative trend created by the age structure from the 1960s onward. In the middle of the 1990s, this trend reversed. Investment shows a similar trend, with the important difference that changes in the demographically induced investment trend lag behind the changes in demographically induced saving. This lag implies that from the beginning of the 1970s up to the beginning of the 1990s, demography had a negative effect on the current account. When the age effect on saving turned to a positive trend in the early 1990s, the effect on investment was still negative, and generated a positive current account effect with surpluses never before seen, both in the trade balance and in the balance of payment.

During the 1990s, the demographic pressure on the government budget lightened considerably. Fertility fell until 1999, and contributed strongly to the improvement of the budget. Although the fertility trend then turned up again, other positive demographic influences have balanced this. The share of the 65–74 age group has decreased by more than one percentage point, and the share of middle aged has increased by more than three percentage points. Together, these changes in the age distribution imply an upward pressure on the saving rate that has not been followed by any corresponding increase in gross investment. This in turn is due to a near moratorium in the residential construction sector during the 1990s. This situation has changed in the last few years, and today residential construction is turning upward again as the increases in the 75+ age group has turned into a decrease.

A demographic interpretation of Swedish postwar economic history is not all that different from conventional accounts with regard to the mechanisms at work, and is not really a competing explanation, but rather a complementary view that deepens our understanding by exposing underlying fundamental trends. The conventional explanation of the overheating of the economy at the end of the 1980s is based on lax fiscal and monetary policies due to influence from excessively strong unions and an excessively big public sector. The age-based explanation strongly indicates that the problems became worse because of policies that were often motivated by these perceived problems, but unintentionally came to work against the demographic pressures. An appreciation of the demographic situation would have made it possible to design policies working with, rather than against, the fundamentals in the Swedish economy – surfing the waves, rather than plunging headfirst into these.

The current account deterioration in the 1970s motivated the adoption of devaluation as a solution. From an age structure perspective, however, a current account deterioration was to be expected as a way to borrow funds to keep investment up as domestic saving sagged. Instead of combating this borrowing, it should have been encouraged, and the inflationary government subsidies to the dying industries of textiles and shipbuilding should rather have been discontinued. The devaluations of the Swedish currency slowed down structural adjustment in response to global competition. This led to overheating of the economy, and undermined long-term sustainability. There is, and will probably always be, controversy concerning the exact details about what caused what, and whose fault it was in this rather dismal story of policy failures. With the final result at hand in the events of the 1990s crisis, it is rather clear that, regarding the goal of stabilizing the economy, this 20-year period of large ups and downs in all the central macro-variables was a failure.

A policy taking due regard of the age structure-induced pressures could have achieved a much smoother path with fewer job losses in the long run, and in terms of the GDP level, and not least the supply of public services. Instead of increasing government debt in the 1970s, as the right wing government did in order to retain dying industries, a moderate increase of government debt in the 1980s to bridge an age-induced temporary imbalance of tax revenue and expenditure could have provided a more painless way to a sustainable recovery. Although such a counterfactual statement is hard to prove, that is what the age models in Fig. 5.3 indicate as a more balanced path.

Finally, a word of caution is appropriate concerning the reliability of the statistical models we have reported here. When fitting age structure variables to time series in a reduced form, as we have done here, overfitting is almost unavoidable, i.e., the model attributes macroeconomic variation to age structure variation that is due to other causes. This problem is much less severe when estimating the relations in a country panel setting. The cross-country variation then allows more efficient controls for this. From experience, we know that although coefficients of cross-country panel estimations show the same pattern, they are in general smaller in magnitude. In particular, there is a risk that our estimates are influenced by some of the large outliers created by failed policies in the 1980s and 1990s, thereby exaggerating the magnitude of the age-caused variations.

The very large current account surplus Sweden is running at the moment may well be an artifact of exaggerated savings in the government sector, in relation to domestic demand for investment. The regression procedure will translate this factor into coefficients that are somewhat too large, and therefore exaggerate both predicted upturns and downturns.[19]

5.7 Concluding Remarks

We have illustrated how changes in the age distribution affect macroeconomic variables like GDP growth, inflation rates, saving, investment, the current account, and the budget deficit. The results are congruent with standard macroeconomic theory, as well as intuition. Introducing a few channels for age effects into a fairly standard textbook model is sufficient to theoretically explain these effects in an internally consistent way. Our theoretical understanding of how different age effects interact in detail is, however, still in its infancy, and more research on this is clearly warranted.

But we think the main message here is nevertheless fairly clear. Age structure matters, and it matters a lot. Policies designed without due recognition of the fact that age structure has a pervasive effect on the whole macroeconomy are liable to make matters worse than intended, and macroeconomic models that are estimated without proper conditioning on the age structure will be biased and misleading. This is not a new insight: "Understanding how to adjust economic policy with respect to future demographic change will be a crucial question for policy makers in the aging industrial countries" (Alvin Hansen (1939), presidential address at the annual conference of the American Economic Association).

But it is unfortunately a largely forgotten insight that we need to actualize again in order not to repeat the mistakes and failures of the postwar period. There is great opportunity for substantial gains by not relying on overly simplistic theoretical steady-state models in the design of policy, when already very simple reduced-form models using age structure can outperform these models in long-range forecasting.

How far would our results generalize? Most European nations have similar welfare systems, similar age structures, and similar economic systems. Country panel regressions tend to show similar age patterns overall in the OECD countries, and so we would expect the general reasoning to apply in most of these. Developing countries are both demographically and economically in another phase, where longevity has not yet triggered the introduction of the welfare

[19] We have here used very simple methods in order to make a point about the necessity to take age structure into account when designing economic policies. If our aim had been good forecasting, then we would have taken care of suspected outliers, and changed the specification of the models separately in order to avoid this overfitting problem that needs specific solutions for each of the variables in question. Lindh (2004) illustrates the procedure to follow by evaluation of out-of-sample forecasts, and recursive estimation to validate the stability of the model.

mechanisms that are so important in this context. Their economic development is undoubtedly also dependent on age structure, but with different mechanisms resulting in different correlation patterns. Conditional on successful implementation of crucial institutions such as education and healthcare systems, their declining fertility now signals a historic opportunity to catch up with the developed countries.

If further research confirms that age structure-driven internal and external imbalances are a general phenomenon, then economic policy will have to be conducted with one eye on the age distribution, in order to avoid problems of the kind that seem so apparent in the later half of the Swedish postwar experience. In particular, deficits following temporary variations in age structure are quite natural life cycle phenomena, and should probably be accepted without policy interventions, unless there is good reason to suspect other identifiable causes.

However, we are on the verge of entering an old age society where social welfare mechanisms will become more, rather than less, important. Changes in age structure will then not be temporary, but may be found to be more or less permanent. Achieving a better understanding of how to adjust economic policy with respect to demography will be a crucial question for policymakers within the coming years. More research and attention need to be devoted to these issues, which especially in Europe for some reason have been marginalized in academic research for a very long time now.

Appendix: Data

This appendix describes sources and definitions of the data. The data for the years 1946–1949 were compiled from a variety of historical sources. GDP at factor costs in current prices 1860–1980, and a deflator from Krantz (1997) were used to link to the GDP at market price from Statistics Sweden 1950–2005. Thus, the years 1946–1949 are slightly different. For the period 1941–1950, the sum of sector GDPs was used since the aggregate for that period is not accurate according to the author. These series were spliced to the latest update from Statistics Sweden by ratio linking in 1950. Real GDP is the deflated series. Due to changes in the National Account system caused by the new European standard having been introduced, data may not be fully comparable backward in the official series either.

The consumer price index is the latest update of annual CPI from Statistics Sweden, and historical cost-of-living indices that go back to 1830. The basic age structure data are 5-year cohort population numbers on annual basis. The series 1911 up to 1967 has been compiled from official statistics by Bo Malmberg. The years 1968 to 2005 are from the latest updates of Statistics Sweden. Projections 2006–2030 are the latest version of the forecasts of Statistics Sweden. Note that all these population data refer to 31 December in the current year, but in the estimations they have been lagged 1 year.

The current account data are among the least reliable. After scrutiny of many different estimates and later revisions, we adopted the following sources: for the period 1950–1993, a series obtained from the Central Bank of Sweden, compiled to be consistent with modern definitions. The missing years 1946–1949 were filled in by data from Ohlsson (1969), Table B:1 column 6 without linking. For the period 1999–2005, data were available to download from the Central Bank, but the gap 1993–1998 was filled by a series based on data from Statistics Sweden downloaded from the National Institute for Economic Research. Since levels were somewhat different in these three sources, ratio linking was applied backward.

The new ENS definitions for gross investment are substantially different from those of previous series. Using the latest ENS estimates for 1993–2005, the series was ratio linked to previous data from Statistics Sweden. The lacuna 1946–1949 was closed by domestic investment in Krantz and Nilsson (1975). The national saving rate was then obtained by adding the current account to gross investment. Strictly speaking, we should have added in net factor income, too, but these are very small numbers. All ratios were computed by using current value estimates. This means that the investment rate is not the real investment rate in terms of goods, but a value estimate consistent with the saving rate and current account, since there is no obviously correct way to deflate these values. Growth rates and inflation have been computed by the logarithmic difference of the level variables.

The series of financial saving of the consolidated public sector was graciously put at our disposal by Lennart Berg (Department of Economics, Uppsala University), who has linked data from Statistics Sweden 1950–1998. Using data according to ENS definitions 1993–2005 downloaded from the National Institute for Economic Research, this series was ratio linked backward to the long series. The measure includes the balances of local as well as central government at all levels, as well as the social insurance sector.

Acknowledgements We are grateful for comments at the workshop "Population Dynamics and the Macroeconomy", the Harvard Center for Population and Development Studies, 10–12 September 2000, in particular from our discussant Bob Schmidt. We also acknowledge comments from participants at the 17th Annual Congress of the European Economic Association, Venice, 21–24 August 2002, and at the Théorie et Méthodes Macroéconomie (T2M) Conference, Lyon, 13–14 January 2005.

References

Allais M (1947) Economie et intérêt (Economy and interest). Imprimerie Nationale, Paris

Bakshi GS, Chen Z (1994) Baby boom, population aging, and capital markets. J Business 67(2):165–202

Bloom D, Canning D (2001) Parsimonious estimation of age structure effects. Research in Economics and Finance, Queen's University Belfast

Bloom DE, Sachs JD (1998) Geography, demography, and economic growth in Africa. In: Brookings Papers on Economic Activity 1998(2), pp 207–273

Bloom DE, Williamson JG (1998) Demographic transitions and economic miracles in emerging Asia. World Bank Econ Rev 12(3):419–455
Bloom DE, Canning D, Graham B (2003a) Longevity and life cycle savings. Scandinavian J Econ 105:319–338
Bloom DE, Canning D, Sevilla J (2003b) The demographic dividend: a new perspective on the economic consequences of population change. RAND, Santa Monica, Population Matters Monogr MR-1274
de la Croix D, Lindh T, Malmberg B (2006) Growth and longevity from the industrial revolution to the future of an aging society. Institute for Futures Studies, Stockholm, Work Pap 2006:9
Easterlin RA (1968) Population, labor force, and long swings in economic growth: the American experience. Columbia University Press, New York
Fair RC, Dominguez KM (1991) Effects of the changing U.S. age distribution on macroeconomic equations. Am Econ Rev 81(5):1276–1294
Fry MJ, Mason A (1982) The variable rate-of-growth effect in the life-cycle saving model. Econ Inquiry 20:426–442
Herbertsson TT, Zoega G (1999) Trade surpluses and life-cycle saving behaviour. Econ Lett 65(2):227–237
Higgins M (1998) Demography, national savings, and international capital flows. Int Econ Rev 39(2):343–369
Higgins M, Williamson JG (1997) Asian demography and foreign capital dependence. Popul Develop Rev 23(2):261–293
Horioka CY (1991) The determinants of Japan's saving rate: the impact of the age structure of the population and other factors. Econ Stud Q 42(3):237–253
Kelley AC (1969) Demographic cycles and economic growth: the long swing reconsidered. J Econ History 29(4):633–656
Kelley AC, Schmidt RM (1996) Saving, dependency and development. J Popul Econ 9(4):365–386
Kelley AC, Schmidt RM (2005) Evolution of recent economic-demographic modeling: a synthesis. J Popul Econ 18(2):275–300
Krantz O (1997) Swedish historical national accounts 1800–1990, aggregated output series. Umeå University
Krantz O, Nilsson C-A (1975) Swedish National Product 1861–1970: new aspects on methods and measurement. CWK Gleerup, Lund
Krueger AO (1968) Factor endowments and per capita income differences among countries. Econ J 78:641–659
Leff NH (1969) Dependency rates and saving rates. Am Econ Rev 59:886–896
Lindh T (1999) Age structure and economic policy: the case of saving and growth. Popul Res Policy Rev 18(3):261–277
Lindh T (2003) The changing age structure and the public sector. In: Andersen T, Molander P (eds) Alternatives for welfare policy: coping with internationalization and demographic change. Cambridge University Press, Cambridge, UK, pp 49–75
Lindh T (2004) Medium-term forecasts of potential GDP and inflation using age structure information. J Forecasting 23(1):19–49
Lindh T, Malmberg B (1998) Age structure and inflation – A Wicksellian interpretation of the OECD data. J Econ Behavior Organization 36(1):19–37
Lindh T, Malmberg B (1999) Age structure effects and growth in the OECD, 1950–90. J Popul Econ 12(3):431–449
Lindh T, Malmberg B (2000) Can age structure forecast inflation trends? J Econ Business 52(1/2):31–49
Lindh T, Malmberg B (2003) Swedish post-war economic development – The role of age structure in a welfare state. Institute for Futures Studies, Stockholm, Work Pap 2003:4
Lindh T, Malmberg B (2004) Demographically based global income forecasts up to the year 2050. Institute for Futures Studies, Stockholm, Work Pap 2004:7

Lindh T, Malmberg B (2006) Demography and housing demand. What can we learn from residential construction data? J Popul Econ, online May 2006, pp 1–19

Lindh T and B Malmberg (2007), Demographically based global income forecasts up to the year 2050. International Journal of Forecasting Volume 23, Issue 4, October–December 2007, Pages 553–567. http://dx.doi.org/10.1016/j.ijforecast.2007.07.005

Lindh T and Malmberg B (2007) "Age structure effects on investment, saving and trade". Chapter 7 in: Population aging, intergenerational transfers and the macroeconomy, Robert Clark, Naohiro Ogawa and Andrew Mason (eds). Northampton, USA: Edward Elgar Publishing, 163–191

Maddaloni A, Musso A, Rother PC, Ward-Warmedinger M, Westermann T (2006) Macroeconomic implications of demographic developments in the Euro area. European Central Bank, Frankfurt, ECB Occasional Pap no 51

Malmberg B (1994) Age structure effects on economic growth: Swedish evidence. Scandinavian Econ History Rev 42(3):279–295

Mankiw NG, Weil DN (1989) The baby boom, the baby bust, and the housing market. Regional Sci Urban Econ 19:235–258

Mason A (1987) National saving rates and population growth: a new model and new evidence. In: Johnson DG, Lee RD (eds) Population growth and economic development: issues and evidence, chap 13. The University of Wisconsin Press, Madison, WI

McMillan HM, Baesel JB (1990) The macroeconomic impact of the baby boom generation. J Macroecon 12(2):167–195

Miles D (2002) Should monetary policy be different in a greyer world? In: Auerbach A, Hermann H (eds) Ageing, financial markets and monetary policy. Springer, Berlin Heidelberg New York

Ohlsson L (1969) Utrikeshandeln och den ekonomiska tillväxten i Sverige 1871–1966 (Foreign trade and economic growth in Sweden 1871–1966). Industriens Utredningsinstitut, Stockholm

Perlman M (1975) Some economic growth problems and the part population policy plays. Q J Econ 89(2):247–256

Poterba JM (2001) Demographic structure and asset returns. Rev Econ Statistics 83(4): 565–584

Samuelson PA (1958) An exact consumption-loan model of interest with or without the social contrivance of money. J Political Econ 66:467–482

Schön L (1991) Development blocks and transformation pressure in a macroeconomic perspective: a model of long-term cyclical change. Skandinaviska Enskilda Bankens Q Rev 3/4:67–76

Schön L (2000) Modern svensk ekonomisk historia: tillväxt och omvandling under två sekler (Modern Swedish economic history: growth and transformation during two centuries). SNS Förlag, Stockholm

Part III
The Relationship Between Key Sustainability Indicators and Intergenerational Justice

Chapter 6
Demographic Change and Sustainability: A Generational Balance

R. Andreas Kraemer, Daniel Blobel, Anneke von Raggamby, Doris Knoblauch

6.1 Introduction: Is Growing Good and Shrinking Bad? Or Vice Versa?

The common perception when considering the link between demography and sustainable development is that an increase in human population aggravates environmental problems. Long before the term "ecology" was coined, there were concerns about the earth's capacity to provide food for the growing number of human beings. At the turn of the 18th century, the English parson and economist Thomas Robert Malthus became a pioneer of this discussion. Although his static way of modelling the development of population and food supply failed to provide adequate predictions, and despite the fact that there are good reasons to denounce his proposed remedies as blatantly inhumane, the basic problem he pointed out remains relevant: an ever-growing human population may at some point exceed the earth's carrying capacity.

One might conclude that the fewer humans there are in a given territory, the less environmental problems there will be. However, this is only one side of the story. Experience from areas with a shrinking population shows that there is no linear correlation between a decrease in population and a corresponding reduction of resource consumption. The reasons for this fact will be discussed in detail below.

Over the past decades, the paradigm of growth has been predominant, most notably in economic issues but also in societal thinking, planning and decision making as a whole. Educated in a school of thought which takes growth, if not as the solution, then at least as a precondition for the solution of most problems, many experts and politicians see the absence of growth, let alone shrinking, as a condition which must be avoided at all cost. But does the main problem really lie in shrinking, or rather in the inheritance of concepts which proved successful in their time but are inadequate to cope with new challenges?

Joerg Chet Tremmel (Ed.) *Demographic Change and Intergenerational Justice*
DOI 10.1007/978-3-540-77084-8

In contrast to the mainstream growth concept, an ecological perspective critical of unlimited growth emerged in the early 1970s, notably with the famous Club of Rome publication "The limits to growth". Since then, the economic notion of growth as a precondition for development and wealth has been opposed by the ecological notion of growth as a fatal phenomenon ultimately threatening to put an end to all human aspirations of development. The concept of "qualitative growth" might serve as an escape from the dilemma; however, to the present its feasibility seems to be more a hypothetical claim than an empirical truth. Nevertheless, while there is a near consensus on the necessity of economic growth, a number of mature industrialised countries are realising that, at least regarding their populations, growth is no longer a fact and it will not be possible to revive it in the future either.

The aim of this chapter is to discuss the sustainability implications of demographic trends in Germany, focusing on resource use and environmental considerations. Our analysis makes reference to the concept of "generational accounting", with a view to broadening it so as to encompass other aspects in addition to the financial dimension. This understanding of a "generational balance" is explained in more detail in the following section. Subsequently, the current demographic trends in Germany are outlined. The main part of the chapter applies the "balancing" approach to a selection of areas associated with, on the one hand, natural resource use (energy supply, settlement and transport) and, on the other hand, nature conservation. Finally, a more general perspective on the topic is given.

This chapter is based on the findings of a project commissioned by the German Council for Sustainable Development "Beiträge zu einer Generationenbilanz Nachhaltigkeit" ("Contributions to Generational Accounting to Assess Sustainability"), carried out by Ecologic in cooperation with the Berlin Institute for Population and Development. The results were published by Oekom Verlag under the title "Unterm Strich" ("Below the line") by Hauff and Bachmann (2006).

6.2 What Does "Generational Balance" Mean in the Context of Sustainability?

The concept of "generational accounting" was originally developed in a fiscal context. It delivers a tool to assess the effects of current fiscal policies on future generations. This is achieved by calculating, separately for different generations (in the meaning of cohorts, i.e. people born in the same year or over a period of a few years), the net benefit or net burden this generation will experience as a result of the state's fiscal activity, over the generation's lifetime.

Without attempting to discuss the merits or problems of this approach, it can at least be said that generational accounting considers only the financial flows between the state and its citizens. Consequently, it does not provide an answer to the question of how other values and goods are distributed, and whether their stock is being enhanced or diminished. The concept of sustainability, however, requires a much broader perspective. This chapter aims to contribute some ideas on the possible elements of a generational balance in such a broader sustainability context. For each of the areas we analyse, we start by looking back and assessing what was inherited from past generations up to the present (distinguishing between "heritage" as an asset, and "legacy" as what is more in the nature of a burden). We then analyse the challenges imposed by the current process of demographic change, along with other major challenges such as climate change and the decline in fossil fuel reserves. Finally, we examine the present generation's options for acting in a responsible way.

Our study understands "generational balance" in a qualitative way, and does not attempt to quantify assets and burdens and balance these against each other. Independently of the fundamental methodological questions which would arise in trying to quantify generational balance in terms of sustainability, and the enormous efforts it would require if at all feasible, democratic decision making will never be achieved by simply filling numbers into a spreadsheet and implementing the results. Although it should be informed by the best available qualitative and quantitative information, it is always about options and preferences, power, and the context of the moment.

6.3 Demographic Development in Germany – Regional Disparities

The changing size of the German population, as well as its changing structure, is influencing our attempts to strive for a more sustainable development. A different distribution of population leads to different infrastructure needs. Furthermore, age, the number of children, and the people moving to and away from a certain region have significant implications on several areas, from the educational system to energy consumption. However, these implications differ heavily when considered at the national level, as some geographical regions grow while others are continuously shrinking. The following sections are based on the 10th Coordinated Population Projection by the Federal Statistical Office, "Germany's Population by 2050".

6.3.1 Germans Don't Like Children?

In the year 2002, Germany had an average of 1.4 children per woman. However, an average of 2.1 per woman is needed for long-term stability of the population (or 1.8 with a certain level of immigration). This means that, in the long term, Germany's overall population is expected to shrink.

There are strong regional differences in the average number of children per woman, ranging from less than 1.2 in several Eastern German regions to more

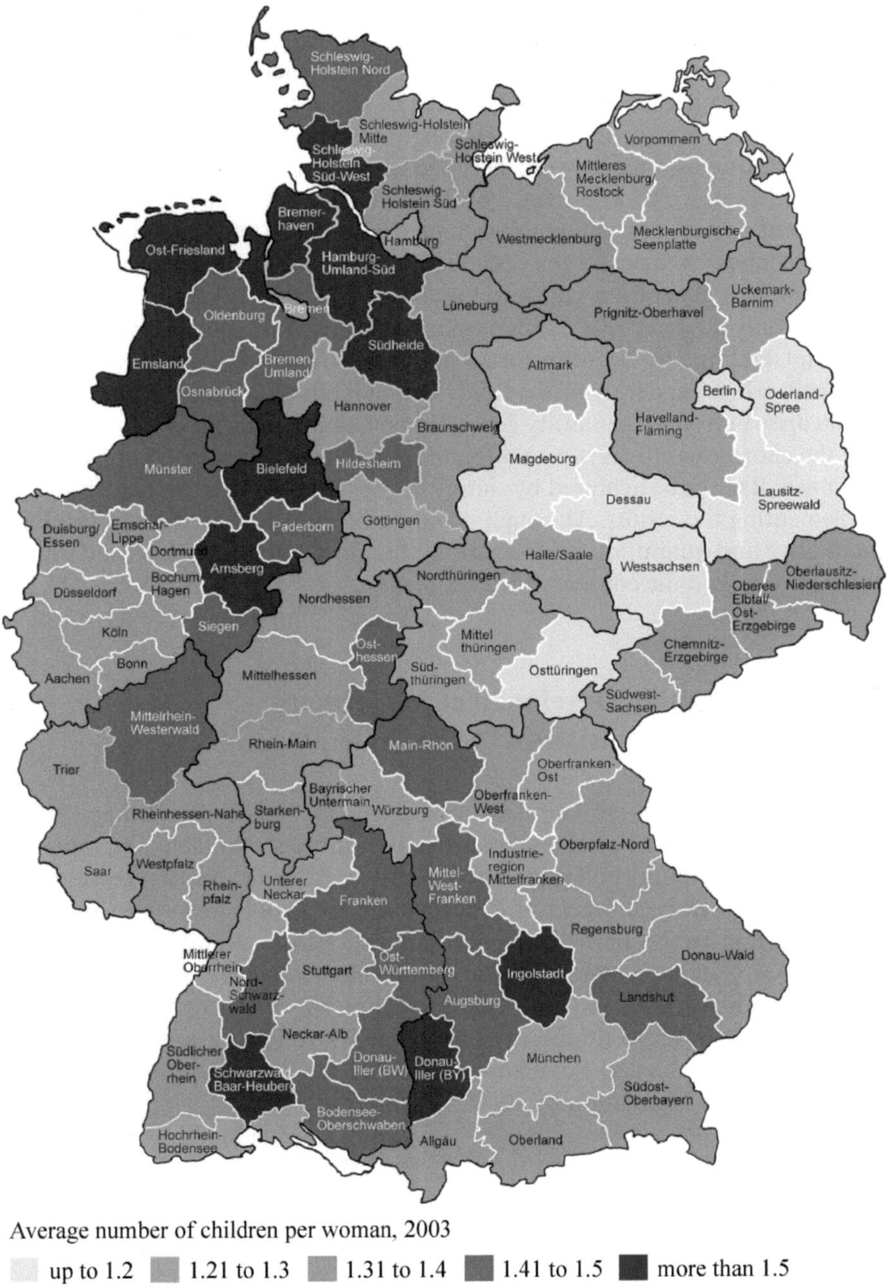

Fig. 6.1 Not a pleasant country for procreation (data source: Statistisches Bundesamt, Federal Statistical Office); graphic: Berlin Institute for Population and Development

than 1.5 in several Western German regions (cf. Fig. 6.1). In East Germany, birth rates are particularly low. However, higher birth rates in West Germany are linked to immigration, as immigrant families there tend to have a higher birth rate. This means that demographic change is expected to strongly vary according to the region, and cause regional disparities between the East and the West.

Moreover, regional disparities can also be observed within the West, namely between urban and rural areas, with more children being born in the latter. This is due to the fact that young people often move to urban areas for education, and then move (back) to rural areas when they start a family.

In summary, Germany's birth rate is in general very low and, as a consequence, the overall population is expected to shrink. This notwithstanding, regional disparities have to be considered: on the one hand, significant differences exist between the Eastern and the Western parts of Germany and, on the other hand, there are great differences between rural and urban areas in both the Eastern and Western parts of Germany. Additional characteristics of how the population is expected to evolve will be specified in the next paragraphs.

6.3.2 Who Should Have a Family ...

With less children being born today, the next generation's potential parents are missing. The proportion of the total population which is made up of potential parents is steadily declining, so that the problem of a shrinking population is expected to worsen. This is a consequence not only of the low numbers of births but also of life expectancy, which has been simultaneously increasing since the early 1970s. The gap between the proportion of the population of the young vs. the old is thus widening.

The situation in Eastern Germany is alarming. Although in the times of the German Democratic Republic the birth rates were not unsustainable, the situation today is characterised by a very low proportion of young people, due to the fact that many of them leave for the Western part of Germany in search of employment.

6.3.3 ... Where Have the Women Gone?

The case of young women is particularly problematic, due to the comparatively few opportunities they have in economically weak, rural areas (i.e. large parts of Eastern Germany). Indeed, many jobs first go to men, as they are still favoured by (male) employers. What is more, young women tend on average to be better qualified than their male contemporaries, so that most jobs in those rural areas are below their level of qualification.

As a result, it is particularly young women who move away to find jobs. The relative lack of young women is particularly marked in Eastern Germany, with up to 14% less women than men between the ages of 18 and 29 years.

The lack of young women can be seen as an early indicator for further economic weakness as well as for further population loss, as young women are indispensable for starting new families.

6.3.4 *Germany's East Is Emptying!*

Prognoses for the period up to 2020, based on migration (immigration as well as internal migration), birth rates and life expectancy, anticipate that in many regions of Germany the population will decline significantly (cf. Fig. 6.2). When focusing on the population distribution in the future, the gap between East and West will be even more marked than today. Although the population of some West German regions will also shrink (like Schleswig-Holstein, the Ruhrgebiet, Saarland and Rheinland-Pfalz), only one Eastern German region is expected to have a population increase of between 0 and 2.5%, namely the region Havelland-Fläming southwest of Berlin. All other regions in Eastern Germany, including Berlin, are expected to shrink both economically and in terms of population.

In the short run, growing regions in the West are benefiting from internal migration. However, this migration is not sustainable. The potential for internal migration is diminishing, as those for whom mobility is a possibility will have already moved westwards. Furthermore, the problem of low birth rates, and the growing gap between the young and old population remain, despite internal migration. Finally, infrastructure has to be adapted to migration flows. New infrastructure has to be built or expanded in growing regions, while existing infrastructure has to be adapted in shrinking regions.

6.3.5 *Consequences of Spatial Distribution Underestimated*

It is still too often the case that the demographic discussion centres on aggregate values, such as the effects of a decline in total population and the change in the age structure of the population as a whole. However, regional population dynamics and spatial distribution patterns of the population are far more relevant in the short term, and even in the present.

As already mentioned, infrastructure has to be adapted for both the regional areas which are growing and those which are shrinking. Internal migration also separates families, so that generation-overlapping tasks, such as grandparents caring for their grandchildren or children caring for the aged, are increasingly becoming more difficult. This has a strong impact on the national level, as public welfare systems are increasingly challenged.

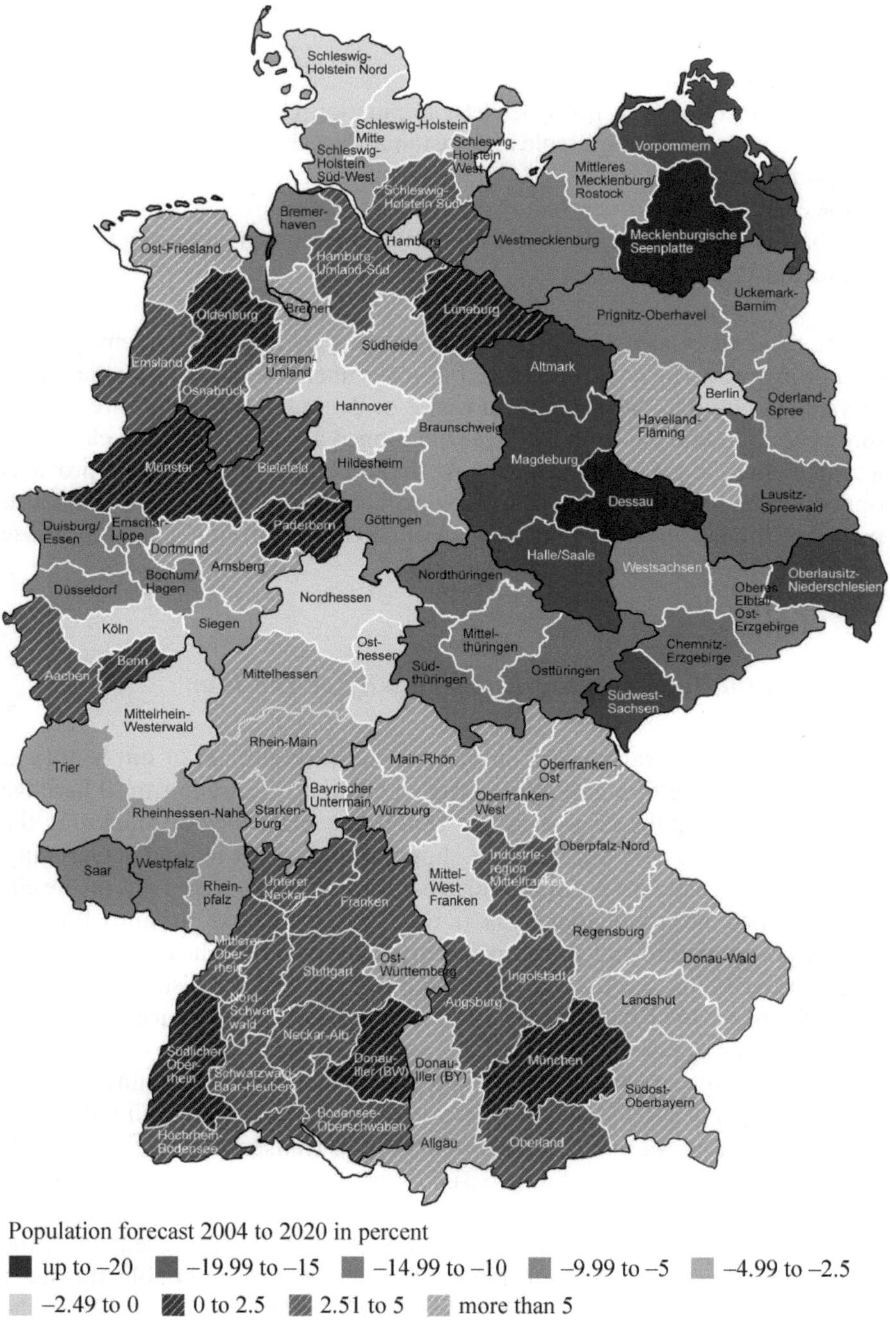

Fig. 6.2 The number of "underdog" regions increases (data source: Statistische Landesämter, State Statistical Offices); graphic: Berlin Institute for Population and Development

6.4 Energy, Settlements, Mobility – Securing Public Utilities and Services

In order to explore the links between population change and our ability to build and maintain an equitable and sustainable society, we focus on three key components:

- the energy economy, centred on oil,
- urban centres and their relationship to the environment, and
- transport and mobility.

All of these three areas are expected to be strongly affected by demographic change in a way which will challenge the government's ability to provide public services and utilities. Since the main trends of demographic change are already foreseeable, and decisions in the areas mentioned are of a long-term character, action should be taken immediately. At the same time, this situation provides opportunities to ease the path towards sustainable development, and could also help government in addressing key environmental problems, including those related to energy, settlement and transport.

6.4.1 Rapidly Changing Lifestyles After the War

The Second World War was not only one of the darkest times of our history in terms of human suffering: it also destroyed much of the architectural heritage of Europe. During the reconstruction period, the 1920s idea of separating the different functions of living, working, shopping and leisure revived in Germany. City centres turned into business and office areas. People moved out of the cities and settled into residential areas. In the 1960s, the idea of urbanity through density grew popular, and skyscrapers started to be built in the outskirts of big cities. In the 1970s, careful city restoration started, and the distances between the different parts of the city (city of short distances) were reduced by mixing their functions again.

In parallel to – and also partly as a result of – these urban planning developments, a boom of individualised transport started which lasts until today, and still shapes our *modal split* (i.e. the distribution of transport services on the different modes of transport; cf. Fig. 6.3). Road building activities starting during the Second World War, and the simultaneous promotion of the Volkswagen ("*people's car*") helped pave the way for this development. Consequently, the railway – as alternative transport mode – lost importance, and public transport was not able to keep its share of prominence, which decreased from 29% in the 1950s to 7% in the year 2000 (BMVBW 2004).

It is in any case worth noting that both trends – people moving to the outskirts of cities, and people increasingly using their cars – became possible only due to the discovery that oil can have other uses than only lighting or heating, such as to power vehicles. This innovation of the early 1920s allowed for much

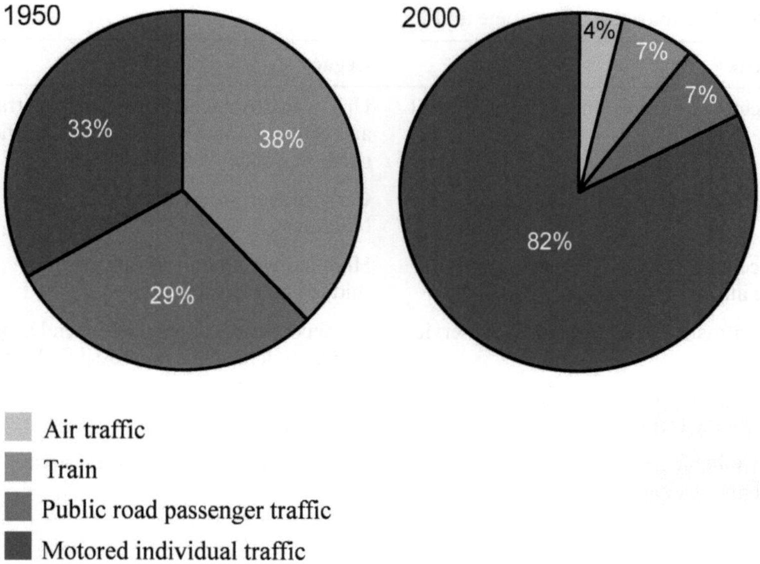

Fig. 6.3 Rate of the traffic performance according to carrier in the years 1950 and 2000 (data source: BMVBW 2004)

progress in mobility and was a precondition for separating the different areas of life. Since the Second World War – when oil prices were much lower than today – energy needs in Germany and other industrialised countries grew constantly. Energy intensity in terms of lifestyles or business was even considered a prerequisite for economic prosperity. The rising oil prices, together with the 1970s oil crises, marked a rupture with this school of thought. As we know, they did not trigger lasting behavioural changes or a dramatic shift from fossil fuels to renewable and clean energies.

6.4.2 Heritage/Legacy

The legacy of these developments for today's generations is mixed (cf. Table 6.1). On the one hand, current generations have inherited dense settlement and centralised supply structures in the cities. On the other hand, those same cities are causing severe ecological and aesthetical problems. Long distances and a modal split dominated by individualised transport not only cause emissions damaging to the environment and public health, but also turn cities and villages into transport corridors uncomfortable to local residents.

This fact, along with the subsidies for purchasing and developing new property on so-called greenfield sites, as opposed to rehabilitating existing brownfield sites, have contributed to a trend for people to move into the suburbs. Thus, energy consumption is expected to increase not only due to the longer distances but also because detached houses are energetically less favourable than apartment buildings.

Table 6.1 Comparison of heritage and legacy

Heritage	Legacy
Municipal autonomy and self-government	Urban environment: pollution (also traffic and oil) and noise, derelict zones, traffic needs and risks
Enough good homes of rising quality	Construction sector focused on new buildings
Multicentred structure/high density of public infrastructure	High individual motorised transport (hidden subsidies)
Good infrastructure and affordable services	Oil dependency, oil import dependency, and also high dependency on fossil fuels and nuclear energy
Good public transport	Low energy efficiency
Highly reliable energy system with increasing share of renewables	High path dependency in these areas

In addition, today's generations have inherited a well-established road infrastructure and a comparably well-working rail and public transport system. As a consequence, today's life is characterized by high mobility – this offers many options but also creates new needs. Mobility, as we know it today, allows us to get from point A to point B faster than ever in history. Consequently, families or friends can live far away from each other but still visit each other regularly. At the same time, high-speed mobility also creates needs, since the gathering of family or friends often implies driving. And one must not forget that high-speed mobility has negative impacts such as greenhouse gas emissions, soil sealing, fragmentation of ecosystems, and noise disturbance (to cite but a few), notwithstanding human injuries and casualties, thus generating considerable external costs. Last but not least, this lifestyle raises oil consumption. Growing fuel needs affect the price of the resources, and today's oil price is already starting to reflect its scarcity. Against this background, the fact that more than one third of the German primary energy use was covered by oil, and more than 80% of the German transport was performed by individualised transport in 2004 is significant (BMVBW 2004). While buildings could theoretically be heated by natural gas, and geothermal and solar energy in the short term if action were taken immediately, the availability of affordable fuels in the long term is expected to be more problematic.

6.4.3 Demographic Change Will Be No Solution

Demographic change will not be a solution for all these problems. A shrinking population does neither automatically lead to energy savings nor does it enhance environmental protection through reduced settlement density or less traffic. On the contrary, it will add new issues to the political agenda which – as will be shown in the following – need to be addressed in order to ensure effective mobility for all citizens, continuity in public services, and a secure energy supply (electricity and fuels).

In the first place, demographic change raises the issue of how public utilities can be maintained when at the same time public resources are expected to shrink. In the debate about demographic change and its effect on national debt, or on the sustainability of pension schemes, the question of municipal budgets is often not considered. However, demographic change might directly impact on the capacity of municipalities to finance public services. Municipalities are responsible for financing capital-intensive utilities such as electricity, water, wastewater treatment, gas or heat provision. Demographic change could make these services harder to offer for public entities which need to make sure they will operate continuously, in a secure and cost-effective way. Financing the services might indeed become highly problematic if the number of users decreases significantly. The reasoning for this is as follows: while the number of users of public services might decrease, the fixed costs of maintaining these, or the interest payments related to infrastructures, will remain unchanged. As a consequence, there will be *fewer* people paying *more* for the same service. As more people leave a particular municipality, the prices for water and water sewage services become correspondingly higher for those who remain. In addition, technical problems might arise because water pipe systems, for hygienic reasons, need to maintain a certain amount of water flow and would need to be rinsed regularly if the number of users decreases. Technical problems may also affect electrical grids which require continuity between the generation, transmission and distribution of electricity, and reliability regarding the number of users. Remarkably, one can anticipate that the people who would stay in their hometowns are likely to be less solvent than those who move, and will suffer if required to pay higher charges.

Another aspect of the problem related to people leaving poor economic and social conditions relates to the market value of houses in these areas. In response to governmental incentives through home purchase savings, many people have invested into homes in these areas, expecting to get pension revenues when they retire. If the market value of their houses decreases, they will lose parts of the expected revenue of their investments. There is already considerable excess supply of housing in many regions, most notably in Eastern Germany (see Figs. 6.4 and 6.5). However, the trend to leave hometowns in rural areas is opposite to the trend that people continue to move into the suburbs of bigger cities. While the latter is contributing to soil sealing and causes ever more traffic, the former sooner or later may even require us to consider abandoning settlements suffering from strong migration (Göschel 2003).

This shows how the important building blocks of public utilities and services, as well as provisions for old age, will be affected by demographic change and it shows that implications of demographic change do not stop in the public sector; at the same time, one must not forget that demographic change is expected to cause severe problems in the private sector as well. An area where providing public services and private living is closely intertwined is the transport sector. The reduction of population density caused by a shrinking popu-

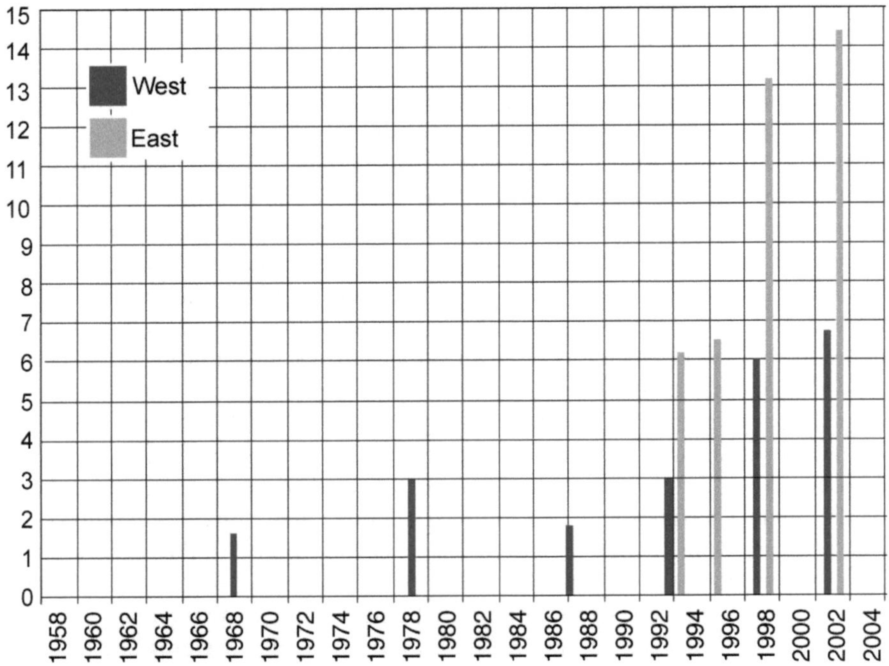

Fig. 6.4 Development of the vacancy rate in Western and Eastern Germany (data source: Statistisches Bundesamt, Federal Statistical Office)

lation due to migration movements and family disruption is likely to generate mobility problems. Since public transport will be used by fewer people, public transport services will be increasingly difficult to finance. In particular in rural areas, where many people without cars depend on public transport, children, old persons and the poor may be condemned to immobility. People owning a car, however, will increasingly use their vehicles and thus contribute to more traffic and more pollution. But driving will not be an easy solution either. It is not only the most environmentally harmful transport mode: in combination with demographic change, it will also become increasingly expensive to support street management and finance new road construction.

Although demographic change in Germany will not directly impact oil consumption, it will also not help solve the global problem of oil scarcity and the negative environmental effects of energy consumption. Given the rapidly growing economies in China and India – a phenomenon closely related to rising energy demand in those countries – these problems are expected to increase.

6.4.4 Options for Future Developments

Though the expected demographic change in Germany will not automatically solve the problems caused by postwar developments, but rather create *new*

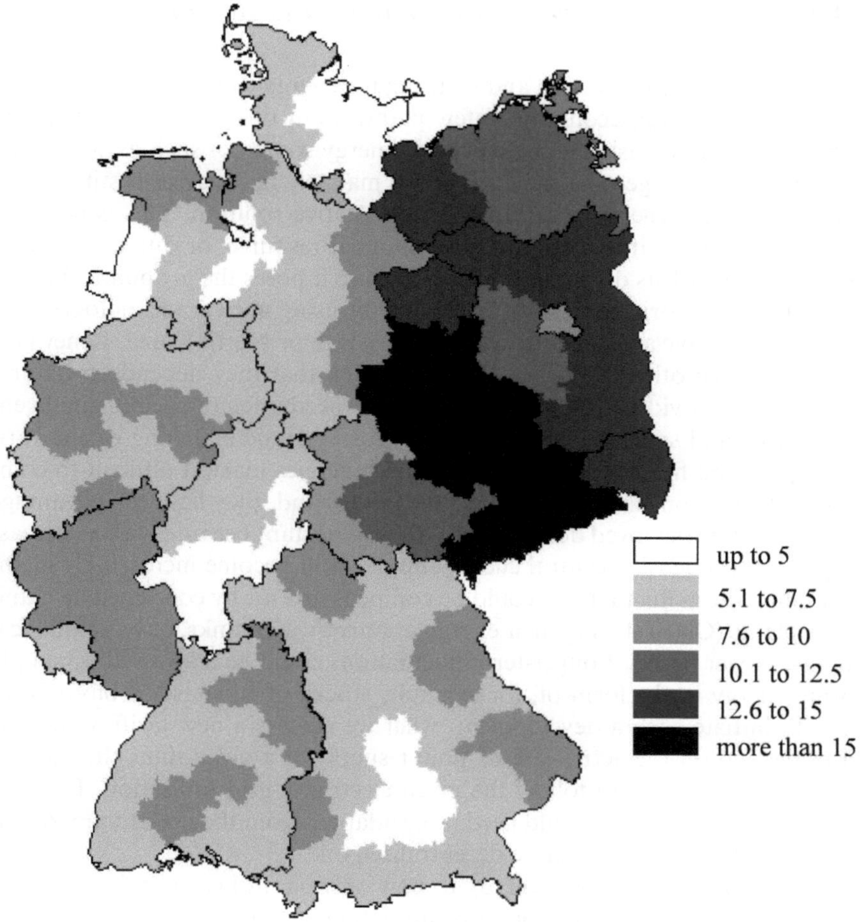

Fig. 6.5 Vacancies (in percent of all flats) in 2002 (data source: Statistisches Bundesamt, Federal Statistical Office – household survey; graphic: Berlin Institute for Population and Development

ones, it will offer the chance to correct current path dependencies and to move in the direction of sustainable development. In other areas which – independently of demographic developments – are already requiring immediate action, demographic change will be *the* dominant framework condition which will not only need to be accounted for when thinking about solutions but which will also considerably shape their form. Demographic change will add pressure on how we organise our energy supply, and it will make us reconsider our settlement structures and offer opportunities for minimising environmentally harmful transport modes. It might lead to large-scale building renovations which will help reduce our energy use (with a view to oil scarcity) and environmentally harmful emissions. The following sections highlight areas where such conceptions might be useful, and sketch the means by which they could be implemented.

6.4.5 A Change in Energy Consumption Is Required

Both active climate protection and securing the energy supply require a radical change in our energy economy. A few pathways in this direction already exist but the target of using climate neutral energy sources – such as sun, wind, water, biomass and geothermal energy – as main energy sources is still unrealistic, and nuclear energy is certainly no alternative solution. This is not only because – like oil – it is a quantitatively limited resource, or due to the unresolved problem of its disposal, but also because it poses the geopolitical issues of a potential terrorist attack, or the risk of diffusing nuclear technologies into politically unstable areas of the world such as Iran or North Korea. Renewable energies, on the other hand, have the drawback that they depend on natural elements and provide variable supply, and thus need interconnected, intelligent power grids and smart end-use appliances for dynamic matching of the variable supply and flexible demand. Renewable energies make it difficult to compensate fluctuations in energy use; on the other hand, they have the advantage that they can be deployed decentrally. This is important because with a decreasing population density, central energy supplies will become increasingly inefficient. Short-term fluctuations could be compensated for by combined heat and power plants (CHP) storing their energy in warm-water tanks, or by small local biomass power plants. Longer-term fluctuations could be addressed by simply storing energy in the form of, for example, stocks of biomass or biofuels. In order to initiate such a development, what we need is a new tariff system: if prices depend on the actual use of power supply at a given time, then use of power will soon start to follow the given electricity grid utilisation. Furthermore, the electricity grid would need to be adapted from the present predominantly central structure to a more decentralised one.

In terms of alternatives to oil, up to now only natural gas has the possibilities of becoming a fully feasible substitute. Similarly to oil, however, natural gas reserves are also expected to come to an end soon (cf. Fig. 6.6). Biofuels such as biodiesel, bio-ethanol, bio-gas and plant oil, in contrast, are expected

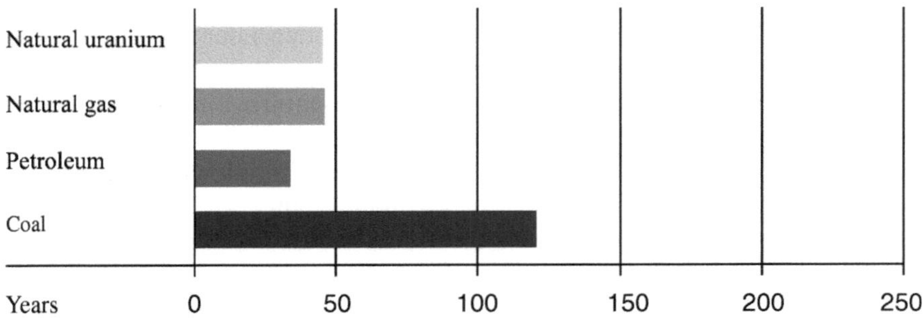

Fig. 6.6 Dynamic lifetimes of non-renewable fuel reserves (source: http://www.learnline.nrw.de/angebote/agenda21/lexikon/fossil.htm)

to be more promising in the long term. These technologies are being used already and still have potentials for maximising their production and minimising costs. The German Federal Government estimates that a 17% share of biofuels in total transport fuel consumption can be achieved by 2020 (BMU 2007). This projection, however, depends strongly on the rapid introduction and development of so-called second-generation biofuels (e.g. biomass to liquid) and essential progress in efficiency in the transport sector. Already in the next few years, hybrid cars with electric or incineration engines could contribute increasingly to fuel saving.

Irrespective of the origin of energy, e.g. whether it comes from fossil fuels or from renewable resources, costs for raw materials for energy are expected to increase. This could trigger innovative solutions and ideas to save or recycle many materials. Too many energy-saving opportunities are still unexplored, ranging from the use of compressed air in the industrial sector to improving energy efficiency in existing buildings. Savings of one third of current consumption seem feasible in the short run without large capital investments, but they may require some changes in our daily relationship towards energy consumption.

How such behavioural changes on the demand side could be triggered can be shown for the case of oil. The use of oil is rarely an aim in itself. Rather, it is expected to serve a particular aim such as getting from point A to point B, or warming an apartment. These uses, however, could already be much cheaper than they are without restraining their use. Energy intensity in Germany (energy use per unit of economic performance) decreased annually by an average of 1.8% from 1990 to 2004 (Deutscher Bundestag 2007). This gives only an idea of what would be possible if the government and the economy gave the right incentives to dramatically improve energy efficiency. A great potential can also be seen in the vehicle technology sector. Innovations such as the three-litre car, hybrid cars or similar existing technologies show that this potential exists but is not yet being fully exploited.

Setting the right incentives for changing behaviour is, therefore, central for adjusting the areas of oil and mobility to a future under changing demographic circumstances, at the same time making these move towards sustainability. For the implementation of this idea, the steering possibilities of energy prices offer several advantages. Political measures such as the ecological tax reform anticipate an oil price increase which will occur anyway due to future shortages. Because in this case price increases can be planned in steps and within foreseeable time frames, they offer planning security and set additional incentives for developing energy-efficient products, new technologies, and alternative energy forms. At the same time, price pressures make an investment into energy-efficient products like machines, power plants, heat insulation or lean cars more profitable, since investments which are initially more costly will soon pay back. Thus, the demand for energy-efficient products and services is also expected to increase. In addition, by making possible the internalisation of external costs, ecological taxes also mean that it is no longer the whole society which pays for the negative consequences of energy use and traffic, such as environmental pollution, injuries and deaths.

6.4.6 Energy, Settlements and Mobility Are Interconnected

But what about the spatial patterns of settlement and transport infrastructures, and their associated problems? Here, a concentration of settlements in the existing structures seems a reasonable way forwards in order to prevent a breakdown of public utilities and services, and to minimise soil sealing.

Concentrating settlements in the existing structures would imply a rediscovery of the city as residential area. While this has long been advocated by experts, a trend of "back to the city" has recently started to become reality (Müller and Siedentop 2004). In part, this is due to demographic trends: for the growing groups of pensioners, singles and single parents, living in the city has specific advantages. Perhaps more surprisingly, young families are also rediscovering the benefits of residing in cities. This is closely related to the good social infrastructure existing in most cities with regard to social services such as medical care, support structures for elderly and children, as well as a higher diversity of learning opportunities for children – but also to the richer cultural life which cities can offer.

However, the reclamation of urban areas is not going to happen on its own. It needs to be supported by an active policy approach aiming to create attractive living spaces, tailor-made for the needs of the aforementioned groups. Where local administrations succeed in attracting people from the middle of society from the outskirts back into the city, there are chances to reverse the vicious circle of inhospitality and social segregation. This could create a number of positive feedback loops:

- Trips needed for covering day-to-day activities, such as moving from home to work, will decrease because people will be able to run their errands within a smaller area. This would maintain the opportunities of mobility while causing less traffic. If prices for individual transport increased at the same time, this would not only result in shorter distances but could also trigger the development of alternative and new work forms, which can be done at home or near the home, such as not-for-profit work, care or education services. This would have as result the minimisation of traffic, and would contribute to making public transport an attractive alternative again.
- A trend back into the city could prevent additional consumption of land and surface. Most cities, even in booming regions, dispose of reserves of space which could be reactivated, provided that an effective space resource management is set in place. Former barracks, abandoned industrial sites or public estates no longer in use could offer new room whilst avoiding the use of new surfaces.
- Moreover, a redesign of urban residential areas could mobilise resources to energetically renovate old buildings. Many buildings could be renovated to a degree which would make them comparable to "passive houses", at costs which are comparably low and which would soon be paid off by the energy savings.

In regions which suffer continued losses of population, public utilities, services and cultural facilities will need to be concentrated at certain locations in order to remain affordable. Such concentration processes are already underway in a number of regions. In order to manage them sustainably, clear decisions would have to be made regarding which locations are to be further developed and which sites should be reduced in their functions, or even abandoned in a long-term perspective. It will also become necessary to explore alternative forms of providing public as well as private services (BMVBW 2005). An effective public transport system will be the precondition to make locations with centralised services accessible for the inhabitants of other communities, in particular those who are the least mobile and may at the same time have the highest need for such services in the region. This, again, will require innovative and flexible solutions – such as shared taxis or on-call buses – in order to satisfy the increasingly decentral demands at lower costs.

From the point of view of each municipality, concentrating inhabitants and functions in certain locations is currently not an attractive option. The tax system (income and business tax) continues to set incentives which lead municipalities to compete for inhabitants and businesses. In practice, such misleading incentives often prevail over planning principles, and prevent an economical handling of land-use matters. In addition, planning law requires municipalities to ensure accessibility of newly built housing areas by car but not by public transport.

In a similar line of thought, the financial equalisation scheme at municipal level could be reformed in a way which sets incentives for stopping the expansion of settlements, and preserving ecologically important and untouched surface areas, rather than basing it on the number of inhabitants and infrastructure offered. Reversing signals in this way could initiate an "economy of surfaces", thereby provoking competition for the best using surfaces among those already in use, instead of using new ones.

While a concentration of settlements may be the appropriate way *within* regions, the increasing imbalance *among* regions in Germany as a whole raises questions of another dimension. The dynamics of growth and shrinking within single regions is due mainly to migration movements from areas which are economically less attractive to areas which are economically more so. Such processes are self-energising. Moreover, shrinking areas are confronted not only with a social and economic downward spiral, but also with a loss of cultural heritage, including buildings as well as cultural landscapes: cultural heritage will decay where there is no one to take care of it, unless it is preserved by costly, museum-like conservation efforts. Likewise, cultural and natural heritage is endangered in growing regions, where a continuously high land-use pressure is exerted by a growing population and an expansion of settlements. Although potential remains to further increase the density of settlements in urban areas, the strategy obviously has its limits: the less semi-natural areas cities provide, the more their population will head for the suburbs. Furthermore, from an environmental and resource economics point of view, it is unwise to demolish buildings in one area, which is costly and creates waste, while using much material and energy to construct new buildings in other areas. Thus, a thorough assessment of options for the further development of regions would have to include all economic, social and environmental costs which would be caused by continued migration between "boom" and "loser" regions, ultimately resulting in a country where the former would be even more crowded than at present, while the latter would be depopulated at a scale far beyond what we are currently experiencing. Institutions like the Federal Office for Building and Regional Planning may be driven not only by self-interest when they criticise that spatial planning capacities are currently being abolished, rather than enhanced, while the opposite would be more adequate to meet the problems the country will face in the future.

The quality of a city as living area can also influence its economic perspectives. In times when the service sector expands, not only do people move to where the jobs are but also jobs move to where people go. So-called perforated cities bring opportunities which neither the city centres nor the suburbs of growth areas can offer. A moderate reduction of density, if well implemented, could generate attractive urban landscapes of completely new characteristics, far different from typical sterile suburbs.

For rural areas, some factors of needed structural change, such as the expansion of renewable energy sources, may also contribute to create new values and jobs. The Austrian regions of Styria and Burgenland provide an example of how regional development can be successfully combined with the promotion of innovative technologies. In these regions, which suffered from severe structural problems, an increased use of the abundant wood reserves for bioenergy had a far-reaching positive influence on overall economic dynamics (ARGE Neue Energie 2004). Maybe we should be somewhat cautious not to adhere to overly static forecasts about "growing" and "shrinking" regions. It is possible that population prognoses in some areas currently suffering from a loss of inhabitants will have to be adjusted in 20 years – upwards?

6.5 Natural Heritage – A Matter of Culture

The preceding section touched upon the question of how current trends affect the use of natural resources, as well as their availability. But beyond the mere "use" aspect of nature, what a society "gives back" to nature in terms of biological diversity should also be taken into consideration. Before discussing current challenges and expected trends in this regard, it is important to take stock of the present state of Germany's natural heritage (cf. Table 6.2).

6.5.1 Our Natural Heritage Is Cultural Heritage

Unlike other regions around the globe, the natural heritage of Germany and large parts of Europe is mostly embedded in cultural landscapes. Ecosystems

Table 6.2 Heritage and legacy in German nature conservation

Heritage	Legacy
Rich cultural landscapes which partly contain a high biological diversity	Almost no "pure" nature left
Strong, elaborated planning system	High levels of land consumption and dissection of habitats
Differentiated system of effectively managed protected areas in place	Monotonous forms and increasing homogenisation of land use
"Green Belt" along former internal border, unique in Europe	Ongoing losses of biodiversity
Strong tradition of voluntary engagement	Few large parks, few interconnections
	Large-area, persistent alterations of ecosystems by pollutants and nutrients

in Germany have been used and shaped by humans for thousands of years, resulting in the development of a multitude of habitats and landscapes. These ecosystems are characterised by the mutual influence of natural conditions and human activity; they reflect many different patterns of land use and expose high dynamics of change (Konold 1998). Agriculture, as the dominating form of land use, has always played an ambivalent role. On the one hand, it pushed back the original ecosystems and, ultimately, eliminated these for the most part. On the other hand, many species have been introduced as a result of agricultural activity, and now depend on specific forms of land use.

6.5.2 *Conservation Versus Development: Leading the Way into the Impasse?*

Nature conservation in Germany has a relatively long tradition. Through its history, its concepts have changed considerably, reflecting changing societal conditions. The origins of the idea of nature conservation lie in the movement for the protection of nature and heritage of the late 19th century, which aimed at preserving individual natural monuments and traditional cultural landscapes within a broader notion of "homeland" preservation. During the second half of the 20th century, the concept of nature conservation became more closely linked to ecological science. The current understanding of nature conservation has developed during the past 30 years. Its predominant goal is to preserve species and biotopes. Its main instruments are of the command-and-control type, combined with voluntary measures such as nature conservation by contract and agri-environmental measures. The focus still lies on the conservation and maintenance of nature and landscapes, rather than on their development and sustainable use. This strategy has undeniably led to certain achievements and contributed substantially to the safeguarding of natural heritage in Germany. On the whole, however, nature conservation measures have not succeeded in halting the unfavourable effects of intensive land use in a densely settled country, such as the continued loss of species and biotopes (EEA 2004).

6.5.3 Forces of Change

A salient feature of the current demographic trend in Germany is that the population increasingly accumulates in certain regions, while its density decreases in others. This will also have consequences for nature conservation. As a general rule, land-use pressure tends to increase in "boom" regions, while it decreases in regions with net losses of people. However, when analysing the impacts and opportunities this implies for nature conservation, other forces of change need to be taken into account.

Agriculture and forestry, which together account for approximately 83% of the total surface of Germany, will undergo dramatic changes as a result of both economic forces and the evolution of the regulatory framework. To start with the regulatory framework, the recent agricultural policy reform in the European Union (EU) has decoupled subsidies from agricultural production, rather granting farmers direct payments for their cultivated land. These payments are coupled with certain production standards recognised as being in the common interest, such as environmentally friendly crop growing, food safety, and animal-friendly husbandry. This change in agricultural policy was also driven by the rules of the World Trade Organisation (WTO), which provide that subsidies may not be paid without any conditions, but only when additional performances are delivered. Having coupled the payments with standards which serve, inter alia, the conservation of landscapes and biological diversity, the EU claims to meet the WTO rules. However, the ongoing WTO negotiations will exert pressure to move even further away from the traditional system of agricultural subsidies.

For which markets will agriculture produce in future? In addition to highly specialised farms, some farms' strategy will be based on a diversification as broad as possible. A combination of food, animal feed and energy crop production, livestock farming, landscape conservation, and rural tourism could develop as a model for a new agriculture. The need for securing future energy supply makes it very probable that the cultivation of energy crops, in particular, will have much more importance than it has today. Biomass may substitute for fossil fuels in transport as well as in heat and electricity generation. Policies to support its use, at least in the areas of transport and electricity generation, are already in place at both national and EU levels, and will certainly be developed further.

In a mid-term perspective which takes ecological aspects into account, the area available for energy crops in Germany is estimated at 2 million hectares, which would correspond to roughly the double of the currently used area. Energy crop cultivation in this order of magnitude would be possible without competing with food and feed crops, and without bringing into question the area needed for nature conservation (Schlegel et al. 2005). However, if more ambitious bioenergy goals are envisaged, 2 million ha will not be enough to guarantee the biomass supply required.

Domestic prospects for future agriculture, including energy crop cultivation, are inevitably linked to global developments (Bringezu and Steger 2005): not only is there a need to feed a still increasing human population, while millions of hectares of fertile soil are lost each year due to desertification; not only is there competition between use of land which provides for meat consumption in rich countries, and the cultivation of food crops which could support a greater number of people in poorer ones. With the need to explore alternative energy sources at a global scale, competition between food crops and energy crops will increase; costs for food and energy will be linked to each other even more strongly than at present, and the costs for both will rise. Meeting the existing bioenergy targets (the European Union's Biomass Action Plan of 2005 sets a target of a 5.75% biofuel share in overall transport-related fuel consumption in 2010) already means that the EU will have to import significant amounts of biofuels from export countries such as Brazil and Indonesia. As there are growing concerns on negative social and environmental impacts in the production of biofuels in these countries, the EU will have a strong interest in producing high proportions of the required biofuels domestically. This will also increase the pressure on agricultural land in Germany, which has – although it has taken the lead in biofuel production in Europe – not yet met the 5.75% target. Meanwhile, in March 2007 the European Council set a target of a 10% biofuel share in overall transport fuel consumption for 2020, while the German Federal Government is evaluating the possibility of a 17% share target for that date (BMU 2007).

To sum up, there is little prospect that the anticipated decrease in population numbers will significantly remove land-use pressure in Germany. It also needs to be taken into account that modern, rationalised forms of agriculture require relatively little labour force and are, therefore, well feasible in regions with a low population density (Heiland 2007).

In addition, the challenges which climate change will pose in the next decades need to be considered. The effects of climate change will not be limited to modifying our patterns of occupying and using space – by forcing us to move settlements, industries, and land transport networks away from river plains and low-lying coastal areas, as well as altering the conditions for agricultural activity. Climate change will also affect the distribution patterns of species and ecosystems. Plant and animal populations which used to be connected with each other may become isolated. Additional stress may be imposed on these populations by competition from newly immigrated species. Ultimately, climate change threatens to accelerate the extinction (at least at the local and regional scale) of wild species as well as domestic animals and cultivated plants. In order to enable species to react flexibly to the aforementioned changes, habitats need to be functionally connected with each other at a large scale (Finck et al. 2005).

Furthermore, the climate change-induced shift of ecosystems will also affect protected areas within their present boundaries. As a consequence, the conservation targets of existing reserves may become obsolete, or they may be more effectively reached elsewhere.

6.5.4 *Preserving Nature by Allowing for Change*

Despite the anticipated decline in total population numbers, many parts of Germany will remain densely settled. In such regions, there will be little scope for establishing new protected areas of significant dimensions: experience shows that one important limiting factor is the opposition from those affected by restrictions of land use (Stoll-Kleemann 2001). Instead of this option, concepts need to be developed for nature conservation in urban areas, which will fundamentally differ from those for rural areas (Millennium Ecosystem Assessment 2005). There are potentials to enhance the ecological value of green spaces as well as wastelands. Even the temporary use of land for nature conservation, before it is reused for new settlements or industry, could make sense. While our present hierarchical system of land-use planning has its undisputed advantages, it may nevertheless impose unnecessary restrictions to such a temporary use of space: the German planning system provides only for "final" use categories, and does not contain the notion of intermediate use. This should be changed by deregulating planning procedures to a certain degree, or at least building some flexibility into existing mechanisms.

With respect to agriculture, the opportunities and limits for nature conservation need to be assessed for both diversified and highly specialised farms. In the context of bioenergy production, there are opportunities for nature conservation in those cases where the crops used do not necessitate intensive cultivation, but rather may also be cultivated with extensive methods. The further development of the technologies which transform biomass into synthetic fuels ("biomass to liquid", BTL) can exert a positive influence because this technology allows a broader range of biomass resources, and whole plants can be used, as opposed to only seeds or fruits. This allows for more extensive farming processes such as mixed crop systems which are less sensitive to weeds. Regionalised processing and use of energy crops are further preconditions for a sustainable bioenergy economy.

In regions with decreasing population, there are chances to reverse some of the detrimental effects of urban sprawl and habitat fragmentation. In some areas of Germany, agriculture and forestry use will diminish, or will be reduced to a level of activity requiring only minimal effort being invested in their maintenance. For such areas, the option of allowing nature's own dynamics to take over should be considered (Bengtsson et al. 2003). This could take the form of a natural succession of ecosystems on formerly cultivated areas, following a "wilderness" model, but also of allowing for some semi-controlled natural river dynamics in flood plains or abandoning certain areas for a limited time. A large-scale “re-dynamisation” of landscapes should be initiated at sites where this is feasible, such as former agricultural land, abandoned mining sites, or military areas. A further development of large-scale reserves, following the concept of biosphere reserves, would be particularly promising as these are based on an integrated concept of natural and cultural heritage. With their explicit inclusion of human activity and its development in accordance with the regional conditions, they allow for the preservation and further development of cultural landscapes, as well as “wilderness” with unrestricted natural succession in their core areas.

Reforming nature conservation for the 21st century, in order to keep it relevant under altered circumstances, can succeed only if there is an increased use of new instruments and if innovative ways are found to mobilise the resources needed. In the long run, it will not suffice to limit the application of new instruments and ideas to isolated pilot projects. Instead, the concepts and instruments of nature conservation should undergo a general overhaul. For some instruments, the experience has so far been obtained mainly abroad, as is the case with the private management of protected sites through rental or leasing (Emerton et al. 2005), or the application of tradable rights for specific forms of land use. Other types of instruments which could be further explored include compensation and transfer payments by the beneficiaries of nature use, incentive-based instruments such as the agri-environment schemes of the European Union, and fiscal instruments such as tax rebates offered for nature-friendly forms of use which go beyond mandatory standards.

In general, establishing economic incentives contributes to an efficient use of public money. In particular, integrating the conservation of biological diversity into the regular production process has proved more effective than any a posteriori corrective measures. Wherever possible, synergies between nature conservation objectives and other interests should be explored so as to create multifunctional forms of land use (OECD 2001). Tourism and leisure industries – which at present are among the most dynamic and flourishing markets in Germany – have a key role to play here. There are, for instance, already examples of “ecological” golf courses.

A model of nature conservation which is almost exclusively financed and effected by government will not be possible to sustain in the future. New ways of cooperation need to be explored which combine governmental with private initiatives to finance and implement nature conservation measures (DNR 2005). An example of how this could be implemented is the transfer of management rights for the “Green Belt” (those areas of high ecological value which developed along the border formerly dividing the two Germanies) to the German Environmental Foundation (Deutsche Bundesstiftung Umwelt). On the whole, it will be necessary to establish the conservation of natural heritage as a task of the whole society, providing more than in the past for an involvement of all relevant stakeholders. Nature conservation can no longer be regarded as a matter to be addressed exclusively by environmentalists and the state.

6.6 Conclusion: The Challenge of Adaptation

Venice and New Orleans have to prepare for it, Winchelsea has already experienced it. Around 1200 a.d., the town was the second largest seaport in the British Kingdom, the home of fishermen, merchants, sailors and pirates. Three decades later, heavy storms began afflicting the town again and again, over five decades. Ultimately, Winchelsea could not continue resisting – but it survived its own destruction by the waves.

The citizens, who repeatedly decided to rebuild a living place in the exact same locality, realised after the continuous repetition that this approach needed to be abandoned. They finally rebuilt their town on higher land. It was from there that, in 1287, they watched their old town being devoured by the sea. They could not rescue their homes and churches but the economic foundations of the seaport remained, and therewith its political and military standing (Pratt 2005).

The lesson to be drawn from this story is twofold: decline does not need to be an inescapable fate, and cherished customs often keep us from taking the right decisions. Much time and money were devoted to reconstructing houses and stores, and to fortifying embankments and docks. The underlying reflexes, formidably depicted by Jared Diamond in his book “Collapse” (Diamond 2005), are familiar to us and are behind our habit of keeping old industries alive through subsidies, and continually rebuilding the same dwellings and commercial buildings on the same sites which are hit by floods.

But the story is not only about the persistence of obsolete structures and habits. The turning point was reached on the occasion of a particularly disastrous storm. From that day on, the repression of uncomfortable truths gave way to a forward-looking view, facing the challenge to build a new, sustainable town. Once it was evident the final catastrophe would come, it took only about 30 years to set the course for a recommencement – not a long time span, in those days. This was helped by a strong local self-government and a good organisation of public matters. Other factors contributing to success were affluence, entrepreneurial spirit, and courage, as well as the discipline shown in the construction of the new town. Last but not least, the municipality received new lands as a gift from the king.

The aforementioned virtues, as well as external support, will also be needed by cities which find themselves at the wrong place in view of global change today. Those same virtues will be necessary for Germany and the whole of Europe to adjust to a change which will demand from us far more than a reconfiguration of our settlement structures. We will also need the courage of that time in order not only to recognise the inevitable consequences of certain latent, long-term developments but also to radically spell these out. A variety of issues must now be tabled with a sober mind, and without inappropriate deference to traditions and vested rights. The more we try to repress the problems and postpone the solutions, the bigger the loss and the larger the expenses which will be incurred to adjust our systems.

Incidentally, structural change, “productive destruction”, is also an invariable sign of economic dynamics. The following example gives a hint at the positive dynamics which may be created when new circumstances are factored in. Since 2005, emission allowances for carbon dioxide (CO_2) have been distributed to companies according to the European Emissions Trading Directive. This has created values which circulate on the market and enter into company accounts. Moreover, a considerable part of the economic activities induced by emissions trading leads to increases in tax revenue, which could in turn be used to finance social security or other matters of public interest.

It shall not be denied that the system still has to surmount considerable problems in order to be recognised as both an ecologically effective and economically efficient instrument, the most serious challenge being the need of a firm commitment to create real scarcity on the market: when it became evident that the overall allocation of emission rights for the first trading period had been far too generous, allowance prices faced a meltdown. In spring 2007, they plummeted to lows of less than 30 cent per tonne of CO_2 – only 1% of their peak-time levels of 2005 and 2006. This should not distract us from recognising that market-based instruments can in principle help transform the economic basis, mitigate the economic consequences of change, and stabilise public finances.

Even though an adaptation of structures will help make the best out of the challenges we are facing, there will be losers and they will require support. This implies that we need not only market transformation but also new burden-sharing mechanisms in our society. In the past century, Germany experienced tremendous economic, social and demographic upheavals – and ultimately managed to cope with these (Miegel 2002). This can be exemplified by the demographic disruptions following the First World War, or the integration of millions of war refugees in the 1950s. At those times, radical measures were taken in order to compensate for cases of hardship.

Even though the idea will not be popular among those in the south and west of Germany, the present financial equalisation scheme between the Federal Government and the States will probably prove inadequate to the challenges ahead. These concern not only public finance: an instrument is needed to provide for some compensation for the differences between those citizens who are lucky and those struck by bad luck. It must be possible to rescue individuals from economically hopeless situations, similarly to the system of financial compensation for losses suffered in the Second World War which helped many people rebuild their livelihoods. In terms of tomorrow's challenges, this could apply to homeowners whose houses have lost their value because they are situated in a "shrinking" region with excess supply of housing space, or to people who live in areas which will be eradicated by sea-level rise.

The phenomenon of shrinking public budgets is only one side of the coin. Capital incomes are growing and many billions of euros are inherited each year by private persons. Moreover, debt and capital income are intimately linked to each other. While there is a common complaint in Germany that not enough money is available to finance desirable action, it should not be forgotten that an incredible amount of wealth has been accumulated in this country during several decades of peaceful and stable development.

However, there will be no acceptance of compensating others for their losses and bad luck if the perception is that the money maintains unsustainable structures. Public money is needed to support transition; it is wasted where it is spent in order to maintain obsolete structures and technologies, in a misguided attempt to avoid, or postpone, transition. A common understanding in society will have to be built regarding the perception of problems (such as demographic and climatic change), and the ways society should respond to these. This means information and communication at all levels, in a sense which enables truly democratic decision making.

The history of environmental policy, in particular, is full of alarming prophecies which did not materialise. But not every such prophecy is wrong: prophecies succeed when they trigger adequate counteraction and, therefore, do not come true. Modern information technologies provide us access to an unprecedented wealth of knowledge. They also enable us to better describe and understand complex systems. We can therefore react earlier and better in our efforts to adapt to future developments than was possible in Winchelsea around 1200 a.d. Just as we can now look back at past decades and centuries to explain how they contributed to shape today's world, we are able to think far ahead. This ability, however, requires practice; and few of us actually think beyond the present.

Moreover, a culture of scrutiny and thinking in alternatives has entered the scientific as well as political practice. It should be much easier for us than it was in past centuries to leave behind outdated truths and misguided dogmas in order to clear the way for new ideas and impulses. Three quarters of a millennium after the events of Winchelsea, we in Germany and Europe are called on to tackle the global and regional problems we are facing, making use of all scientific and technical instruments at our disposal, and to create the necessary political, legal and economic frameworks.

References

ARGE Neue Energie (2004) Stadt mit neuer Energie. Stadtentwicklungskonzept: Gräfenhainichen. Zwischenbericht, Dezember 2004. http://www.dr-kegler.de/sek_04_12_13.pdf

Bengtsson J, Angelstam P, Elmqvist T, Emanuelsson U, Folke C, Ihse M, Moberg F, Nyström M (2003) Reserves, resilience and dynamic landscapes. AMBIO 32(6):389–396

BMU (2007) Klimaagenda 2020: der Umbau der Industriegesellschaft. Hintergrundpapier, Bundesministerium für Umwelt, Naturschutz und Reaktorsicherheit (BMU), Berlin, 26 April 2007. http://www.bmu.de/files/pdfs/allgemein/application/pdf/hintergrund_klimaagenda.pdf

BMVBW (2004) Verkehr in Zahlen 2004/2005. Bundesministerium für Verkehr, Bau- und Wohnungswesen (BMVBW), Berlin/Bonn, pp 216–217

BMVBW (2005) Öffentliche Daseinsvorsorge und demographischer Wandel, Erprobung von Anpassungs- und Entwicklungsstrategien in Modellvorhaben der Raumordnung. Bundesministerium für Verkehr, Bau- und Wohnungswesen (BMVBW), Berlin/Bonn

Bringezu S, Steger S (2005) Biofuels and competition for global land use. In: Berger H (ed) Bio im Tank: Chancen, Risiken, Nebenwirkungen. Dokumentation Fachtagung, 15. April 2005, Berlin. Heinrich-Böll-Stiftung 2005, pp 64–79

Bruns E, Herberg A, Köppel J (2005) Flächen- und Massnahmenpools in Deutschland. Konzepte, Management und naturschutzfachliche Standards. Natur Landschaft 80(3):89–95
Deutscher Bundestag (2007) Antwort der Bundesregierung auf die Kleine Anfrage der Abgeordneten Dr. Reinhard Loske, Hans-Josef Fell und der Fraktion BÜNDNIS 90/DIE GRÜNEN. Drucksache 16/4655. Energieeffizienz voranbringen, Drucksache 16/5026 vom 18.04.2007
Diamond J (2005) Collapse. Penguin, New York
DNR (2005) Langfristige Finanzierungsansätze zur Sicherung des nationalen Naturerbes. Deutscher Naturschutzring (DNR) Berlin, p 132
EEA (2004) The state of biological diversity in the European Union. European Environmental Agency (EEA). Paper EU Stakeholder Conf Biodiversity and the EU – Sustaining Life, Sustaining Livelihoods. Malahide, May 2004
Emerton L, Bishop J, Thomas L (2005) Sustainable financing of protected areas: a global review of challenges and options. IUCN, Gland, Switzerland
Finck P, Riecken U, Ullrich K (2005) Europäische Dimension des Biotopverbundes in Deutschland. Natur Landschaft 80(8):364–369
Göschel A (2003) Stadtumbau – zur Zukunft schrumpfender Städte vor allem in den neuen Bundesländern. In: Bundesamt für Bauwesen und Raumordnung (ed) Informationen zur Raumentwicklung 10/11. Bonn, pp 605–616
Hauff V, Bachmann G (eds) (2006) Unterm Strich. Erbschaften und Erblasten für das Deutschland von morgen. Eine Generationenbilanz. Oekom, München, http://www.oekom.de
Heiland S (2007) Demographischer Wandel – (k)ein Thema für die Zukunft des Naturschutzes? Natur Landschaft 82(1):2–5
Konold W (1998) Raum-zeitliche Dynamik von Kulturlandschaften und Kulturlandschaftselementen. Eugen Ulmer, Stuttgart, Naturschutz Landschaftsplanung 30(8/9):279–284
Miegel M (2002) Die deformierte Gesellschaft. Propyläen, München
Millennium Ecosystem Assessment (2005) Ecosystems and Human Well-Being: Synthesis. Island Press, Washington, DC
Müller B, Siedentop S (2004) Wachstum und Schrumpfung in Deutschland – Trends, Perspektiven und Herausforderungen für die räumliche Planung und Entwicklung. Deutsche Zeitsch Kommunalwissensch 43(1):14–32
OECD (2001) Multifunctionality: towards an analytical framework. Organisation for Economic Co-operation and Development (OECD), Paris
Pratt M (2005) Winchelsea: the tale of a medieval town. Malcolm Pratt, Bexhill-on-Sea, http://www.winchelsea.net
Schlegel S, Kraemer RA, Schaffrin D (2005) Bodenschutz und nachwachsende Rohstoffe. Gutachten im Auftrag der Kommission Bodenschutz. UBA FKZ 360 13 006
Stoll-Kleemann S (2001) Opposition to the designation of protected areas in Germany. J Environ Planning Management 44(1):109–128

Chapter 7
Intergenerational Justice in an Extreme Longevity Scenario

Ulrich Feeser-Lichterfeld

7.1 Introduction

Justice between generations has always been regarded as a thorny issue. Complex and unstable intergenerational relations call for continuously revised definitions. At present, the demographic challenge of low fertility and increasing longevity requires a new debate about intergenerational justice. The fear of an unjust burden for younger and future generations resulting from the altering ratio between the age groups in society needs to be addressed. At the same time, we need to strengthen the arguments regarding the value of aging and the continuity of intergenerational solidarity.

This chapter presents an attempt to pursue these issues by focusing on a key aspect: the extreme longevity scenario caused by biogerontological intervention. Life expectancy has been increasing steadily for the past 150 years, and there is no indication as to when this trend will end. Moreover, several anti-ageing strategies, exploring possibilities to postpone ageing and extend the human lifespan, may further contribute to this development. It is an open question as to what the consequences for the intergenerational relationship would be in the wake of the hypothetical dissemination of life-extending techniques. In this context, I challenge the common convictions that prolongation of the human lifespan would primarily be an advantage for the elderly. However, life extension and rejuvenation research strives for the benefit of people in the middle of their life and the so-called young elderly, and not for the benefit of people in their last period of life. It is with respect to these former groups that aging tends to be defined as a treatable disease. My argument is that frailty and finiteness may fall prey to a new kind of ageism at the expense of all generations.

Joerg Chet Tremmel (Ed.) *Demographic Change and Intergenerational Justice*
DOI 10.1007/978-3-540-77084-8 © Springer 2008

7.2 The Truth About the Fountain of Youth?

In Jonathan Swift's best-known novel "Gulliver's Travels", the protagonist meets a citizen of Luggnagg who tells him that in his country a child is born every few years with a distinctive mark signifying that he or she will never die. Such births are extremely rare, so that no more than 1,100 immortals – called "Struldbruggs" – live in Luggnagg. The family into which such a person is born is a mere coincidence. Furthermore, the children of the Struldbruggs are as mortal as the rest of the population. Gulliver responds to this enthusiastically: "Happy Nation where every Child hath at least a chance of being immortal! Happy People who enjoy so many living Examples of Ancient Virtue, and have Masters ready to instruct them in the Wisdom of all former Ages! But, happiest beyond all comparison are those excellent Struldbruggs, who being born exempt from that universal Calamity of human Nature, have their Minds free and disengaged, without the weight and depression of Spirits caused by the continual Apprehension of Death" (Swift 2003).

However, Gulliver's conversational partner assesses immortality in a completely different way: he points out that the system of living, contrived by Gulliver, is unreasonable and unjust because it supposes a perpetuity of youth, health and vigour, which no man can be foolish enough to hope for however extravagant his wishes may be. In his view, the question therefore is not whether a man would choose to always be in the prime of youth with prosperity and health, but rather how would he spend a perpetual life under all the usual disadvantages brought by old age. Swift describes the Struldbruggs above all as melancholic and stingy, as people with failing memories and ugly bodies, despised and hated by all others. As soon as they have completed the term of 80 years, they are legally considered dead; the heirs immediately obtain their estates and only a small pittance is reserved for their support.

Is the situation in Luggnagg simply a masterpiece of fiction or a serious outlook on future generations? Without doubt, Jonathan Swift was referring in his novel to the eternal dream of conquering the effects of time and continuing life, even infinitely. Written in 1726, Gulliver's journey to Luggnagg appears satirical against the background of contemporary efforts in the search for the fountain of youth. About 100 years earlier, for example, Francis Bacon illustrated special research centres in "New Atlantis" (1624). These centres perform experiments on the prolongation of human life, leading to unforeseen prosperity and satisfaction. Only a few years later in his "Discours de la méthode" (1637), René Descartes argued for medical progress, resulting in a considerable reduction of senescence.

Such goals seem to be the historical background for current endeavours under the label of "biogerontology". Intensive attempts to explore the biological basis of aging and modulate the aging process have been undertaken. For example, on the basis of remarkable results from animal experiments (e.g. Austad 2002; Arking 2005), the following approaches are under discussion.

- Consistent caloric restriction – this procedure has protected the animals involved from many causes of illness and extended their lives by 40% or more (e.g. Roth 2005).
- The use of the human growth hormone seems to increase muscle mass and strengthen the immune system, two factors which may facilitate a longer lifespan (e.g. Walker and Bercu 2002).
- Antioxidants such as vitamins A, C and E are largely used to fight the harmful effects of free radicals (see Arking 2004).
- Major recent achievements in the effort to prolong the human lifespan include different forms of gene therapy allowing for an extension of the cell capacity to divide before dying. In this context, telomeres play a very prominent role. These ends of chromosomes potentially trigger the process by which cells progressively exhaust their capacity to maintain and repair themselves.
- Finally, another discussion focuses on the possibility to genetically program embryonic stem cells in order to repair and rejuvenate specific tissues or organs (e.g. Ho et al. 2005).

Some proposed interventions seem so moderate that any effects would likely be minor. However, others aim at radical changes in the familiar aging process. How far towards immortality can biomedical technology take us still remains to be seen. However, we need not wait for this promise to mature before considering more closely what it would mean to live significantly longer than we do at present. In my view, the hypothetical longevity scenario helps to find a well-defined position in relationship to age and the elderly. In this sense, it can serve the necessary discussion of intergenerational relationships.

7.3 Ethical Issues in Biogerontological Endeavours

The proposal of extreme longevity raises many individual and societal issues. This chapter will not focus on the so-called war on anti-aging (Binstock 2003), in which mainstream biogerontologists try to defend the acquired "credibility of serious scientific research efforts on aging" (Olshansky et al. 2002) from proponents of the idea of prolongevity and immortality. The central point of the following short presentation on the ethical debate is rather concerned with the question of whether it is morally acceptable to enhance human beings by means of biotechnology. There is an intensive dispute about the differences between the use of biotechnology for, on the one hand, treating the ill or relieving suffering and, on the other hand, applications "beyond therapy" (cf. The President's Council on Bioethics 2003; Fuchs et al. 2002).

Regarding the prospect of an extra long life (cf. Fuchs 2006), there is a debate on the naturalness of age and aging. Prima facie, prolongation is a clear form of enhancement. The idea that most people could live 150 years or more appears to be a perfection of human nature. If we interpret aging as evolutionarily senseless and in no way as an intrinsic part of human life, then "there is no reason why it is intrinsically wrong to try to reserve or cure aging" (Caplan 2004). At the level of genetics and biochemistry, there simply does not seem to be a meaningful distinction between "processes predisposing to or constituting disease" and "normal aging" (Bostrom 2005). Furthermore, according to this view, "any delay in the development of rejuvenation therapies means that thousands of people, who could have been saved, will get cancer, Alzheimer's disease, heart disease, arteriosclerosis, and other age-related ailments, and will die as a result" (ibid. sic.). This position shows how aging is inextricably linked to age-associated diseases.

Moderate scientists emphasise the compression of morbidity (Fries 1980, 2003) as the desirable therapeutic goal and potential practical payoff of aging research, according to the motto "adding life to years, not years to life". The aim of successive postponement of the onset of morbidity is to improve the ratio of "healthspan" to "frailspan". In the view of more ambitious biogerontologists, this strategy of better treatment for particular diseases is likely to yield only a modest increase in health expectancy. Only by slowing or reversing the underlying biological processes of senescence would significant gains in healthy lifespan be possible (see, for example, de Grey et al. 2002).

Opponents of anti-aging caution against the attitude that medicine has a duty to cure all diseases and to combat all causes of death. Rather, Daniel Callahan, for example, pleads for an imperative to accept aging as a part of life in order to make dying as tolerable as possible (Callahan 2000).

7.4 Consequences for Intergenerational Justice?

In the following, this chapter aims to draw attention to possible social consequences of a hypothetical future dissemination of life-extending techniques, in particular to some intergenerational justice issues. For the lack of an elaborate theory of justice with a view to such an extreme longevity scenario, a fragmentary list of critical points and open questions is given below.

1. The foreseeable demographic change in Western societies will force an ever smaller percentage of young people to work and create a basis for the medical care and social security taxes for an ever larger percentage of elderly people. Potentially, lifespan-enhancing technologies could strengthen this trend in a fatal way. Instead of research on life extension, so the argument is often heard, there should be a debate on the allocation of health resources. These should give all people the opportunity of reaching the normal lifespan, within a limit natural to our species. In contrast, the elderly who have passed it would be an appropriate and justified target for withholding such resources (e.g. Callahan 1995).

   Richard Miller labels such an argument with the term "gerontologiphobia". He notices "an irrational public predisposition to regard research on specific late-life diseases as marvellous but to regard research on aging, and thus on all late-life diseases together, as a public menace bound to produce a world filled with nonproductive, chronically disabled, unhappy senior citizens consuming more resources than they produce" (Miller 2004). Furthermore, it has to be emphasised that such a phobia ignores the real goal of biogerontology: to prolong the productive and healthy periods of life – not to promote a "national nursing home" (Fukuyama 2002).

2. At present, the elderly are the main recipients of public income transfer programs, whereas children, for example, are to a large part privately financed by their parents. Such an unequal allocation of public resources among age groups may be considered "unfair" but it seems to be perfectly legitimate. All individuals potentially progress through the life course from one age group to the next. As a consequence, treating people differently at different ages, provided we do so systematically over the lifespan, does not seem to create inequalities across persons (Daniels 1988, 2006; for a detailed critique, see Hübner 2001).

   However, this concept must be questioned with regard to an extreme longevity scenario. It seems very likely that only a small part of society will be able to test and enjoy the benefits of life-extending techniques. As a consequence, the dispersion of life expectancy around the mean would noticeably increase, and the age-relative fair share of opportunities would become increasingly impossible. Apart from the ethical issue of an appropriate access to these technologies, the question arises as to whether groups with shorter "natural" life expectancy should help finance the benefits for those living significantly longer. This point shows the close connection between questions of intergenerational and intragenerational equity (cf. Kohli 2006).

3. In contrast to the changing membership in age groups, one cannot leave a generation in the sense of a birth cohort. Most people will agree that the intergenerational sharing of burden and reward is fair to the extent that each generation, as it moves up through the stages of life, can expect to receive the same treatment as the preceding and the following ones. On the other hand, the continuously changing context already limits such a claim of equal treatment. Biotechnologies, for example, which were not available for the elderly when they were young but will be available over the lifespan of those now young, pose a special problem of intercohort equity (Daniels 2006).

4. Today, it seems to be that most of the intergenerational conflicts focus on the distribution of resources between, on the one hand, the "baby boomers" and their parents and, on the other hand, the proponents of the younger birth cohorts. Public issues of aging are at present, above all, issues of social security and the welfare state. The opinion is growing that the elderly have been the recipients of an unfairly high share of public resources at the expense of younger and future generations.

   In this view of generational equity, the varied experiences of generation interdependence and solidarity cannot be adequately considered. For example, the public resources flowing to older adults have often enabled them to transfer resources to their offspring in turn. The public generational contract is partly balanced by a private one in the opposite direction (see Kohli 2006). The significant extension of the human lifespan would bring forward multi-generational families and put the voluntary transfer functions at risk. In an extreme longevity scenario, thinking and acting in categories such as "generation" can only make limited sense. Where people live open-ended, there may be less interest in families or intergenerational relations and, for example, in their part in providing assistance and support.

5. Finally, there is a more emotional or psychological question: is the aim of prolongation with the idea of being "forever young" perhaps a fundamental mistake? Who is going to produce fresh inputs and innovative proposals, given such a long lifespan? Relationships and interactions between different age groups and generations seem to be the best protection against rigidity and the vital condition for generativity.

7.5 Anti-aging or Acceptance of Frailty and Finiteness? – A Question for All Generations

The desire to live "forever" is not predominantly "an expression of [a] childish and narcissistic wish" of the already elderly and, for this reason, "incompatible with devotion to posterity" (Kass 2004). Rather, life extension and rejuvenation research tends to emphasise the negative aspects of growing old, rather than differentiating aging processes from age-associated diseases. Many results in gerontology are opposed to the assumption that adulthood is the apex of life, for which childhood is the preparation and of which old age is merely the decline. With this background in mind, attempts to stop, slow or reverse aging are in the full literal sense an expression of anti-aging medicine which promotes a new kind of ageism. If we take the view that growing old is a pathological process which calls for prevention or cure, we are questioning the existential limits of the human condition, its frailty and finiteness. However: "Aging [...] offers opportunities (though not equal opportunity) to become more fulfilled as human beings" (Cole and Thompson 2001/2002).

In my opinion, the cultural discussion on the future of aging, as well as biogerontological research, has to reflect the "goodness of fragility" (Parens 2003) and the "blessing of mortality" (Jonas 1992). Anti-aging seems to point in a dehumanising direction and to aggravate generational conflicts. Furthermore, the preservation of the dignity of the life cycle, including age and old age, is in the interest of all generations, the present and the future – subject to the condition of persisting temporality and mortality of human beings. For this reason, issues of intergenerational relationships need to stabilize the solidarity within society, especially between the different age groups. This implies the respect for all age groups and the different stages of life. In this context, I see the benefit of discussing such a hypothetical extreme longevity scenario in order to face the problems of justice between the generations.

This scenario demonstrates the fatal consequences of the attempt to postpone or defeat old age and to modify the human life cycle in a fundamental way. Radical anti-ageing strategies cannot provide a basis for intergenerational solidarity and intergenerational justice. Nevertheless, both principle denial and unconstrained promotion of biogerontological techniques cannot allow for adequately dealing with the complex process we call "aging". It is not only a biological process but also a psychological and cultural one. For this reason, the question of how to reflect multidimensional aging requires more than a biological or a medical answer. I am convinced that only a broader discussion on the future of aging will be able to protect against fatalism as well as age discrimination.[1]

References

Arking R (2004) Extending human longevity: a biological probability. In: Post SG, Binstock RH (eds) The fountain of youth: cultural, scientific, and ethical perspectives on a biomedical goal. Oxford University Press, Oxford, pp 177–200

Arking R (2005) Biology, fruit flies, and humans: can extended longevity stretch from one to other? The Gerontologist 3/2005:418–425

Austad SN (2002) Adding years to life: current knowledge and future prospects. http://www.bioethics.gov/transcripts/dec02/session1.html. Rev 12 Dec 2006

Binstock RH (2003) The war on "anti-aging medicine". The Gerontologist 1/2004:4–14

Bostrom N (2005) Recent developments in the ethics, science, and politics of life extension. Ageing Horizons 3/2005:28–33

Callahan D (1995) Setting limits. Medical goals in an aging society, 2nd edn (1st edn, 1987). Georgetown University Press, Washington, DC

Callahan D (2000) Death and the research imperative. New Engl J Med 9/2000:654–656

Caplan AL (2004) An unnatural process: why it is not inherently wrong to seek a cure for aging. In: Post SG, Binstock RH (eds) The fountain of youth: cultural, scientific, and ethical perspectives on a biomedical goal. Oxford University Press, Oxford, pp 271–285

Cole TR, Thompson B (2001/2002) Anti-aging: are you for it or against it? Generations 4/2001/2002:6–8

Daniels N (1988) Am I my parents' keeper? An essay on justice between the young and the old. Oxford University Press, New York

Daniels N (2006) Equity and population health: toward a broader bioethics agenda. In: Hastings Center Rep 4/2006, pp 22–35

de Grey ADNJ et al. (2002) Time to talk SENS: critiquing the immutability of human aging. Ann New York Acad Sci 959/2002:452–462

Fries JF (1980) Aging, natural death, and the compression of morbidity. New Engl J Med 303/1980:130–135

Fries JF (2003) Measuring and monitoring success in compressing morbidity. Ann Internal Med 5/2003:455–459

---

[1] The preparation of this chapter is based on my work in the research project "Life Prolongation and Deceleration of Human Aging", which has been carried out under the direction of Dr. Michael Fuchs and Prof. Dr. Georg Rudinger, Institute of Science and Ethics and Centre for the Cultures of Ageing (both University of Bonn, Germany).

Fuchs M (2006) Biomedizin als Jungbrunnen? Zur ethischen Debatte über künftige Optionen der Verlangsamung des Alterns. Zeitsch med Ethik 4/2006:355–366

Fuchs M et al. (2002) Enhancement. Die ethische Diskussion über biomedizinische Verbesserungen des Menschen. Deutsches Referenzzentrum für Ethik in den Biowissenschaften, Bonn

Fukuyama F (2002) Our posthuman future: consequences of the biotechnology revolution. Farrar, Straus & Giroux, New York

Ho AD, Wagner W, Mahlknecht U (2005) Stem cells and ageing. The potential of stem cells to overcome age-related deteriorations of the body in regenerative medicine. EMBO Rep 6/2005 spec issue:S35–S38

Hübner D (2001) Justice over time. Zum Problem der Gerechtigkeit zwischen den Generationen. In: Honnefelder L, Streffer C (eds) Jahrbuch für Wissenschaft und Ethik 6/2001, pp 39–66

Jonas H (1992) The burden and blessing of mortality. In: Hastings Center Rep 1/1992, pp 34–40

Kass LR (2004) L'Chaim and its limits: why not immortality? In: Post SG, Binstock RH (eds) The fountain of youth: cultural, scientific, and ethical perspectives on a biomedical goal. Oxford University Press, Oxford, pp 304–320 (first published in First Things 113/2001:17–24)

Kohli M (2006) Aging and justice. In: Binstock RH, George LK (eds) Handbook of aging and the social sciences, 6th edn (1st edn, 1976). Academic Press, Amsterdam, pp 456–478

Miller RA (2004) Extending life: scientific prospects and political obstacles. In: Post SG, Binstock RH (eds) The fountain of youth: cultural, scientific, and ethical perspectives on a biomedical goal. Oxford University Press, Oxford, pp 228–248 (first published in The Milbank Quarterly 1/2001, pp 155–174)

Olshansky SJ, Hayflick L, Carnes BA (2002) Position statement on human aging. J Gerontol Biol Sci 8/2002:292–297

Parens E (2003) The goodness of fragility: on the prospect of genetic technologies aimed at the enhancement of human capacities. In: Beauchamp TL, Walters L (eds) Contemporary issues in bioethics, 6th edn. Wadsworth, Belmont, CA, pp 548–554

Roth GS (2005) Caloric restriction and caloric restriction mimetics: current status and promise for the future. J Am Geriatrics Soc suppl 9/2005:S280–S283

Swift J (2003) Gulliver's travels. Edition with an introduction and notes by Robert Demaria Jr (original edn, 1726). Penguin, London, p 192

The President's Council on Bioethics (2003) Beyond therapy. Biotechnology and the pursuit of happiness. The President's Council on Bioethics, Washington, DC

Walker RF, Bercu BB (2002) Growth hormone therapy in aging: is aging a treatable disease? J Anti-aging Med 1/2002:3–6

Part IV
Intergenerational Justice and Population Policies

Chapter 8
An Ethical Assessment of the Legitimacy of Anti-natalistic Birth Policies

Joerg Chet Tremmel

8.1 Introduction

Governmental regulations on permissible number of births raise profound ethical questions. Undoubtedly, they are a form of interference in individuals' and families' freedom of choice. Having a baby is an intimate, private affair but, at the same time, it is also a process of great relevance to society as a whole. This dual character is one of the key reasons why debates on this subject are so explosive and emotionally charged. The ethical questions are serious and intractable. Is it acceptable for a government to influence how many children its citizens have, for instance, by offering incentives? Or is freedom of choice always of greater value than the positive effects hoped for future generations? Does this in itself mean that birth policies can never be ethically legitimate? Are reproductive decisions an individual right to such an extent that the individual may reach a decision while completely disregarding other factors? If not, to what degree may the family, clan, government or even world community intervene?

This chapter offers a train of thought on how to assess the ethical legitimacy of birth policies.

8.2 Focus on Anti-natalistic Birth Policies

Demographic change and the wellbeing of the next generation are intimately linked because it is the size of a generation that determines a great share of its fate. But for better or for worse?

The relationships are not one-directional. Both rapid population growth in developing countries and projected population decline in developed countries are considered a threat for future generations in the respective countries.

Joerg Chet Tremmel (Ed.) *Demographic Change and Intergenerational Justice*
DOI 10.1007/978-3-540-77084-8 © Springer 2008

Although shrinking societies are usually growing older, and growth processes usually go hand in hand with juvenescence, for analytical purposes the elements of demographic change can be separated into changes in population size (growth, shrinking) and changes in median age (ageing, juvenescence). Each of these four developments has different effects on policy fields and indicators relevant for the wellbeing and the quality of life of a generation. Table 8.1 shows some of the impacts and their relative strength. Regarding the quality of the environment, food safety, job opportunities and access to educational institutions, each member of the next generation is better off if his generation is smaller than the previous one. However, for other sustainability indicators (e.g. stability of the social security system, or the reduction of state debt per head), it is better for a member of the next generation if his generation is bigger than the previous one. The same complexity applies to ageing and juvenescence. Some sustainability indicators are aided by an ageing population (e. g. democratic stability) whilst others benefit from a juvenescent society (e. g. ability to innovate).

Table 8.1 Impact matrix showing possible impacts of facets of demographic change on certain sustainability indicators (source: present author)

Explanation:

–3: strong negative influence;
–2: medium negative influence;
–1: weak negative influence;
0: no influence;
+1: weak positive influence;
+2: medium positive influence;
+3: strong positive influence

Demographic change	**A. Environmental factors: CO_2 emissions, etc.**	**B. Food security**	**C. Competitiveness**	**D. Pay-as-you-go retirement system**	**E. Funded retirement system**	**F. Opportunities on labour market**	**G. Efficiency of education systems**	**H. Financial solidity/public debt**	**I. Stability of the democratic system**
1. Ageing of population	0	–1	–2	–3	–1	–2	–1	0	+1
2. Juvenescence of population	0	+1	+2	+3	+1	+2	+1	0	–1
3. Shrinking of population [a]	+2	+2	0	-	-	+2	+1	–2	0
4. Growth of population	–3	–2	0	+2	+1	–2	–1	+2	–1

Source: present author. Note that this line describes the effects of shrinking, all else being equal. Only if a country could move from one state (for instance, 30 million people) to another (20 million people) without increase of the median age would the effects have the tendency shown in Table 8.1. It is, however, difficult to envisage a society which is shrinking without ageing. The reader should bear in mind that most industrialized societies are shrinking *and* ageing.

Explanations for Table 8.1

1 affects A	Ageing – unlike growth or shrinking – does not directly and strongly affect the environment. Minor indirect effects can occur because the consumption habits change with age
1 affects B	An ageing population might be less able to produce food than a younger one
1 affects C	An ageing population is less competitive because innovative ability and risk appetite will decrease. The (increasing) experience also influences competitiveness, but to a lesser extent
1 affects D	A pay-as-you-go system is negatively affected by ageing
1 affects E	A funded system is less prone to demographic changes but also negatively affected by ageing
1 affects F	Employers prefer young staff. Older people also have a lower tendency to become self-employed or to set up businesses. Therefore, the opportunities on the labour market become worse in an ageing society
1 affects G	Assuming that the median age of students rises, this will deteriorate the efficiency of education systems, as older students will have more problems to find jobs, esp. in an international competition
1 affects H	An ageing (but steady-state) population will not or hardly suffer from public debt, because the debt per capita ratio does not raise
1 affects I	"It is the young men that shatter states", Cicero said. There is, in fact, empirical evidence that older societies become calmer, less inclined to wage war, to make revolutions or upheaval. This is the flipside of the coin of less risk appetite. Another aspect of the relationship between age structure and democracy is the growing overbalance of elders in political decision making
2 affects A–I	The results are more or less mirror-inverted
3 affects A	According to the PAT formula, people are a driving force in environmental problems like resource depletion, CO_2 emissions, and loss of forests and biodiversity. But the effects of a shrinking and a growing population are not mirror-inverted. The rate of species goes down when population grows rapidly; however, the number of species hardly increases when a population shrinks
3 affects B	A shrinking population usually has less problems to feed itself
3 affects C	A smaller population is by itself not more or less risk-averse than a bigger one
3 affects D	If a country with a pay-as-you-go retirement system would shrink without ageing, then the yield would not go down. But as this situation does not apply to any country with such a retirement system, there is no entry in this field
3 affects E	See above
3 affects F	Most studies project a lower unemployment rate or even a shortage of workers in a shrinking society
3 affects G	Less students could use the existing infrastructure (university buildings, etc.)
3 affects H	A population decrease implicates that a given amount of debt has to be paid back by less people

(continued) Explanations for Table 8.1

3 affects I	If all else stays equal, there is no direct influence
4 affects A–I	The results are more or less mirror-inverted but exceptions apply, as described in "3 affects A"

This chapter confines itself to a discussion of anti-natalistic birth policies. This is because leading international environmental research institutes emphasize that we are unlikely to succeed in creating an ecologically sustainable world unless we further reduce worldwide population growth (UNEP 2000; World Resources Institute 2000; American Association for the Advancement of Sciences 2001; World Wide Fund for Nature 2004). If we assume a world population, in line with UN projections, of 9.1 billion in 2050 (United Nations 2005, p. 6)[1], the pressure on renewable freshwater, arable land, woodland, fishing zones, biodiversity and the atmosphere will be greater than at any point in human history. The current trend in world population growth, which stands at 76 million people per year at present, will diminish only slowly and continue far into the future. While sinking birth rates on a global level have caused some to sound the all-clear on this issue, the increase in worldwide population of around 40%, or 2.6 billion people, makes serious consideration of anti-natalistic policies an urgent necessity.

On a country level, one cannot ignore the fact that many developing countries still suffer from very high birth rates. According to UN Population Division projections, the population of the following countries will triple between 2005 and 2050: Afghanistan, Burkina Faso, Burundi, Chad, Democratic Republic of Congo, East Timor, Guinea-Bissau, Liberia, Mali, Niger and Uganda (United Nations 2005, p. 7). China and India, which make up for more than a third of the world's population, also regard their population growth as too high. India, with a population growing by 16.5 million people every year, accounts for around 22% of annual world population growth (Government of India 2005; United Nations 2005, p. 52). To ensure a decent life for these additional Indians, 6–7 million new jobs, 16,000 primary schools and around 400,000 new teachers would be necessary (see Bronger 1996, p. 87). India is unable to cope with these developmental needs. China, of which the territory consists largely of mountains and deserts and only 10% cultivable land, fears that rapid population growth may lead to famine. As Lester Brown of the Worldwatch Institute

[1] The experts in the Population Division work from the premise that the total fertility rate (TFR) will fall to 2.05 children per woman by 2050. If the TFR will be 2.53, we could expect 10.6 billion people by 2050 (maximum variant), while a summarized birth rate of 1.56 would produce 7.7 billion (minimum variant). If TFR will remain constant, then world population would be 11.7 billion in the mid-21st century.

has shown in the study "Who will feed China?" (Brown 1997), such fears are not without foundation.

Alongside the economic and social burdens, rapid population growth also causes ecological problems, ultimately affecting every one of us. Besides deforestation, depletion of natural resources, and greenhouse gas emissions, the extinction of animal and plant species is another effect intensified by population growth in many developing countries (Rolston 1998; Tremmel 2005, pp. 75–94).

Many governments in the Western world are more preoccupied with their own low total fertility rate nowadays. And rightly so, as Table 8.1 shows. A rapidly shrinking and ageing population can create stress for the welfare state and the social security systems. Whether or not an increasing or a decreasing population size is beneficial to the next generation depends on the specific situation a nation is in. Hence, the reasons which could possibly justify a pro-natalistic policy differ from those which could legitimate an anti-natalistic policy. To discuss both kinds of cases would be beyond the scope of this chapter. The questions are difficult enough. Being able to choose to have a high number of children is undoubtedly a matter of elementary self-determination, closely bound to an individual's personal happiness. If we can assume that the wellbeing enjoyed by future generations would increase if one had fewer children, one would have to balance the interests of those individuals living now against those of future generations. Without an endless supply of people, our species would have been unable to survive or develop. Fertility has therefore been valued greatly since Biblical times. Yet, if the inhabitants of specific regions' food security and environment are threatened, then their rights to freedom and self-determination are also at risk.

Ecologists often believe that the next generation will be better off if it grows at a smaller or even a negative rate compared to its predecessors. Economists believe the opposite (Simon 1998). How many of the 200 countries worldwide are currently in a position which requires an anti-natalistic birth policy? An ecologist might count 80, an economist only eight, and they could debate this question for a long time, each one with good arguments on her side. I do not discuss this question in my chapter. Instead, I offer a non-contextualized principle which is meant for the hypothetical case that a government has good reasons to devise and implement an anti-natalistic birth policy. For the sake of the argument, we assume that the members of the next generation would clearly benefit if the state imposed an anti-natalistic birth policy on the members of the present generation. But even good ends do not justify all means. The social and economic rights and interests of the members of the next generation must be weighted against the rights and interests of the members of the present generation, including the right to self-determination and the right to choose freely the number and spacing of one's own children. This chapter thus asks if political intervention in family planning can be reconciled with ethical norms.

8.3 The Human Rights Discourse and the Ethical Discourse

Before entering into my line of argument, I want to explain my notion of the complex relationship between ethical norms and laws in the field of population ethics. I do not frame my line of thinking in human rights language, so often employed when it comes to population policies. The nationally oriented population policy discourse, and its attendant institutionalization in the global arena, sets forth norms for states to adopt, embed in the jurisprudence of national and international law (Barrett and Frank 1999, p. 199). Bentham (1824) has put forward the opinion that real (or enforceable) rights come from real (or legislated) law, recognisable by the duties imposed on others, not by normative contents of aspirational documents. But most ethicists nowadays employ the term "rights" in the ethical sphere ("moral rights") and the legal sphere ("legal rights"). The legal and the ethical discourse overlap, but they should be distinguished. It is thus something different to say that something is "ethically unacceptable" or a "human rights violation". The two intersecting circles in Fig. 8.1. show the relationship between laws and ethical norms.

Firstly, there are moral commandments or, alternatively, moral obligations (left circle). This is the realm of ethicists reflecting on population issues. Not all ethical norms can be embedded in positive law – some will be non-contextualized, others could be codified into legal terms but the political majority is not (yet) willing to do so. Taking a bird's eye view, the codified law is usually sooner or later adjusted according to the changes in the moral convictions within a society.

Secondly, there is the group of ethical norms regarding population policies which are at the same time legal norms and vice versa (cf. intersecting part of the two circles). In international law, this legislative body regarding population policy consists, among other, of the Universal Declaration of Human Rights (1948), the International Covenant on Economic, Social and Cultural Rights (1966), the International Covenant on Civil and Political Rights (1966),

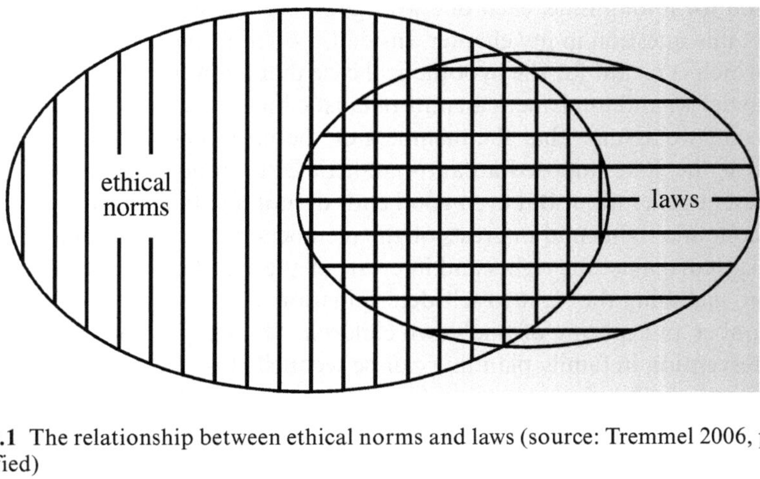

Fig. 8.1 The relationship between ethical norms and laws (source: Tremmel 2006, p. 199, modified)

the Convention on the Elimination of All Forms of Discrimination Against Women (1979), the Programme of Action of the International Conference on Population and Development (1994) and the Declaration on the Elimination of Violence Against Women (1999) (for an overview, see Babor 1993).

Most *national* laws on population issues are also ethically legitimated.

The third case (non-overlapping part of the "law" circle) are legal norms which are not ethical. For example, the Nuremberg Racial Laws of Hitler's Third Reich are laws which are blatantly unethical. Nevertheless, they were codified in positive law. Another example (still not comparable to the Nuremberg Racial Laws, but bad enough) are the apartheid laws in South Africa until 1994. They made apartheid legal, but not moral. Some of the population laws currently in force in China are also unethical, as this chapter will show.

I will confine my reflections on the sphere of ethical norms in this chapter.

8.4 The Dissemination of Birth Policies

This section deals with the argument that all types of birth policy are unethical. If this is accepted, follow-up questions concerning the ethical assessment of specific birth policy measures become trivial – these would then also lack legitimacy.

The widespread use of birth policies underlines the importance of their ethical assessment. The member states of the United Nations report regularly to the Population Division any active birth policy they may be pursuing. The most recent figures (cf. Table 8.2) show that this applies to 131 of 193 states (68%). In all, 77% of developing countries have implemented such policies, 59% of these anti-natalistic, 8% pro-natalistic, and 19% of policies are intended to maintain the current fertility level.

In all, 43% of the "more developed countries" pursue a natality policy (31% pro-natalistic, 2% anti-natalistic and 10% intended to maintain current fertility rates). Approximately 4.8 billion people (75% of the world population) are affected by birth policies.

8.5 The Role of the State

In liberal theory, the state should not interfere in any way with the decisions of its citizens concerning procreation. A laissez-faire state providing only for security will not take a stand regarding a desired population development–and definitely not take actions to carry it into effect. But it is now widely recognized that governments have a responsibility to try to increase their citizens' wellbeing and prosperity. "Population policy" is a generic term for the three subterms "birth policy", "health policy" and "migration policy". The modern state pursues social, economic, educational and environmental policies. Through migra-

Table 8.2 Birth policies by country (source: United Nations 2003, p. 4)

States aims with regard to level of fertility						Percentage				
	Raise	Maintain	Lower	No intervention	Total	Raise	Maintain	Lower	No intervention	Total
Africa										
1976	2	2	12	32	48	4	4	25	67	100
1986	3	3	21	24	51	6	6	41	47	100
1996	2	3	36	12	53	4	6	68	23	100
2001	1	3	38	11	53	2	6	72	21	100
Asia										
1976	2	9	14	12	38	5	24	38	32	100
1986	8	6	13	11	38	21	16	34	29	100
1996	7	6	19	11	46	15	20	41	24	100
2001	8	7	20	11	46	17	15	43	24	100
Latin America/Caribbean										
1976	2	0	10	15	27	7	0	37	56	100
1986	0	0	15	18	33	0	0	45	55	100
1996	1	1	18	13	33	3	3	55	39	100
2001	1	1	19	12	33	3	3	58	36	100

tion policy and health policy (improving health and thus increasing life expectancy), the government is in fact already pursuing population policy, without arousing moral controversy. But what about birth policy? In 1976, the ethicist Daniel Callahan wrote on the role of governments:

> "It is only fairly recently, however, that governments have taken a leading role in an anti-natalist control of fertility (…). While many countries still do not have such policies, few international objections have been raised against the right of nations to develop them. So far, most government population policies have rested upon and been justified in terms of an extension of freedom of choice. Increasingly, though, it is being recognized that, since demographic trends can significantly affect national welfare, it is within the right of nations to adopt policies designed to reduce birth rates and slow population growth. (…) Is there any special reason to presume (…) that governmental intervention in the area of individual procreation (…) raises problems which, *in kind*, are significantly different from other kinds of interventions? (…) I see no special reason to think that the formation of interventionist, anti-natalist, national population policies poses any unique *theoretical* difficulties. (…) In any case, the premise of my discussion will be that governments have as much right to intervene in procreation-related behaviour as in other areas of behaviour affecting the general welfare" (Callahan 1976, p. 26 f.).

The legitimacy of a government's claim to pursue birth policies is also embodied in the "Programme of Action" drawn up at the World Conference on Population held in Cairo in 1994 (Bib 1994). At the same time, some measures were classed as impermissible. The international community demands that governments refrain from making the subordinate civil servants who implement family planning programs pursue set targets, although governments themselves may work towards demographic objectives. The final text from Cairo+5 painstakingly captures this apparently controversial issue: "In attempting to reach this benchmark,[2] demographic goals, while legitimately the subject of government development strategies, should not be imposed on family planning providers in the form of targets or quotas for the recruitment of clients" (United Nations 1999b, par. 58).

On this view, a country like China may continue to proclaim national goals with respect to population growth and size. But if it wishes to act in accordance with international law, it must not stipulate target figures for local family planning services. One has to bear in mind that specific target figures may lead lower-level civil servants to behave inappropriately. Governments do not need to be indifferent. It would be preposterous to forbid a state on course to doubling its population from pursuing official birth policies of any kind.

We may provisionally conclude that a government may have demographic goals but may pursue these only by means of specific birth policy measures.

8.6 The Democratic Proviso

In my opinion, a government should be allowed to devise and implement a birth policy only when it is a democratic regime. It makes a great deal of difference whether birth policies are developed and implemented by a dictatorial or democratic government. Objectives are discussed and questioned constantly within democratic governments. The stance of a minority may become that of the majority. In his famous essay "The tragedy of the commons", Garrett Hardin argues that reproductive behaviour is an example of how the selfish deeds of individuals can wreck the entire system. He posits that a government in a democracy will not be able to execute an effective birth policy (Hardin 1968, pp. 1243–1248).

Under this assumptions, utility-maximizing parents have more children than is necessary for a stable population. Does this mean that the democratic proviso is wrong?

There is plenty of empirical evidence that *democratic* developing countries are able to impose anti-natalistic birth policies, despite the fact that the vast major-

---

[2] The target is described in the preceding sentence: "Where there is a gap between contraceptive use and the proportion of individuals expressing a desire to space or limit their families, countries should attempt to close this gap by at least 50 per cent by 2005, 75 per cent by 2010 and 100 per cent by 2050."

ity of citizens would like to have more than two children. Likewise, reasonable individuals accept the necessity for taxation, although no one likes paying taxes. And compulsory military service – and sending people to war – is a much more severe intervention of the right to self-determination than restricting numbers of children. Nevertheless, many democracies continue to have military draft. This shows that the statement that democracies by their very nature are unable to have birth policies is wrong. There are thus good reasons why only democracies should be permitted to formulate population targets and birth policies. In India – unlike China – it has proved possible to correct abuses, as evident, for example, in the resignation of Indira Gandhi's administration as a result of its forced sterilization policies. Being a democracy has weakened the efficiency of India's birth policy, but it has increased its ethical legitimacy.

On the basis of the discussion thus far, we can conclude that birth policies in democracies are not generally ethically inadmissible. The crucial factor is the means deployed.

8.7 The Link Between Severity and Efficiency

A correlation evidently exists between severity and efficiency. A single empirical example will suffice to illustrate this – a comparison between the birth policies of China and India.[3] At the beginning of the 1950s, both states felt compelled to introduce measures to reduce population growth. The need to ensure food security played a particularly important role in both states.

Initially, both China and India tried to achieve their population policy objectives exclusively by means of appellative approaches combined with provision of a plentiful supply of contraceptives. In light of the unsatisfactory results from the Chinese perspective, the (in)famous "One Child Policy", designed by Deng Xiaoping, was introduced in 1979. Between 1979 and 2004 (when this policy was significantly relaxed), couples required official approval if they wished to have children. Being married was also a precondition.

After the birth of the first child, the "One Child Policy" prescribed the use of contraceptives, mostly diaphragms and sterilization, as these were consid-

[3] It would be a digression from my topic to pursue this subject in detail here. For an in-depth look at China's population policy, which has been studied thoroughly, see Zhang (1990), Qu and Li (1994), Scharping and Heuser (1995), Schultz and Yi (1995), White (2000), Xie (2000), McElroy and Yang (2000), Merli and Raftery (2000), Peng and Guo (2000, pp. 105–123), Wong (2001), Scharping (2003), Meulenberg (2004), and announcements made by the Chinese government (see, for example, http://www.npfpc.gov.cn/en/en2005-01/enews20050106-4.htm). For an in-depth look at the population policy of India, see Bronger (1996), Haub (2003), Gans (2005) and announcements made by the Indian government (at http://www.mohfw.nic.in/dofw%20website/Health%20&%20Poulation%20indicators/hpi%20frame.htm)

ered cost-effective and reliable. Abortion was a lawful means of contraception, and unauthorized pregnancies were to be terminated by means of it. Officially, this required the consent of the woman, yet in some provinces women had been forced to comply. The "One Child Policy" was intended to combine sanctions against offenders with incentives for those who stick to the rules.

However, because the family planning authorities were anything but well-funded, sanctions predominated. Should couples refuse to abort unauthorized pregnancies, both parents faced the prospect of sanctions, such as pay cuts of 10–20% extending over 3–14 years.

Second-born children, moreover, were excluded from the state education system and had to be sent to expensive private schools. Possible sanctions also included one-off fines, discontinuation of grain rations, or disadvantages such as expulsion from the party. After the birth of the second child, sterilization was recommended, officially without compulsion, though some reports attest to the opposite. In the month of January 1983, a massive propaganda campaign resulted in record 2.68 million new cases of sterilization and 210,000 other preventative measures. The rather rarely granted incentives consisted of a "one-child bonus" of 60 Yuan per annum since 1980, enhanced welfare benefits, and help getting a job.

India, the second most populated country in the world, took a different approach. Though the strict Chinese birth policy has been relaxed several times (1984, 2001, 2004), from 1979 onwards India's birth policy has always been more liberal than that of China (apart from the 1975–1977 period).

At this point, it is intriguing to look at the difference in the extent to which these countries have achieved their objectives. In 2005, the population of India was around 1.03 billion. The growth rate is 1.5% and the total fertility rate is 3.01 children per woman. Estimates suggest that India will overtake China in terms of population by 2050. It already ranks first in terms of absolute increase in population. Only 46.2% of families are covered by family planning programs.

China has a population of 1.3 billion people. The yearly growth rate is 0.7% and the fertility rate 1.83 children per woman. According to Chinese sources, 95% of the Chinese population are involved in the family planning system. The price of efficiency was (and to some extent still is) more coercion. To sum up: the more severe the measures, the more efficient the birth policy but, at the same time, the more ethically problematic they are.

8.8 The Classification of Birth Policies

Demography is faced with the challenge of classifying and assessing birth policies. Such policies may be categorized as pro- or anti-natalistic, depending on their aims. If one examines anti-natalistic policies only, as in this work, a large number of additional classificatory criteria exists. They may be classified, ac-

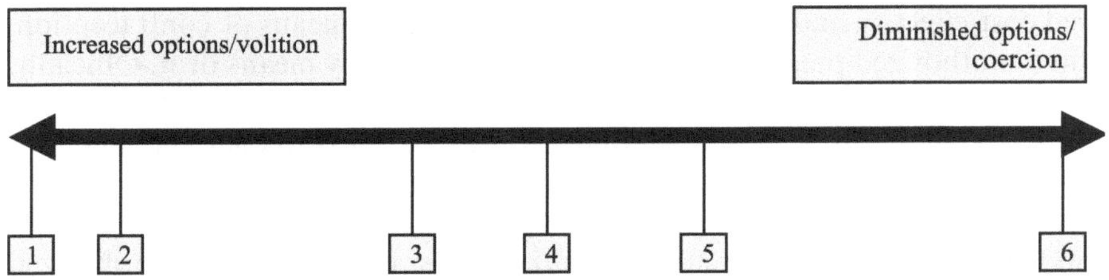

Fig. 8.2 Continuum of birth policy measures. Types *3–5* are financial steering measures (source: present author)

cording to how pervasive they are, as fully or partly established, as supply- or demand-oriented, depending on the underlying motivation, and as governmental or non-governmental.[4]

In the present context, the criterion of ethical legitimacy is of greatest interest. The borderline between ensuring freedom of choice and coercion, and between ethical and unethical measures is unclear. The following continuum, which reflects their degree of ethical legitimacy, appears as sensible means of categorizing anti-natalistic measures (cf. Fig. 8.2).

8.8.1 The Indirect Approach

Here, the government refrains entirely from directly influencing how many children its citizens have. Instead, it attempts to influence other factors in order to reduce the birth rate. This includes improving health services and educational levels, and providing more job opportunities, especially for women. Making contraceptives universally available enables individuals to decide how many children to have and how long to wait between births. All necessary steps are taken to ensure that freedom of choice is real, rather than on paper only.

If one can call this a "birth policy" in the first place, it is simply because the government aims to determine demographic development or, at least, has an opinion about whether the birth rate is too high, too low or appropriate. However, it pursues these quantitative goals only indirectly.

---

[4] The reader is referred to Wingen (1975, p. 19), Görres-Gesellschaft (1985, pp. 764–770), Hauser (1991, pp. 601–655), Feucht (1999, p. 21), Gauthier (1999) and Hummel (2000, p. 103).

8.8.2 *The Appellative Approach*

Here, the government actively encourages people to have a specific number of children. Roadside billboards featuring happy couples with two children, and slogans such as "small family = happy family" are a common sight. Individuals are called upon to voluntarily refrain from exceeding a specific number of children. Citizens are informed about the negative effects of rapid population growth for development and the environment. This is accompanied – as with all the approaches described here – by provision of a plentiful supply of contraceptives.

8.8.3 *The Financial Incentives Approach*

The government offers positive financial bonuses which influence reproductive behaviour. This may include incentives[5] for sterilization or the use of contraceptives effective over long periods of time (such as "Norplant"), compensation for longer breaks between pregnancies, lower interest loans for small families, and awards and public commendations for responsible parenthood.

8.8.4 *Restricting Financial Incentives*

The government restricts existing financial bonuses to a specified number of children. Direct financial subsidies or tax reductions, free school education, paid maternity leave, childcare payments and similar incentives are, for instance, available only for the first child.

8.8.5 *Imposition of Financial Disincentives*

The government demands "negative" financial incentives, or disincentives[6]. Those who have too many children have to pay extra taxes or a specified fee per child.

---

[5] I use this neutral word instead of "rewards" or "benefits".

[6] I use this neutral word instead of "penalties" or "sanctions".

8.8.6 *The Rationing Approach*

In the case of "rationing", no one is allowed to exceed the specified number of children, even if someone is prepared to pay a hefty fee for this.

If a couple has already had the permissible number of children, a new pregnancy is classified as illegal and the woman is forced to have an abortion. Rationing laws may also result in forced sterilization.

8.9 Reaching Ethical Decisions

What does an individual assessment of the six identified categories of birth policy in the continuum look like? The indirect approach is ethically unproblematic. It embodies the principle, first adopted in Teheran in 1968 and reiterated in Cairo in 1994, which affirms the "fundamental right of all couples and individuals, to decide freely and responsibly the number and spacing of their children and to have the information and means to do so and to ensure informed choices and make available a full range of safe and effective methods" (UNFPA 1994, par. 7.3 or 7.12). In the second part of this formula, the state is brought in because it is its task to come up with solutions if couples have no access to contraceptives. In fact, family planning programs should not only guarantee access to one or more types of contraceptive, but must also make available "an entire choice of harmless and effective methods" (UNFPA 1994, par. 7.12). In 1994, it was ascertained that "the full supply of modern family planning methods for at least 350 million couples in the world is still not available" (UNFPA 1994, par. 7.13). To ensure that, despite a rising world population, the same proportion of people continue to use contraceptives, about 300 million additional users are needed between 2000 and 2050. Already at present millions of people are unable to obtain the contraceptives they want. In all cases in which individuals, in their own words, are forced to have more children than they would like because of a lack of other options, contraceptives or sex education, there is no ethical dilemma; the interests of individuals and those of future generations are entirely in sync. Here, it is doubly ethically imperative that both developing and developed countries do everything they can to cover people's need for contraceptives within the framework of high-quality health services and advice.[7]

---

[7] The fact that the notion of being "free to choose how many children one has" is problematic does not stand in the way of this imperative (Tremmel 2005, pp. 166–170). Even in rich countries, individuals have to reach agreement with their partners on how many children to have. The choice is thus not completely "free". Moreover, how many children a person wishes to have can only be assessed subsequently as it also changes following the birth of a child (Goldstein et al. 2003, p. 8). Furthermore, how many children a person wishes to have also depends on the values which prevail in the specific culture as well as biological factors. Couples can thus choose how many children to have only within the framework of these external factors.

The second approach, straightforward appeals, also involves no coercion. One has only to think of governmental campaigns on organic produce, smoking, soot filters on cars and so on. Why should billboards encouraging people to have no more than two or three children involve greater pressure than those promoting other goals?

Assessing measures at the other end of the continuum is also relatively easy: there are good reasons for regarding rationing as unethical.[8] It is a clear violation of the human rights identified by the United Nations, which states that nobody may be tortured or subjected to cruel, inhuman or degrading treatment or punishment (13, Article 5). Rationing almost inevitably has a negative impact on society, as people, for example, live in fear of the consequences of unauthorized pregnancy. The implementation of a rationing law would require intense surveillance, and encourage informers to report anyone failing to comply. As a result, many women whose pregnancy "breaks the rules" will experience anxiety and psychological pressure. The harm done may include suicide. The potential disruption to society ranges from selecting gender by means of ultrasound to child murder. The rationing approach entails many risks for children. It is incompatible with human dignity and self-determination.

Let us assume that the state permits only one child per family. Anyone whose happiness or wellbeing depends entirely on having one more child is unable to fulfil his or her wish. He or she cannot even swap with somebody who does not want to have children. From a utilitarian point of view, this is obviously a poor solution.

A rationing policy, the most rigid of the birth policy types listed here, in recent human history was adopted only in China.

The Indian birth control law, drawn up at the beginning of 2003, may be regarded as a regulation of this type. Men and women who have more than two children are barred from running for election. The ban is intended to force politicians to set a good example in terms of family planning. This law excludes individuals who have more than two children from a specific career, in line with a rationing approach. This is rationing of a particular type. While rationing strictly applied to all citizens generates a great deal of unhappiness, as people are unable to live their lives as they would wish, in this case they are faced with a difficult decision. Do they compromise in terms of their career or their preferred number of children? To generate such dilemmas is unethical. The most interesting aspect in terms of population ethics is the assessment of financial control mechanisms, which is the topic of the following section. The aforementioned reflections thus far are summarized in Fig. 8.3.

---

[8] A rationing strategy often seems to lead to abuses. This may and ought to be taken into consideration in making an ethical assessment. However, for analytical purposes we need to distinguish between *legally regulated* birth policy and excesses and abuses. Corruption is bad in general, and corruption in relation to birth policy is no worse than in other contexts. The risk of abuse, moreover, is not an exclusive feature of rationing strategies.

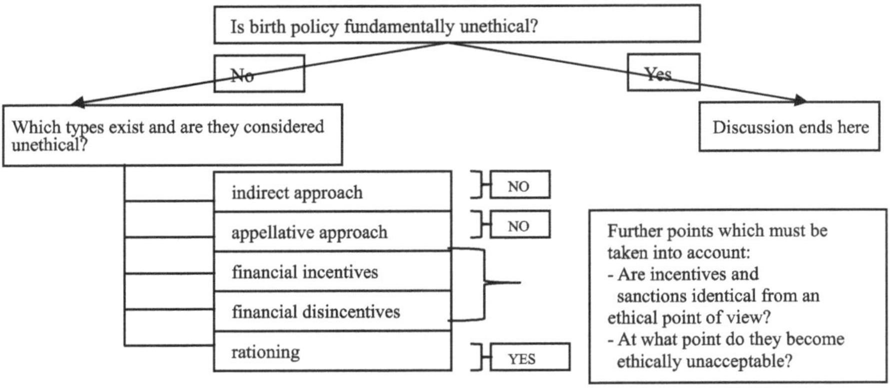

Fig. 8.3 Making ethical decisions on birth policy (source: present author)

8.10 Incentives and Disincentives

Most states pursuing an anti-natalistic birth policy deploy *financial or material* incentives and disincentives. Let us look at some real-world examples. In China, parents must pay a fine for every additional child. The population and natality planning law, passed in 2001 and implemented in 2002, stipulates that married couples of reproductive age must practice family planning. Citizens who have unauthorized children "must" according to the law, pay maintenance contributions, i.e. to the society which raises the children' (§41). In Vietnam, families with more than three children are not allowed to move to town centres or industrial zones, and additional taxes and "community work" may be imposed on them (Haub 2003, p. 1). In contrast, at the discretion of the local authorities, one-child families may receive free building land, be exempted from taxes and community work obligations, and may receive child benefit and other financial rewards. In Bangladesh, the allocation of food support depends on proof of sterilization (Kasun 1988, p. 91). In Laos, an official told the village elder that his community would be provided with a well if all the villagers refrained from having a third child over a 5-year period (Schockenhoff 1996, p. 51). In many developing countries, micro-credit programs and income-generating projects are linked with family planning. In the south Indian state of Andhra Pradesh, families receive cheaper loans and subsidized seeds if they can present proof of sterilization (Randeria 1995, p. 121).

8.11 Are Bonuses and Maluses Equal from an Ethical Point of View?

The question of how bonus and malus systems differ is of key ethical importance. For *a homo oeconomicus*, no difference exists between the two systems.

This may be elucidated through the example of the remuneration system applying to the employees within a firm. Let us assume that half the employees have their salary increased by 5%, the other half by 4%. From an economic perspective, it makes no difference whether one speaks of a bonus for one half or a malus for the other. However, psychologically it makes a great deal of difference how one justifies these differing increases. If this difference arises from the fact that the less efficient employees have 1% deducted from the general salary increase of 5%, they will be far more angry than if the more efficient half of the employees receive a bonus of 1% on top of a general salary rise of 4%. People are more willing to do without a bonus, if they dislike the conditions attached to it, than to accept financial maluses. For the same reason, however, financial bonus systems are less effective.

Philosophers disagree over whether bonuses (i. e. incentives) and maluses (i. e. disincentives) are ethically equivalent. Some hold the view that offering people incentives involves coercion, while others maintain the opposite (Bayles 1976, p. xiv). The ethicist Callahan regards bonus systems as ethically unproblematic. He writes: "In principle, incentive schemes are noncoercive; that is, people are not forced to take advantage of the incentive. Instead the point of an incentive is to give them a choice they did not previously have" (Callahan 1976, p. 29). Bayles develops this notion further: "For example, if Jones is trying to decide whether to take a position with employer A or B and A increases the salary offered, A has not limited Jones' liberty to decide" (Bayles 1976, p. 42). By definition, bonuses are in addition to the normal level of compensation.

But for many critics of birth policies, not only financial disincentives are unacceptable. For them, incentive systems also have a subtly coercive character. As shown, it makes no real difference to couples' economic situation which system exists. The principles of freedom of choice and self-determination may be threatened if the economic situation means that no alternatives exist (Hummel 2000, p. 109). The power relations are less visible, but this does not mean they are absent (Schlebusch 1994, p. 162).

We may conclude that financial disincentives seem less legitimate than bonus systems, and are thus located further on the right side of the continuum (see Fig. 8.3). Restricted bonuses occupy an intermediate position. An example of this is seen when a state provides a financial bonus only for the first two children.

8.12 The Four-fifths Rule

The ethical acceptability of financial instruments is not primarily a matter of whether they are bonuses or maluses. It is rather a matter of how radically these affect the couple's financial position. The higher the positive or negative financial incentive, the more one may justifiably speak of coercion. Financial steering instruments involving small amounts of money cannot be considered an offence against freedom of choice or the right to self-determination – even in the case of a disincentive system. Raising the tax on cigarettes or on fuel oil also affects individuals' freedom of choice. Yet all these attempts to shape behaviour allow individuals varying degrees of freedom, without transgressing the coercion threshold.

If *moderate* bonuses and maluses pertain, those who want a certain number of children – whether or not this differs greatly from the governments' desired number – are not forced into a lower income bracket. If the bonuses and maluses are *substantial*, a couple's economic position will change tremendously if they have more or fewer children than the state would like.

It is difficult to determine at precisely what point a financial burden ceases to be ethically neutral. However, a line must be drawn somewhere. The following rule of thumb seems reasonable: *the lifetime income of those who choose to have more children than officially approved must not decline by more than 20% compared with the income of those who have the approved number of children.* Admittedly, this four-fifths rule provides us with no more than a rough guide to action. It can be seen as the middle value of a corridor. In many discussions, people have told me that a fifty-fifty rule would not be ethically legitimate because it would be a blatant intrusion of the government into free choice. On the other hand, most people felt that a one-twentieth rule would only slightly influence the overall financial or material situation of the families concerned, and have no effect on their actions at all.

Hence, the four-fifths rule seems to be middle ground. Rather than rejecting it out of hand, those who accept that financial birth policy measures must at some point be deemed ethically inadmissible but are unhappy with the four-fifths threshold could play a constructive role by proposing alternative fractions. This is in line with the broadly accepted principle of constructive criticism, which holds that a solution should be rejected only if a better alternative exists. In my opinion, according to the principle of commensurability, the four-fifths rule allows just enough freedom to individuals such that one cannot talk of coercion.

What does the four-fifths rule mean in practice? If, for example, the democratically elected government of India wishes to implement an anti-natalistic population policy establishing a norm of two children per couple, according to the four-fifths rule it must go about this in such a way that couple A, who choose to have six children, should not suffer an income reduction of more than 20%. If, for example, the couple has to pay a monthly malus of 15% of their income from the fourth child onwards, school fees are not paid from the third child onwards (for which couple A must use, say, 5% of their income), while two-child families receive cheaper loans (which cost couple A 6% of their income), then the overall amount of money involved is substantial. In this example, the financial disadvantages suffered by couple A amount to 26%. Couple A is more than 20% worse off as a result of state birth policy measures and, thus, disadvantaged to an unethical degree. One could argue that couple A, with six children, enjoys higher lifetime income than couples with two children, because their offspring help pay to cover their needs in old age. This, however, depends on various factors and is not included in the calculation.

Table 8.3 One anti-natalistic population policy based on the four-fifths rule and a malus system (source: present author)

Number of children	Negative child benefit (as % of lifetime income, not cumulative)
1	–
2	–
3	5
4	10
5	15
6 or more	20

According to the four-fifths rule, China's current birth policy, for example, is ethically illegitimate. Town dwellers in many provinces suffer pay cuts of 20% for both parents per "surplus" child. This is permissible according to the four-fifths rule, but additional monetary disadvantages apply (in comparison with one-child families), constituting a violation of the rule.

The easiest way to make such calculations is to compare scenarios in which a couple decides to have more children than the government deems favorable. If we compare two different couples A and B, we must assume that the differences in the couples' income is due solely to the number of children.

Paul Ehrlich suggested in 1968 that parents with an income of $ 25,000 should pay additional tax for the first two children ($ 600) and $ 1,200 for all additional children (Ehrlich 1968, p. 108). If we assume a rate of personal taxation of 15%, a couple with no children would have an available income of $ 21,250[9]; a couple with four children would have $ 17,650[10]. This would be compatible with the four-fifths rule[11]. As soon as this couple has a fifth child, however, the state would intervene too starkly, leaving them with only $ 16,450[12].

Ehrlich's system of financial control has one main disadvantage: there is no upper limit on the maluses imposed on couples with a large number of children. It is preferable for financial steering systems to calculate financial maluses in relation to income. These must exclude the income necessary to ensure the minimum acceptable standard of living. Let us assume that newly industrialized countries in Asia, with an average annual income of € 10,000, introduces the fee shown in Table 8.3 within the framework of an anti-natalistic birth

[9] $25{,}000 - (25{,}000 \times 0{,}15)$

[10] $25{,}000 - (25{,}000 \times 0{,}15 + 2 \times 600 + 2 \times 1200)$

[11] $21{,}250 \times 0{,}8 = 17{,}000$

[12] $17{,}650 - 1200$

Table 8.4 One anti-natalistic population policy based on the four-fifths rule and a bonus system (source: present author)

Number of children	Positive child benefit (as % of lifetime income, not cumulative)
1	20
2	20
3	Discontinuation of bonuses paid for 1st and 2nd child

policy. A couple's relative income status would vary no more than 20%, no matter how many children they have.

Of course, a suitable system could be designed featuring positive, rather than negative financial incentives. Bonuses could be awarded as in Table 8.4.

Financial incentives, though the term sounds positive, are not free of coercion. In the example mentioned above, a middleclass couple with two children and an annual income of € 10,000 receives state benefits of € 2,000 per annum. If they have a third child, they loose this support. Since bonuses are clearly less ethically problematic than maluses, one might propose an upper limit of 22.5% or 25% (rather than 20%). As mentioned before, however, the four-fifths rule is a rule of thumb only. The crucial point is that people are coerced into refraining from having children even by positive incentives, once these reach a certain level. If positive child benefit amounts to 50% of annual income and is valid only for two-child households, this puts huge pressure on couples who wish to have a third child; they would probably refrain from having a third child as a result.

Another point is that negative and positive incentives differ in their consequences for state finances. While financial malification systems increase the income of the state, bonus systems are a drain on its budget. Here, international donors have a duty to help developing countries convert disincentive-based systems into the ethically less problematic incentive systems.

8.13 Arguments Against the Four-fifths Rule

1. *Financial bonuses or maluses are socially unjust because it is easier for rich people to have the number of children they want.* This argument applies with greatest force to one-off financial bonuses or maluses. It does not apply, for example, to the birth policies described in Tables 8.3 and 8.4 because here the financial bonuses or maluses are income-related. However, one might still argue that it is easier for a person with an annual income of € 1 million to pay € 200,000 as malus than for a person with an annual income € 100,000

to pay € 20,000. As a rule, the income necessary to a minimum acceptable standard of living (in a particular country) should therefore be tax-free. In other words, governmental birth policies should never cause poverty. A situation in which the birth policy would not apply to the poor could be avoided by introducing a system combining bonuses for the poor with maluses for the rest of the population. This is ethically unproblematic as long as the four-fifths rule is observed.

The four-fifths rule could also be adapted to produce a system of progressive taxation. However, the broader issue of whether a progressive or linear tax system is fairer is subject to heated debate the world over. Lack of space prevents me from discussing this subject further here.

2. *The four-fifths rule is not practicable for the least developed societies because they lack a monetary system.* This objection is valid to a certain extent. If in a country like Laos a village is promised a well if all its members refrain from having a third child for a 5-year period, the material changes in living standard is hard to quantify. But with some assumptions and calculating, it is still possible. The four-fifths rule might be primarily applicable to monetarized societies but not solely. The train of thought is the same for non-monetarized societies; it is only more difficult to calculate when it comes to implementation.
3. *The four-fifths rule will make the poor poorer because it is designed for developing countries.* This is not true. It is designed for every country of which the government thinks that it would be beneficiary for the future citizens to belong to a smaller generation than be without an anti-natalistic policy. I left the question open to which countries this pertains. But the assumption that countries with the biggest ecological footprint are currently overpopulated, as posited by Paul Ehrlich, is debatable.
4. *It is impossible, given the labyrinthine nature of current financial incentive systems in most states, to assess whether two contrasting decisions on how many children to have would lead to a difference in income of more than 20% as a result of state birth policy.* It is true that most states currently have extremely complex negative or positive incentive schemes in their family or birth policies. This would appear to be an argument for more transparency in relation to birth policy, rather than against the four-fifths rule.
5. *Financial steering mechanisms are unnecessary because there are equally effective and ethically less problematic alternatives.* A state should, of course, always utilize indirect and appellative anti-natalistic birth policy measures before turning to financial steering mechanisms. However, it is unlikely, for instance, in those countries of which the population is set to triple by 2050, that such measures would be sufficient. The notion that the various options open to states are equally efficient is, as we have seen, incorrect. There is no doubt that more inflexible, strictly implemented measures are more effective.
6. *Coercion can never be ethically legitimized.* Anyone raising this objection has failed to understand the purpose of the present work, which was to investigate at what point financial steering mechanisms may be described as coer-

cive. Those who claim that *all* bonuses and maluses aimed at influencing citizens' behaviour, severe or not severe, are "coercive" are simply misusing the concept of coercion. The question of where coercion begins and ends will, however, be debated by demographers and ethicists well into the future.

References

American Association for the Advancement of Sciences (ed) (2001) AAAS Atlas of Population and Environment. Edited by Harrison P, Pearce F. University of California Press, Berkeley, CA

Babor D (1993) Population growth and reproductive rights in international human rights law. 14 Conn. J Int Law 83:93

Barrett D, Frank DJ (1999) Population control for national development: from world discourse to national policies. In: Boli J, Thomas GM (eds) Constructing world culture: international nongovernmental organizations since 1875. Stanford University Press, Stanford, pp 198–221

Bayles MD (1976) Limits to the right to procreate. In: Bayles MD (ed) Ethics and population. Schenkman, Cambridge, pp 41–55

Bentham J (1824) The book of fallacies. From unfinished papers of Jeremy Bentham. By a friend. J & HL Hunt, London

Bronger D (1996) Indien – Größte Demokratie der Welt zwischen Kastenwesen und Armut. Justus Perthes, Gotha

Brown L (1995) Who will feed China? Edited by the Worldwatch Institute. WW Norton, New York

Callahan D (1976) Ethics and population limitation. In: Bayles MD (ed) Ethics and population. Schenkman, Cambridge, pp 19–40

Dasgupta PS (1998) Population, poverty and the local environment. In: VanDeVeer D, Pierce C (eds) The environmental ethics & policy book. Thomson, London, pp 404–409

Ehrlich PR (1968) The population bomb. Ballantine, New York

Feucht R (1999) Beeinflussung demographischer Tatbestände durch den Staat. Eine Analyse zur bevölkerungspolitischen Kennzeichnung ausgewählter Politikbereiche in Deutschland. Nomos, Baden-Baden

Gauthier AH (1999) The state and the family: a comparative analysis of family policy in industrialized countries. Oxford University Press, New York

Goldstein J, Lutz W, Testa MR (2003) The emergence of sub-replacement family size ideals in Europe. Vienna Institute of Demography, Vienna. European Demographic Research Papers no 2, 10.08.2004. http://www.oeaw.ac.at/vid/publications/EDRP_No2.pdf

Görres-Gesellschaft (ed) (1985) Staatslexikon: Stichwort "Bevölkerungspolitik". In: Recht, Wirtschaft, Gesellschaft, vol 1. Herder, Freiburg, pp 764–770

Government of India (2005) Department of Family Welfare. http://www.mohfw.nic.in/dofw%20website/Health%20&%20Poulation%20indicators/hpi%20frame.htm, accessed 18 Jan 2005

Hardin G (1968) The tragedy of the commons. Science 162:1243–1248

Haub C (2003) Bevölkerungspolitik in Vietnam. Online-Lexikon des Berlin-Instituts. http://www.berlin-institut.org/pdfs/Haub_Vietnam.pdf, accessed 20 Mar 2004

Hauser JA (1991) Bevölkerungs- und Umweltprobleme in der Dritten Welt, vol 2. Haupt, Bern

Hummel D (2000) Der Bevölkerungsdiskurs. Demografisches Wissen und politische Macht. Leske und Budrich, Opladen

Kasun J (1988) The war against population. The economics and ideology of population control. Ignatius Press, San Francisco, CA

McElroy M, Yang DT (2000) Carrots and sticks: fertility effects of China's population policies. Am Econ Rev 90 2/2000
Merli MG, Raftery AE (2000) Are births underreported in rural China? Manipulation of statistical records in response to China's population policies. Demography 37 1/2000:109–126
Meulenberg C (2004) Probably one. A generation comes of age under China's one child policy. Worldwatch Mag September/October 2004:31–33
Peng X, Guo Z (eds) (2000) The changing population of China. Blackwell, Oxford
Qu G, Li J (1994) Population and the environment in China. Lynne Rienner, London
Randeria S (1995) Die sozio-ökonomische Einbettung reproduktiver Rechte: Frauen und Bevölkerungspolitik in Indien. Feministische Studien 13 May 1995:119–132
Rolston H III (1998) Feeding people vs. saving nature. In: VanDeVeer D, Pierce C (eds) The environmental ethics & policy book. Thomson, London, pp 409–421
Scharping T (2003) Birth control in China 1949–2000. Routledge, Oxford
Scharping T, Heuser R (eds) (1995) Geburtenplanung in China. POD, Hamburg
Schlebusch C (1994) Bevölkerungspolitik als Entwicklungsstrategie. Historisches und Aktuelles zu einem fragwürdigen Argument. IKO, Frankfurt am Main
Schockenhoff E (1996) Bevölkerungspolitik und Familienplanung in der Dritten Welt. In: Berichte aus den Sitzungen der Joachim-Jungius-Gesellschaft der Wissenschaften, March 1996, vol 14. Vandenhoeck und Ruprecht, pp 3–69
Schubnell H (1990) Bevölkerungs- und Familienpolitik – Definitionen, Bezug zur Gesamtpolitik und Probleme der Wirkungsanalyse. In: Birg H, Mackensen R (eds) Demographische Wirkungen politischen Handelns. Campus, Frankfurt am Main, pp 33–53
Schultz TP, Yi Z (1995) Fertility of rural China: effects of local family planning and health programs. J Popul Econ 8(4):329–350
Simon JL (1998) The ultimate resource, vol 2. Princeton
Tremmel J (2005) Bevölkerungspolitik im Kontext ökologischer Generationsgerechtigkeit. Diss, Deutscher Universitäts-Verlag, Wiesbaden
Tremmel J (2006) Establishment of intergenerational justice in national constitutions. In: Tremmel J (ed) Handbook of intergenerational justice. Edward Elgar, Cheltenham, pp 187–214
UNEP (2000) Global environmental outlook. United Nations Environment Programme, New York
UNFPA (1994) Programme of Action Int Conf Population and Development. http://www.unfpa.org/icpd/icpd_poa.htm#top, rev 24 Feb 2007
United Nations (1999) Schlüsselmaßnahmen zur weiteren Durchführung des Aktionsprogramms der Internationalen Konferenz über Bevölkerung und Entwicklung. Resolution der Generalversammlung. 21. Sondertagung. A/RES/S-21/2. New York
United Nations (2003) Fertility, contraception and population policies. United Nations Population Division (UNPD), New York
United Nations (2005) World Population Prospects. The 2004 Revision. United Nations Population Division (UNPD), New York
White T (2000) Domination, resistance and accommodation in China's one-child campaign. In: Perry EJ, Selden M (eds) Chinese society: change, conflict, and resistance. Routledge, New York, pp 102–119
Wingen M (1975) Grundfragen der Bevölkerungspolitik. Kohlhammer, Stuttgart
Wong J (2001) China's sharply declining fertility: implications for its population policy. Issues Studies 37, vol 3. US Census Bureau, http://www.census.gov/cgi-bin/ipc/idbsprd, accessed 12 Sep 2003
World Resources Institute/UNEP/UNDP/World Bank (2000) World Resources 2000/2001. Washington, DC
World Wide Fund for Nature (2004) Living Planet Report 2004. http://www.panda.org/news_facts/publications/index.cfm, accessed 1 Dec 2005
Zhang J (1990) Socioeconomic determinants of fertility in China. J Popul Econ 3(2):105–123

Part V
The Implementation of Long-term Thinking

Chapter 9
Changing the German Constitution in Favor of Future Generations – Four Perspectives from the Young Generation

Marco Wanderwitz, Peter Friedrich, Anna Lührmann, Michael Kauch

translated by Michelle Wenderlich

9.1 Introduction, by Joerg Chet Tremmel

In Berlin, 100 Representatives of the Bundestag have introduced a bill to add the principle of intergenerational justice to the Constitution (http://dip.bundestag.de/btd/16/033/1603399.pdf). Since autumn 2003, the Foundation for the Rights of Future Generations (FRFG) has fought both inside and outside of Parliament for this bill. In more than a dozen workshops between autumn 2003 and spring 2005, representatives of the foundation met with young Representatives to work on its formulation. The proposed bill (16/3399) was introduced by 27 Representatives of both the CDU und SPD, as well as 25 Greens and 21 Representatives from the FDP. The first reading took place in October 2007. As a result, the bill was transferred to the legal committee. At present (Feb. 2008), it awaits further examination. With a new Article 20b, the state will be bound to better protect the interests of future generations. The text is as follows: "The state must consider the principle of sustainability and must protect the interests of future generations in its decisions". In addition, Article 109 of the state's financial guidelines would also be expanded to limit the national debt.[1]

The younger Representatives in Parliament have thus started a new "generational project". They will no longer accept that the costs of today's actions (or lack thereof) are laid on future generations. It is they who will be held responsible for today's policies, after their older colleagues have long retired. For the first time the Left-Right spectrum is being replaced by a Young–Old spectrum. This alliance is limited, however, to this single effort.

---

[1] In the German original: Article 20b: "Der Staat hat in seinem Handeln das Prinzip der Nachhaltigkeit zu beachten und die Interessen künftiger Generationen zu schützen". Article 109, Paragraph 2: "Bund und Länder haben bei ihrer Haushaltswirtschaft den Erfordernissen des gesamtwirtschaftlichen Gleichgewichts, dem Prinzip der Nachhaltigkeit sowie den Interessen der künftigen Generationen Rechnung zu tragen".

DOI 10.1007/978-3-540-77084-8 © Springer 2008

The representative of each party for this initiative was requested to answer the following two questions:

1. Why, from your (Christian democratic/Christian social, social democratic, green, liberal) perspective, does the anchoring of intergenerational justice and sustainability make sense?
2. How would you evaluate the process of cooperation on the initiative up to this point?

9.2 Intergenerational Justice from the Perspective of the Christian Democrats/Christian Socials, by Marco Wanderwitz, Member of the German Bundestag (CDU)

For years, demographic change and intergenerational justice have stood in the center of the work of the younger Representatives of the Youth Caucus of the CDU/CSU ("Junge Gruppe"). We see intergenerational justice and sustainability not only as principles of environmental policy – that is, of course, a main point – but also as part of social and financial policy. Demographic change, with continually lower birth rates, family politics is another field of politics, that we are willing to handle with much more intense by the way not only from that point of view, are leading to a social security system where the needs of the older generation must be met by an ever smaller group of wage earners. At the same time, the burden of taxes and repayment of state debt are falling on ever fewer shoulders.

This situation requires not only substantial reform and revaluation of the social security system and budget process to enable us to support them over the long term, but also a comprehensive inclusion of principles of intergenerational justice in all facets of the political system.

In day-to-day work in a democracy, there is a tendency to prefer the needs of the present, and today's voters and special interests. This structural problem has the consequences that today's policies are made mostly to the detriment of future generations. In addition, our Constitution currently effectively protects only the rights of present generations. Together with the bias toward the present, this policy leads to the end outcome of visible and ever more immanent state indebtedness. Time and time again, our burdens are pushed onto the future. The freedom and flexibility of future generations to shape their own policies and world is nearly being taken away. Despite the fact that Article 115 of the Constitution contains intended checks on debt accumulation, a mountain of debt can still be acquired without direct consequences.

The anchoring of intergenerational justice in the Constitution, as an aim of the state through a new Article 20b and a revision of the existing Article 109 in the budget policy, should make the state consider and protect the interests of future generations in its policies. With the adoption of intergenerational justice in the Constitution, all branches of government, but especially the legislative, will be charged with institutionally implementing intergenerational justice. It should then be possible to anchor generational accounting and further assessments of intergenerational justice in the consciousness of politics and society. We politicians then must be conscious that the younger and coming generations in Germany need a sign of a change of course in the direction of intergenerational justice, in order to have a viable future for our country. Its definition as a goal of the state would be such a sign.

The common goal of the sponsors of the constitutional reform is to create a fair balance between individual responsibility and solidarity for each generation, and also between generations. All of the four parties agree on this goal, albeit not on how to achieve it. The adoption of the change is not primarily a question of which party one belongs to, and the crossing of party lines and cooperation that has lasted now over years show the seriousness and commitment of the Representatives. This is not glorious work. The long and intensive process of unifying the format of the changes has shown that Representatives are willing to lead constructive discussions, and reach compromise independently of their party membership. Our work is above all goal-oriented and pragmatic. Nevertheless, is it clear to the 100 co-sponsors that each party has its own priorities, and thus will also differ in opinion over the implementation of the reform. We prefer, however, to first pass the reform, before we discuss these issues.

9.3 Intergenerational Justice – The Social Democratic Perspective, by Peter Friedrich, Member of the German Bundestag (SPD)

Together with other parliamentary groups, the SPD re-launched the nonpartisan initiative to implement the principles of intergenerational justice and sustainability in our Constitution in the summer of 2006. The initiative has been suspended in the last parliamentary term due to the reelection in 2005. About 100 members of the parliament from different generations support the project to change our Constitution in order to make intergenerational justice and sustainability an aim of our state. The initiative is based on the belief that the adjustment of politics to support intergenerational and sustainable policies needs a broad consensus among all parties. For this reason, representatives of four of the present five parliamentary parties support the initiative: the Social Democratic Party (SPD), the Christian Democratic Union (CDU), the Free Democratic Party (FDP), and the Alliance 90/The Greens. Only the Left Party rejects the idea entirely. The broad consensus of four political parties is rather unusual in German politics, and emphasizes the importance of the project. We are unified in the goal – even though we differ in opinions how to reach it. I witnessed the cooperation between the young members of parliament of all parties to be very constructive and collegial.

The bill aims to introduce a new Section 20b into our constitution, within the section where the aims of our state are defined, and to change Section 109, where the national budget policies are laid down, as follows:

- Section 20b: the state must consider the principle of sustainability, and must protect the interests of future generations in its decisions.
- Section 109, Paragraph 2: in managing their respective budgets, the Nation and the Länder shall take due account of the requirements of the overall economic equilibrium, as well as the principle of sustainability and the interests of future generations.

The needs of the present generations have to be reconciled with the life prospects of future generations. Political action must be sustainable and intergenerationally just. But in political day-to-day business, the costs of our decisions are often transferred to future generations, a fact that can easily be seen in our enormous national debt. This indebtedness restricts the opportunities of future generations to design policies, and narrows their freedom to create their own future. The constitutional amendment would obligate all branches of government, especially the legislative, to respect the interests of future generations, and to consider the long-term effects of present actions.

We understand intergenerational justice as part of an extensive concept of sustainability, which applies to all political fields in a way similar to the principle of the welfare state as stated in Section 20a.

We must grant future generations the opportunities to make their own decisions, to design their own future. That should not be limited to eco-policy and energy policy. It also should comprise the sphere of finance, education, the labor market, and healthcare. And to base this sustainable and responsible policy on a solid and long-term foundation, we advocate the constitutional amendment.

Like the requirements of the welfare state, the concepts of intergenerational justice and sustainability are far from clear. They are, in fact, quite vague in their meaning. But that is no reason to abandon these concepts. And, of course, our initiative is not undisputed, even among our own ranks, especially with regard to the relation between sustainable financial policy and the consolidation of the national budget. But it is, and has always been, the specific legal and political applications of our laws that make these living and relevant to our time.

In my opinion, social democratic politics is based on at least two fundamental principles. The first is the strong conviction that the concept of justice has to be a guiding principle in politics. Persons, facts, and issues have to be treated equally under equal or similar circumstances. Second, we believe that one significant condition for the survival of our community, and to maintain the human face of our society is that every part of our society, especially the leaders of politics and economy, must show solidarity with one another. When shaped by solidarity, our society keeps a promise to everyone: no matter what will happen, we will not let you down, you will not be alone, and we will help you out. Solidarity is the only kind of insurance that is able to forgive personal failure. With these two concepts in mind, it should be clear that we will always need a system that balances between the poor and the rich, between the generations, between the young and the old, and between healthy and sick persons. Therefore, intergenerational justice is part of a broader concept of justice, as one fundamental pillar of social democratic politics. The vision of social democratic policy is made up of the realization of the political, social, and economic basic rights through their effective institutionalization.

Modern civilizations can not be governed only by appeals to personal conscience. In order to substantiate our moral values on a stable, reliable, and lasting foundation, we have to lay these down in the general conditions and rules of our society. And the most important framework of our society is our basic constitutional law. With the implementation of intergenerational justice and sustainability in our Constitution, all branches of government, especially the legislative, would be charged to realize intergenerationally just and sustainable policies. Every political decision-making process would have to be vetted to meet the requirements of the principles of intergenerational justice and sustainability.

Beside the institutionalization of these basic rights, we have to ensure that all members of our society have the feeling that the distribution of achievements, life prospects, social participation, education, etc. are just in our society. The degree of the realization of justice in our society serves as the legitimizing factor of our politics. Our decisions today directly affect the lives of future generations, and are often made to their detriment. With the implementation of intergenerational justice and sustainability in our Constitution, a first important step would be made to put an end to this injustice.

Intergenerational justice demands that the present generation fulfils its needs without risking that future generations can not fulfill theirs. In my opinion, the indebtedness of our state, for example, contains a deep injustice, even outside of the burden it presents to future generations. The debts of today are the taxes of tomorrow. Moreover, the national debts, and the payments of interests correlated with these work as a reallocation from bottom to top. The money for interest payments is acquired from the national revenue. Consumption tax and wage tax amount to 75% of our tax budget. Every fifth Euro from the tax budget is spent on interest payments. So, we burden the working people in order to pay the interest of wealthy people. And that can not remain that way. Beside the question how to consolidate the national budget, it is in the interest of the next generation to reduce the national debts in order to break through this reallocation.

Intergenerational justice is also always linked with the conflict between the poor and the rich. Future generations want to know what kind of society they will be born into. They ask how just the society is, and how wealth and property are distributed in it. The incomes of private households have been going down for years. Furthermore, the incomes are unevenly distributed. The poorest 20% of the population have only 10% of the total income. The richest 20% have 36%

of the total income. The picture is similar with respect to the distribution of wealth and assets in our society. The wealth of private households correlates directly with their income situation. The poorest 50% of private households have only 4% of the total wealth at their disposal. By way of contrast, the richest 20% possess about 70% of the total wealth in our society. Available income and wealth both define the position of our citizens in society. Thus, one major task is to create jobs, and to improve the chances for the next generations on the job market. In order to achieve this goal, we have to increase our investments in education and research.

Furthermore, the additional costs of demographic change have to be reflected in our tax system. In my opinion, wealth tax and inheritance tax play a crucial role in this formulation. Moreover, we have to adjust the taxation of the various kinds of wealth. In this context, I also want to mention that the financial elite are able to manage their lives without their own effort, simply by investing their capital. It is not their business ideas, not a new product or service, not their own work that are the source of their wealth. If you assume further that inheritance is one of the most significant kinds of wealth formation, the financial elite are able to live from the efforts of their ancestors. But this diminishes the innovative ability and strength of our society.

Campaigning for the weak, for the poor, and for unprivileged people has always been part of the self-conception of social democratic policy. Yet the needs of future generations are hardly borne in mind in the decision-making processes of today. They have no voice. With the implementation of intergenerational justice and sustainability in our Constitution, we will ensure that the needs of future generations will be considered in the political decisions of today.

9.4 "We Have Only Borrowed the Earth from Our Children" – The Green Perspective, by Anna Lührmann, Member of the German Bundestag (Green)

This slogan, which was already on the campaign posters of the Greens 20 years ago, is today more current than ever. Intergenerational justice was a part of the conception of justice of the Greens from the beginning. This concept makes the original green conviction clear that only politics geared toward the future can be good politics. Political decisions must be sustainable, meaning that they may not have negative consequences for future generations. Future generations should have at least the same opportunities in life as people living today.

In the public debate, however, intergenerational justice is being used ever more frequently as a synonym for "the younger generation wants to take the retirement system away from the older". With sound bites designed to provoke, colleagues in my generation aim to get media attention, but so garner only fears from the older generation.

But this is not about a "war between the generations". Of course, the younger generation wants things to go well for their parents and grandparents. We have a lot to thank them for – growing up in peace and prosperity, our upbringing and education, and much more. And by the same token, the older generation of course wants their children and grandchildren to have a secure future. So, we should not let the Mißfelders[2] and Hirrlingers[3] of this world convince us to start a generation war. We have collective problems that we can solve only collectively.

The future of our children has been jeopardized by ecological depletion, as well as short-sighted social, economic, and financial policies for a long time already. It is high time to act.

Intergenerational justice offers the chance to take a long-term look at politics. Our democracy now obviously has a deep-seated structural problem: its bias toward the present, and disregard for the future. Only people living today take part in elections, and in the majority, from politicians they want answers only to the problems that face them today. It is thus rational for politicians to satisfy first the wishes of the populace that were expressed in the last elections, or perhaps those that will be issues in the next. The flaws of the government can so be explained, but that does not excuse placing burdens on the future with an excessive national debt. In environmental and energy policy, the effects of today's actions can extend particularly far into the future, as some policies can cause irreversible damage. We need to invest in sustainable education and research, instead of concentrating on these short-sighted programs, which will not be sufficient to solve our problems.

We are making the same mistakes as previous generations. Many problems that will face us in the future are already known. Measures to solve these problems early, however, are not politically feasible, because they do not currently have direct effects on the lives of voters.

Intergenerational justice in the Constitution should put an end to short-sightedness in German politics, and institute an equality of opportunity between generations.

Some examples from current political debates illustrate this problem.

- Researchers have been warning us for decades about global warming. The Alliance 90/The Greens have been fighting just as long for initiatives in this field. Earlier, we were laughed at by the other parties – now, they are trying to address the issue, but with inadequate copies of our original propositions. Even so, political initiatives up to this point have been insufficient. We have

[2] Philipp Mißfelder, a former speaker of the "Junge Union" (the youth organisation of the Christian Democrats), generated a media outcry when he said: "I don't like the idea that an 85-year old can receive money from the social security system for hip replacements. Earlier they just used a cane".

[3] Walter Hirrlinger, born in 1926, is the president of the "Sozialverband VdK Deutschland", a pressure group advocating for the rights of veterans and retired persons.

not instituted necessary reforms like the removal of tax exemptions from air travel, the introduction of strict global CO_2 limits for trucks and vehicles, or the institution of a trading system for industrial pollution.
- For decades, the national debt of Germany has been growing ever larger. In principle, there is nothing against state debt, but these debts must be paid back in good economic times. At the moment, a large part of the interest payments of around 45,000,000,000 Euros a year is paid with the taking up of new loans. Our current options of how to deal with debt policy are already being limited. And the debt burden itself grows at a rate of 2,113 Euros per second, further limiting the options of future generations.
- The unemployment rate of older workers has been above the national average for years. However, there are still no retraining and lifelong learning programs that could effectively work against these problems.
- The left within the SPD is arguing against the initiative of younger Representatives for the implementation of intergenerational justice in the Constitution, stating that "the interests of future generations cannot be known to us".

These examples make frightfully clear the importance of an all-encompassing commitment to the rights and opportunities of future generations. The 2002 platform of the Alliance 90/The Greens already addressed this issue comprehensively, and took the principle of intergenerational justice as a foundation in various policy areas. Therefore, we are very happy to have reached a preliminary decision about the development of the bill with the SPD, CDU, and FDP in October of 2006.

Many of the suggestions of The Greens dealing with intergenerational justice over the past decades did not have public opinion on their side. However, our constant demands for sustainable policies, once a political disadvantage, have now become an advantage. We can show that long-term sustainable environmental policy helps our children's children, even when it brings with it some unpopular measures. The best example for this is the introduction of the eco-tax as part of the ecological financial reform. Green ideology has been decried for years, but few today doubt its effectiveness.

In addition, the SPD-Green coalition has already succeeded in instituting a sustainable, climate-friendly energy provision during the last legislative period. The Renewable Energy Bill is an important building block for generationally just energy and environmental policy. By supporting the development and use of renewable resources and energy, we protect our natural resources. At the same time, renewable resources have turned into an important factor for the economy. The national allocation plan is a precondition for the trade of emissions as a central element of a climate policy that is based on market forces, rather than government regulation. Moreover, environmental protection creates jobs. Already today, more than 200,000 people are working in the renewable energy industry – more than in the coal and nuclear energy industries combined. Through ecological modernization, we can invest in, and export innovation. Whoever sees environmental policy as a hindrance to growth is stuck in the past, because building a sustainable economy offers us a chance to create new economic sectors, jobs, and prosperity for the future.

But there is still much more to be done – also outside of environmental policy. In social policy, no solutions are currently being found to deal with the burdens of the retirement and pension system. Moreover, demographic change will burden all future generations more than that of the present. Other examples come to mind concerning budget policy, when we have to take out a credit to pay off debts that earlier generations accumulated. All of these aspects should at long last gain the importance they deserve, through a foundation of intergenerational justice in the Constitution.

One goal of our initiative is to generate a wide public discussion on the issue, and gain further support for the goal of sustainability. Of course, not all the details of the bill have yet been clarified, and the content of the changes to the Constitution will necessitate further political compromise.

But by and large, we can evaluate the whole process as a productive one. Also within the core group of supporters, a new type of political understanding has developed: young, pragmatic politicians who can agree on collective measures to address future-oriented policy. To be sure, the media has viewed the process as a curiosity, convinced that it must be led along party lines. But in the long-term green perspective, we view this consensus as a constructive basis on which to build sustainable ideas of intergenerational justice in the future.

9.5 Intergenerational Justice in the Constitution – The Liberal Perspective, by Michael Kauch, Member of the German Bundestag (FDP)

The Constitution protects the freedom of today's citizens, and sets limits on state actions. There are no limits, however, on constraining the freedom of future generations. It is even politically attractive to deliver goods to today's voters, but foot the bill to our grandchildren and great-grandchildren.

Intergenerational justice mostly takes place today as compensation for the different interests of the present generation. The interests of future generations, however, are hardly considered in the political decision-making process. To be sure, we set "sustainability" and "intergenerational justice" as goals in the discussion of political and social issues, but this rarely translates to actual application in laws. We need effective, long-term politics. Sustainable politics will work for our grandchildren as well. It is not only an insurance of the future of coming generations, but also a recognition of the achievements of the older generation.

For liberals, intergenerational justice is the fulfillment of the social, ecological, and economic interests of current generations, without incommensurately encroaching on the prospects of future generations. The FDP has recognized the principle of responsibility for coming generations since 1997 in its Wiesbaden resolution, as well as advocating a socially and ecologically oriented market economy.

We face large challenges, particularly in the area of securing our natural basis of existence. We especially need to protect the climate, develop an energy system designed for the future, and protect biological diversity, and thus preserve the genetic reproduction potential of our planet. To act to protect the interests of today's youth and future generations, we need to invest in research and development of these areas, and institute market incentives and a legal framework for dealing with these issues.

Social and financial sustainability is particularly endangered today. National debt, and a social system without financial backing lead to exploitation of coming generations. The financing of the social security system is in danger especially when one considers the effects of demographic change. The system must be reformed. The problems of financial support for retirement, health, and old age care are above all questions of finding a balance of contributions between generations. Of all parties, the FDP sees the largest role for individual responsibility within the context of intergenerational justice: only when the social security system moves toward private accounts can the system truly be sustainable. Only this efficient and consistent approach to financial backing of the retirement, health, and old age care systems will present an answer to demographic developments.

The liberals want an ordered withdrawal from the overburdened and heavily indebted state. Thus, the "modest state" must be constitutionally anchored. The heaviest burden of future generations is the ever more quickly growing national debt, which translates into higher taxes and contributions in the future. This terrible debt takes away from future generations the freedom and opportunities, and possibility to shape politics. The alteration of Article 109 in the Constitution will hinder the ability of the Nation and Länder to borrow more.

The FDP is also the only party to speak for a reform of the limits to debt in the state's financial guidelines, to stop the path toward a nation of debt. Those who want to permanently abolish state debt must forbid the uptake of new debts in the Constitution. The FDP supports at least a further reform of Article 115, implementing the application of the Maastricht criteria in the Constitution. Additionally, the possibility for exceptions to the prescriptions of Article 115 contingent on economic conditions should be reduced.

The implementation of intergenerational justice and sustainability in the guiding principles of the Constitution will present the state with legally binding impacts. Every government is responsible for respecting and adhering to its laws and decisions. As a directly specified goal of the state, the principles of intergenerational justice and sustainability would receive a higher priority. They give a clear charge to lawmakers to implement future-oriented policy.

The liberals also emphasize intergenerational justice as part of the national sustainability strategy. For a long time, we have advocated the creation of official balance of accounts between generations. In this intergenerational accounting, the contributions and burdens of society in regard to coming generations should be compared. Thus, we could see the relationship between, on the one hand, contributions in education, support for children and youth, and investments in infrastructure, and on the other hand, social security, national debt, the pension system, and environmental damage. This would create transparency, and form the foundation for a systematic evaluation of the intergenerational contract for lawmakers.

In our nonpartisan initiative to introduce intergenerational justice in the Constitution, our aim is to codify intergenerational justice as a goal of the state, and as a foundation for the national and Länder budget processes. We are unified in the goal to require the protection of future generations within the Constitution. A new Article 20b will be added: "The state must consider the principle of sustainability and must protect the interests of future generations in its decisions". This would be an expansion on the 1994 addition of Article 20a mandating ecological sustainability.

The anchoring of intergenerational justice and the principle of sustainability in the Constitution would allow coming generations a greater influence on political decisions. The important thing for now is introducing the debate of intergenerational justice into the political arena, so we can later address ways to reach this goal.

The young representatives in the German Bundestag have succeeded, despite political differences, in creating a central goal of future-oriented policy. This is promising for the development of a national sustainability strategy. It hopefully will also mean that the parliamentary committees on sustainable development can orient themselves toward long-term goals, not only those focused on the next election.

Chapter 10
Demographic Pressure and Attitudes Towards Public Intergenerational Transfers in Germany – How Much Room Left for Reforms?

Harald Wilkoszewski

How a minority,
Reaching majority,
Seizing authority,
Hates a minority.

Leonard H. Robbins,
on the elderly

10.1 Introduction

Intergenerational transfers transmit goods (money, time, education) from a member of one to another generation. These transfers can be split into two main categories: public sector transfers, where the state reallocates, e.g. money via taxes and benefits between different generations; and intra-family transfers where, e.g. a grandfather is supporting his grandson by financing part of the grandson's university education, or a daughter is taking care of her disabled mother. The last two examples show another dimension of intergenerational transfers: they can be directed either upwards, i.e. from the younger generation to the older one, or downwards (vice versa). For centuries, the direction of the net transfer (both public – in its early forms – and intra-family) has been downwards: generally speaking, the generation of parents and grandparents invested more in their children than they received from them when they where old (Lee 2003).

Both public and private intergenerational transfers are large and have an enormous impact on the wellbeing of all societies. Each young generation has to rely on the resources which the older members of the respective society devote to their health, education and sustenance. In the modern society, too, the wellbeing of the elderly depends on social programs which provide healthcare and income support (Mason et al. 2006).

DOI 10.1007/978-3-540-77084-8 © Springer 2008

Demographic change is radically altering this relationship between generations, especially when we look at public sector transfers: longevity and low fertility rates are exerting increasing pressure on all Western European social security systems. As the percentage of older people grows, ever more money has to be spent on benefits for the elderly, in particular pensions. In Germany, the share in the total population of people aged 60+ is expected to rise from 27.2% in 2000 to 49.2% in 2050 (Adolph and Heinemann 2002). As the number of people of working age declines, the financial burden for each member of this group increases significantly. National budgets may also be affected in terms of increasing deficits, if governments cannot simply transfer all costs to the younger taxpayers immediately.

In 1984 this issue was broached by Samuel Preston, who claimed that higher benefits for older people in the USA were financed by cutting benefits for children and younger people (Preston 1984). An OECD report on educational systems lends support to this hypothesis as far as Germany is concerned: the German national budget is providing ever fewer resources for education whereas the costs for pensions are exploding (OECD 2004).

In addition to the situation described above, there has been a trade-off between public sector and intra-family transfers: in Germany, for example, intergenerational transfers have been moved gradually into the state's sphere of responsibility by implementing the Bismarckian system of public social security. Consequently, people relied less on intra-family transfers than they did previously.

In the light of recent demographic changes, social systems have to be reformed substantially, but room for reforms may be small. Benefits for older people will have to be cut to a certain extent (e.g. by further increasing the retirement age). Whether older people will be willing to accept reductions in their benefits or an increase in the benefits for the younger generation depends largely on their political and social attitudes and preferences: are older people driven by "altruistic" motives and willing to contribute to the reduction of burdens on children by lowering transfers to themselves? Or are they "egoistic", in the sense that they prefer to maintain or even increase the level of transfers to themselves? Are these preferences determined by age or membership of a certain generation? What role do other factors, such as socioeconomic status or the number of children, play? In fact, the question of whether a person remains childless or not may determine the extent to which this person is "altruistic", i.e. accepts public sector transfers to the younger generation.

As the electorate is aging even faster than the whole population – in Germany, the median age of the electorate today is 47 years and is projected to be 54 in 2030 (Sinn and Übelmesser 2000) – and at the same time voting turnouts in older age groups are generally higher than those for younger age groups, the question is whether there is only a small "window of opportunity" left for policymakers to implement necessary reforms. Another limiting factor for reforms may be the level of the self- and special-interest organization of the elderly in the political system (Leisering 2000). In early 2005, roughly 2 million people – i.e. a relatively small group, compared to the total population of Germany – voiced strong opposition to the labour market reforms in Germany. Continuous demonstrations were organized by this group, forcing the government in the end to change some elements of the reform. This may foreshadow what might happen in the future concerning the implementation of reforms of pensions and other social benefits. However, the scope for public transfer reform is also dependent on whether the older generation is capable of putting its interests through in the political system.

In terms of research, the question of intergenerational transfers and demographic change has been addressed mainly by economists aiming at measuring the extent and direction of transfers between generations, as well as by sociologists and psychologists analyzing the underlying motives of transfers. The latter two, however, focused on private intergenerational transfers, rather than public ones. This chapter aims not only at complementing the few existing studies on preferences towards public transfers in Germany, but also at developing a wider research perspective by adding a political science approach: The central question addressed here is to what extent growing numbers of older people, combined with their possibly unified preferences concerning public transfers, may limit the scope of necessary social policy reforms.

An analysis of this question has the potential to contribute to the scientific understanding of transfers in a policy-relevant way in the sense that the (political and social) interests of different groups in the modern welfare state depend largely on rights and duties to which they are entitled according to chronological age. The factor of age, in a system where access to and restriction of benefits is so heavily based on this variable, can be disregarded only as long as the system is stable, i.e. every age group is treated in the same way as its counterpart in the past or in the future. However, demographic change poses major challenges to all modern welfare states. Unequal treatment of different age groups, therefore, is to be expected in the future and, in turn, this may result in the group's refusal to accept political reforms.

The structure of the chapter is as follows: we first give theoretical considerations on the wider context of the research question (Sect. 10.2) and focus particularly on reviewing the importance of preferences within the analysis of intergenerational transfers, including a summary of existing findings (Sect. 10.3). On the basis of recent survey data, we then provide descriptive as well as analytical statistics to investigate whether there is an age effect in transfer policies in Germany (Sect. 10.4). Section 10.5 summarises the findings briefly and gives suggestions for directions of future research.

10.2 Theoretical Starting Point – Mannheim's Concept of Political Generations

Whereas most of the studies dealing with the determinants of intergenerational transfers argue that these transfers are the result of private cooperation and social contracts which are guided by altruism and efficiency concerns (Becker and

Murphy 1988), there has been research work which models transfers as the outcome of political processes in which the magnitude and direction of transfers reflect the political power of the elderly relative to other demographic groups (Preston 1984; Galasso and Profeta 2002; Razin et al. 2002). In these models, the existence of social security is theoretically explained by political competition between two groups – young vs. old – each of these putting pressure on political decision makers in order to make gains in the transfer exchange with the other group. Thus, the final policy outcome – in this case, the intergenerational transfer – depends on the groups' sizes.

With regard to a broader theoretical perspective, Karl Mannheim's concept of "political generations" seems to provide a useful framework; it is derived from his seminal theory of generations (Mannheim 1964). The core idea is that a generation can be the focal point of common interests and, therefore, has the potential to be the basis for collective mobilization: a common generational positioning within the social sphere may be transformed, through the influence of a historical, political or social change, into a generational context and, eventually, form generational units of which the members not only identify themselves through a collective consciousness but also can form a powerful societal group under certain conditions. One of these conditions is the identification with the other members of the same generation, which can be tested empirically by the level of (political) self-organization of the respective generation (Kohli 1996; Dunham 1998).

Even though exposed to some critiques (e.g. Attias-Donfut and Arber 2000), Mannheim's concept has experienced a revival in sociological studies on transfers over the past decade (Kohli 1996, 2003b, Rosenmayr 2000; Szydlik 2000; Dallinger 2002; Niethammer 2003). Dunham (1998), for example, points out that "most of the research has tested the notion of a generation gap as a gap between parents and children [...] rather than reflected in a sense of common identity with one's age group and a general distrust of all of those who are older or younger. [...] There is little research examining the role of this type of consciousness in producing political action".

We propose a research framework which aims at contributing closure of this gap with an analysis in the field of demographic change. According to Mannheim's theory, the formation of a political generation occurs in three progressing steps (Kohli 1996), from (1) a common social location and experience, to (2) consciousness of this shared reality, and to (3) getting together to form a unified political actor. In a corresponding analysis, the first step would be formed by the changing demographic realities in Germany, as well as their public perception, which has become ever more intense over the past years. Especially the current generation of elderly seem to be more exposed to fundamental critique than the ones before. Rather cold-blooded claims by seemingly uninhibited young politicians to, for instance, exclude hip replacements for individuals at advanced ages from the benefit catalogue of public health insurances appear more often in the public discourse. Partially due to the extensive discussion in Germany on demographic change and possibly shared preferences concerning the relation between generations, the elderly might have been able to develop a common consciousness, which could be identified by observing possibly unified political preferences amongst older people; whether this has made the elderly a more powerful group within the political system might then become apparent by the degree to which they organize themselves in interest groups.

One critical point in this application of Mannheim's theory could be that demographic change is not comparable with the characteristics of a war or a sudden social event with high impact, but rather the opposite, because it evolves gradually and is at first barely noticeable. However, the effect which initiates the formation of a generation does not necessarily have to be short and sudden, as Pilcher (1994, p. 491) illustrates with the example of the women's movement: "There has not been a "Wall Street Crash" in women's lives; the changes in women's lives have not occurred in a sharp, easily delineated manner". The same attributes of a slow, gradual alteration of the social situation applies to the example of demographic change.

Another theoretical consideration which we already mentioned in the Introduction deserves closer scrutiny in this context: the question of how an age group's size, intergenerational transfers and political power are interconnected.

Parsons (1982) points out – actually 2 years before Samuel Preston confirmed this guess (Preston 1984) – that due to the then expected sharp rise in the ratio of the elderly relative to the working-age population, transfers to the older generation were likely to increase, leading to greater tax burdens for the welfare state which, in turn, were expected to exert pressure on public policymakers to reduce pension benefits again. However, demographic change increases also the voting participation of the aged, contributing to even more generous benefits for the elderly. Galasso and Profeta (2002, p. 7) stress that "this size effect has often been neglected in the social security literature [...], although it may be crucial in analyzing the impact of demographic changes on the political equi-

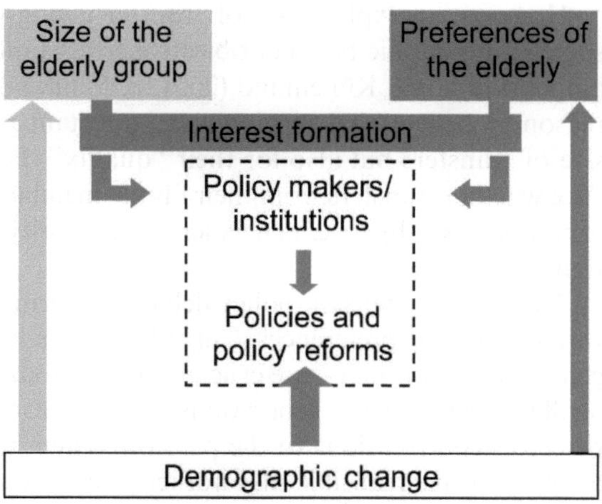

Fig. 10.1 Theoretical framework

librium". In this context, Kohli (2005, p. 4) makes clear that in modern societies, age groups are not given naturally but are "socially constructed through the institutionalisation of the life course. "The elderly" as a category are today directly predicated upon the institutionalised age boundary of retirement". In other words, these age boundaries can be changed – even if at some cost – and according to the hereby created new relative sizes of age groups, the distributional balance would be altered, too. Recently, the mandatory age of retirement has been changed in Germany, and will be increased stepwise by 2 years from 65 to 67. However, this evidently marginal modification will not be able to significantly affect the relative sizes of the age groups. Figure 10.1 illustrates the theoretical framework developed.

10.3 Preferences Towards Public Intergenerational Transfers

Why is it important to consider preferences and their underlying attitudes and motivations when we want to analyze public transfers? In fact, taking into account preferences brings in its wake three main methodological problems. As information on preferences can be retrieved solely by asking individuals, there is the danger – as with all other survey data – that the expressed attitudes are unsystematic and contradictory. Furthermore, it is not clear to what extent people's preferences comply with their actual behaviour. Finally, people may answer sensitive questions in accordance with social desirability, rather than their actual beliefs (Swift et al. 1995).

Apart from these conceptual difficulties, it would be possible to explain behaviour between generations – within the family as well as in the public context – by more reliable socio-demographic variables such as income and wealth of the giving generation, or by the needs of the receiving generation. Relational aspects such as geographical distance, emotional closeness, or the frequency of contact between the young and the old also may serve as explanatory variables for transfers.

However, an explanation of transfer giving which is based solely on these socio-demographic or other objective criteria must remain incomplete. For example, Kohli and Künemund (2001, p. 5) have pointed out that there is "good reason to believe that motives are important not only for the incidence and size of transfers but also for their "quality". For recipients, it makes a difference whether transfers from their family members are motivated by self-interest (only) or (also) by love, benevolence, generosity or a sense of personal obligation".

The ongoing pension policy debate in Germany provides an apt illustration why motives or preferences – in this case, public acceptance of the so-called generational contract – are crucial not only for family but also for public transfer flows between the generations. As long as the generation of working age perceives contributions to the pension system as insurance rates – and not as taxes – it seems plausible that workers are more willing to make these contributions to the elderly. On the other hand, a perception of pension contributions as being pure taxes creates welfare losses by lower support for these transfers, e.g. in the form of an increase of illegal activities in the economy (Börsch-Supan and Reil-Held 2001). Surveys show that at the beginning of the current German pension system in the early 1960s, most workers perceived pension contributions as fair rates, whereas now the majority consider pension benefits as transfers to the generation of the elderly which are linked only loosely to their own contributions (Boeri et al. 2001).

A further reason for the importance of motives and preferences arises from their relevance in structuring social relations as well as the political process. If the outcome of public transfer policies is conceptualized as a result of negotiations between generations, changes in the preferences of large social (or age) groups – such as in the aforementioned example – serve as a crucial factor in forming the preferences of a generation towards certain policies. Thus, motives and preferences are critical because they affect the acceptance of taxes and contributions imposed by the state at the individual level. They also condition the public acceptance of social security reforms on the collective level (Kohli 2005). With regard to the research framework developed above, this is of high relevance: if the preferences and interests of the elderly comply with what the interest groups for these generations formulate towards policymakers, then one could speak of the emergence of a political generation in Mannheim's sense.

On the basis of these considerations, the following section will first present theoretical considerations of the underlying concepts of motivations and preferences for transfers in general. These considerations will provide the basis for identifying the main motives for public intergenerational transfers. We then conclude with an overview of the current state of research on preferences, with a special focus on age-related differences.

10.3.1 Beyond the Dichotomy of Altruism Versus Exchange: Motivations for Intergenerational Transfers

The two main motivations referred to in the research on both public and private transfers (e.g. Feinerman and Seiler 2002) have been, on the one hand, self-interest (exchange between generations) and, on the one hand, altruism (Becker 1974). Depending on the research field, altruism is to a greater or lesser extent favoured over self-interest as the explanatory framework – or vice versa. Some sociological studies tend to interpret all seemingly pro-social behaviour as indication of altruism – for example, contributing money and providing volunteer work for charities, non-cash gifts at social occasions, or all other transactions through which the donor does not gain directly or immediately (e.g. Opaschowski 2004). Also in the area of public transfers, where at first glance surprisingly high levels of support for transfers to the elderly can be observed among younger age groups, altruism serves as the explanatory basis (Kohl 2003). On the other hand, economic studies have the tendency to reduce all motivations – even seemingly altruistic ones – to egoism; this is indeed not in the sense of a direct quid pro quo, but some economists argue that transfer donors still may gain in the longer run, e.g. because they expect reciprocal action at a later stage when they themselves need help (Cox et al. 1998).

However, as Schokkaert (2006) points out, it should be common sense that neither a strategy of reducing pro-social behaviour to a somewhat advanced version of egoism nor a one-sided view on altruistic preferences help to understand the mechanisms of transfers. Consequently, he proposes not only to treat both motives as of equal explanatory value for transfer analysis, but also to extend this dichotomy by two further motives or by several subcategories. Below, this rather comprehensive concept of transfer motives will be briefly presented and discussed in light of the concepts of other authors. It has to be noted that there is no consensus about alternative sets of motivations and the relations among these in the existing literature – apart from the model of altruism vs. exchange (Kohli and Künemund 2001).

The first main motivation in Schokkaert's concept is self-interest, which is divided into two subcategories: material self-interest and social prestige. Material self-interest can be considered as the "pure form" of self-interest, since the donor gives money and/or time because he expects direct consumption benefits from it (e.g. donations made solely in order to increase the donor's tax refund). The hope to gain in social prestige by giving transfers might not be a plausible motive with regard to public transfers, as e.g. paying taxes is not directly linked to social prestige. On the other hand, being able to make transfers may be particularly important for older people whose status in society is threatened by their withdrawal from the labour market (Kohli 1999).

Another version of the self-interest motivation – and the second main transfer motivation – is reciprocity, which is not always clearly distinguishable from the first motivation because, like in the pure egoism model, donors give in order to receive. However, in the case of reciprocity, the transfer has the form of an exchange: all partners benefit from the transfers made. The expectation that donors as well as recipients gain in this interaction is also a necessary condition for them to further participate in the social interaction.

Within the family, public transfer returns from the older to the younger generation provide a plausible example for the reciprocity hypothesis. As Kohli (1999, p. 111) points out that "the high acceptance of the public old-age pension system even among middle and young adults that is (still) demonstrated by survey data can partly be attributed to these return transfers in the family. Middle and young adults know that the public pension system [...] allows them to expect material support [from their parents] in times of need and/or bequests at the time of their parents' death".

Further support for the concept of reciprocity may come from findings of a study on generational accounting in the US welfare system, by Bommier et al. (2004). Its results challenge the common view in the contemporary public discourse on transfers that the distribution of modern welfare burdens is stacked against the younger generation. Although the study confirms large lifetime losses for all generations born after 1972 caused by public transfers to the elderly, it also states that these losses are more than levelled out by gains for the younger generation through the educational system. As a result, there is a net positive balance for generations born up to 2043. Even the generations born afterwards will experience only relatively small lifetime losses, according to the study. The authors conclude: "It no longer appears that we are exploiting the now and future young generations [...]. Indeed, the elderly of today have negative NPV's [net present values], while a baby born today is projected to have a positive one, directly counter to the prevailing view" (Bommier et al. 2004, p. 17).

This could further explain the high support levels among younger people for public transfers towards the elderly: given that the younger generations actually are aware of their potentially favourable position (which might not be the case, due to incomplete information), they may be more willing to pay relatively high taxes and/or contributions to the welfare state in exchange for high investments by the older generations in their future through a good educational system.

The third set of motives in Schokkaert's concept is called "norms and principles". Here pro-social behaviour is explained by the obedience of a donor either to personal principles or to norms set up by society, which impose altruistic rules for social interaction. Thus, a distinction between dutiful altruism and social pressure can be made. Dutiful altruism is based on the internal norms of a person, which lead to a "sense of duty". This person feels committed to pro-social behaviour on the basis of a set of internal moral principles, generally simply called the conscience. As a consequence, the actor behaves altruistically even if the recipient is not expected to return pro-social behaviour. Whereas a dutiful altruist will act pro-socially even if this behaviour can not be observed or rewarded, social compensation is essential to explain behaviour in a setting of social pressure, since the norms are exposed by society, i.e. externally. Sanctions imposed by society on an individual who does not obey to its norms are blame or disapproval. Even though the differences between the two concepts may be clear from a theoretical point of view, Schokkaert stresses that the motivations may not be clearly distinguishable in practice, since one cannot observe whether the norms which an individual obeys are externally or internally imposed.

"Pure altruism", i.e. pro-social behaviour which is driven solely by one's empathy for someone else, represents the fourth main concept of transfer motivations. Supported by recent results in psychological research, which now considers empathy as a motivating aspect for social interaction, pure altruism has been also used in economic utility modelling, in which the recipient's utility enters the donor's utility function.

In conclusion, there are two main drawbacks in the typology presented above: first, it is comprehensive, yet incomplete, since it does not include the concept of justice and intergenerational solidarity, as proposed by Andreß and Heien (2001) or Kohli (2005), especially in the context of public transfers. Even though Schokkaert acknowledges the importance of justice and solidarity, the two aspects are not included into the set of motivations.

This is striking, as they form a dimension of their own, not clearly distinguishable either from norms and principles or from reciprocal behaviour. Justice, for instance, can serve as an externally imposed norm by society with impending sanctions for those who do not obey this norm. At the same time, beliefs surrounding justice always contain an element of "fair", i.e. reciprocal exchange between partners or members of a society. In a society where social justice plays an important role and its manifestation through a more or less generous welfare state becomes visible, people may also be led by strong considerations of "justice" in their social interactions, e.g. the attitude that it is not "just" if children have to suffer from poverty (especially in a rich society), or that older people should not receive optimal healthcare, even at very advanced ages. In Germany, the connection between social norms and justice becomes very clear when we look at the provisions for family support: the family is regarded as a social institution having a role which is central to the state; therefore, Article 6 of the German Constitution places the family under special protection. From this, state support for the family can be derived as a second step. At the same time, the family is regarded as being very important to the German society, thus representing a "social norm".

The second drawback of Schokkaert's set of motivations is that it does not distinguish between motivations for public intergenerational transfers and preferences with regard to private/family transfers. As this chapter focuses on public transfers, it is necessary to endorse Schokkaert's model of motivations correspondingly, which will be done in the following section.

10.3.2 A Set of Motivations for Public Transfers

Are individuals participating in private intergenerational transfers, and transfers between generations on the welfare state level driven by the same motivations? Parsons (1982) calls attention to the fact that

> "the forces that determine the magnitude and even the direction of public transfer payments are not well understood. Some economists have argued that public transfers are simply a reflection of the charity motives of taxpayers. Other economists have stressed the importance of voting power while suggesting that altruism has little to do with most public transfer programs. Of course, these behavioural models are not mutually exclusive; both may capture important elements of the transfer process".

One form of Schokkaert's motivations, pure altruism, is a good example illustrating how difficult it is to distinguish between motivations for public and private transfers. Pure altruism first seems to be an appropriate explanatory variable of transfer interaction solely on the family level, since empathy for another person represents a relatively personal dimension of human life. Compared with childless people, however, people with children – thus, persons with strong empathy to one or more representatives of the younger generation – may also favour public transfers (e.g. education) towards the whole group of younger people in the society to a greater extent. This question is neither addressed by Schokkaert nor has it been analyzed in research work on transfers up to this point. Likewise, it plays no role in the set of motivations proposed by Andreß and Heien (2001) which, however, offer – in one of the few studies in economic research which does – a special framework for the preferences concerning public intergenerational transfers.

Starting from the analytical problem of how to identify individual characteristics which lead to variations in attitudes towards public transfers, their concept introduces four dimensions: motivations concerning the welfare state and (1) its functions, (2) its means (institutions, programs, actors), (3) its (intended and unintended) effects and (4) its financing. Within these dimension, there are four determinants of welfare state attitudes: self-interest, values and norms, different socialization patterns, and national welfare cultures.

Self-interest motivation corresponds to Schokkaert's definition but adds another aspect to it, namely the different roles of the individual in the welfare state: as consumers of public intergenerational transfers, citizens are expected to support these regulations much more than would taxpayers, who actually have to pay for these. Consequently, the older generation does not support transfers to the younger age cohorts, such as child benefits, as it does not profit from these directly.

With regard to values and norms, the difference from Schokkaert's set of motives is that Andreß and Heien do not differentiate between social pressure and dutiful altruism. Additionally, they focus this dimension of motives exclusively on justice beliefs: "In terms of attitudes towards the welfare state, values and norms that concern the question of how material and non-material goods should be distributed between the members of a society are of particular interest. Since this question is connected with the problem of a just society, we call these values and norms *justice beliefs*" (Andreß and Heien 2001, p. 340). Special attention is paid to the distinction between egalitarian vs. non-egalitarian attitudes: justice beliefs can be sorted along a continuum of transfer regulations from absolute equality to absolute differentiation. Egalitarian-oriented actors are expected to show more support for public transfers than would non-egalitarian ones. This rather one-sided understanding of societal values is problematic, however, as other social norms, such as (economic) efficiency, which might be helpful to understand transfer interactions are excluded.

Another conceptual weakness in the concept presented arises from looking at the third and fourth determinants of welfare state attitudes: differential socialization and national welfare cultures. Andreß and Heien (2001) have stressed that values and norms are not given naturally but that they are influenced by socialization processes at the individual (social milieu) as well as the aggregate level (welfare state organization). Consequently, these processes form a different category of determinants – since they are the ground on which observed attitudes are built on – and should not be treated on the same level as self-interest and values and norms. This "distinction of quality" is not included in the concept presented.

In order to analyze the specific socialization processes, Andreß and Heien refer to several individual characteristics: age, gender, education and employment sector. With regard to the explanatory capacity of age – which is of particular interest in the context of the question addressed in this chapter – the authors rely solely on Inglehart's theory of materialistic and post-materialistic values (Inglehart 1977). According to this theory, younger generations, influenced by socialization experiences different to those of their parents and grandparents, are expected to have post-materialistic values such as self-fulfilment, environmental protection, and solidarity. This is an approach which interprets age as an explanatory variable for transfer motivations, based exclusively on cohort considerations and, therefore, problematic. In sociology as well as political science, a rather vast literature exists on the hypothesis of age conservatism; even though there is consensus that the influence of chronological age on changing social and political values should not be overestimated, the hypothesis that age has no effect at all does not hold in the light of empirical results (Rattinger 1994). It also has to be critically noted that the family situation of the individual, i.e. the question of whether the person has one or more children or remains childless, is not included in Andreß and Heien's set of characteristics, even though it might have a crucial impact on attitudes towards public transfers, as argued above.

10.3.3 Empirical Findings on Preferences Towards Public Intergenerational Transfers

10.3.3.1 Studies on the Magnitude and Direction of Transfers

Whereas the analysis of preferences has been broached only recently in a relatively elaborate way (Kohli 2003a), most of the economic and sociological research work which has been done on the relation between generations has dealt with the magnitude and direction of intergenerational transfers. Generally, these studies come to the conclusion that family transfers exist to a significant extent and are given mostly from the elderly to the younger generations (e.g. McGarry and Schoeni 1997), whereas public transfers have been directed upwards (Lee 2003), even though recent generational accounting studies have added support to the hypothesis that – in the case of the USA – the net present value over the life cycle is positive for current younger generations (Bommier et al. 2004). According to Schokkaert (2006), one of the most remarkable findings in the empirical work on the magnitude of transfers is the significant effect of age and education in terms of voluntary work and charitable giving: highly educated, older people give more of their resources than do the less educated and younger members of society.

10.3.3.2 Studies on Preferences Towards Public Intergenerational Transfers

When we look at preferences, it has to be noted that most studies dealing with the analysis of attitudes focus on private intergenerational transfers in specific social interactions in the family context (e.g. Cox and Soldo 2004). Far less research has been devoted to the analysis of preferences towards public intergenerational transfers. This is partly due to the fact that the necessary survey data are available only to a limited extent. The most recent overview of studies on attitudes towards public intergenerational transfers is given by Kohli (2005). However, these studies all focus on the so-called generational contract, i.e. they deal exclusively with upward transfers in form of pension contributions and – with the exception of one study (Smith 2000) – do not contrast this with attitudes towards downward transfers, e.g. to families (children's day care) or the young (education).

Two data sources were used in these studies (Smith 2000; Hicks 2001; Andreß and Heien 2001; Kohl 2003; Blekesaune and Quadagno 2003; European Commission 2004), focusing on international comparison: (1) the International Social Survey Program (ISSP), a rather extensive (in terms of sample size) yearly survey with additional topical modules at larger intervals and (2) the Eurobarometer, the regular survey of the European Union covering all member and candidate countries, although with smaller sample sizes than the ISSP, which make the analysis of preferences according to age groups more difficult.

Concerning the general picture of preferences towards transfers (regardless of the effect of age), all recent studies basically offer the same findings: the analysis of Hicks (2001), which is based on ISSP data, shows that the majority in all countries oppose reductions of old age benefits. Furthermore, when asked if government spending on pensions should be increased "more" or "much more", even at the cost of a general tax increase, considerable fractions of the analyzed populations agree with this policy option. In Germany, 13.5% of the population opt for "much more", even a third for "more" public spending for the elderly, whereas only 3.9 and 0.4% support "less" and "much less" expenditures respectively. With regard to the responsibility for the provision of pensions, the study finds high support in all countries, claiming that the state should be responsible for the income of the elderly. In Germany, this view even gained support during the last decade of the 20th century (38% in 1992, 40% in 1999).

More recent findings on these issues are provided by a special Eurobarometer in late 2001 covering public attitudes to the welfare state's tasks, such as a guaranteed minimum pension or the pay-as-you-go system, which both can rely on the support of a large majority of citizens throughout the EU, showing very little difference between countries (European Commission 2004). This Eurobarometer also asked for preferences towards a set of three concrete policy options which aim at lowering the burden of increased expenditure for the pension systems: raising the age of retirement, maintaining contributions at the cost of lower benefits, and maintaining current benefits at the cost of higher contributions or taxes. The first option, raising the age of retirement, distinctively receives the least public support among EU citizens (23%), whereas 69% strongly or slightly disagree with this option. In contrast, clear majorities in all EU member states are in favour of maintaining current pension levels. This result is particularly striking because the current European working-age population is sceptical regarding future benefit levels of the state pension, even though public pension is still perceived to be the main income of the elderly in the future (Kohl 2003).

The drawback of the studies mentioned is clearly to be identified by the fact that they do not contrast pension transfers for the elderly with government spending on other policy fields, which potentially benefit younger generation. As people obviously tend to perceive the state as being the most responsible actor for social care (see above), it is plausible that the majority might support transfers to all age groups, regardless of the cost. The explanatory power of the respective questions would be much higher if the respondents had to make a choice, e.g. between transfers for the elderly and transfers for the family under the framework of a limited budget. Unfortunately, most surveys ask this kind of "either–or" questions, at least with regard to transfers, only to a limited extent, presumably because these questions tend to be rather complex and, thus, time-consuming and not suitable for a questionnaire.

Smith's study somewhat addresses the gap in the research described above by focusing – apart from other sets of questions – on preferences concerning government expenditure on different policy fields (elderly, education, police, education, health), using ISSP data from 1985, 1990 and 1996 (Smith 2000). The main results of this study show that, on average, an increase in public spending for the healthcare sector is favoured over increased retirement benefits which, in turn, ranks above all other government sectors. However, there exist relatively large country-specific differences. (West)German respondents in 1985 and 1990, for example, enormously favoured raises in expenditure for environmental protection (81.1 and 89.5% respectively), even at the cost of higher taxes.

Even though this study points into the right direction, its results have only limited explanatory use – as the government expenditures which were included in the ISSP modules cannot be directly connected to the interests of either the young or the older generation. The exception is education, which however was not analyzed in Smith's study in the context of differences in age groups.

10.3.4 Socio-demographic Influence on Preferences Towards Public Transfers: Does Age Matter?

Whether age has an influence on attitudes towards public intergenerational transfers remains a controversial issue in the recent literature. Kohli (2005, p. 19), for example, draws the conclusion that "most attitude studies to this point show a level of acceptance of welfare policies that is much higher than the discourse on generational equity would lead us to think, with pensions being the most popular part of the welfare state. There is some differentiation along the age dimension, but much less than one would expect from an interest-based model of political preference".

This conclusion follows the argument presented by Hicks (2001) and Blekesaune and Quadagno (2003). The former claims that there are only few age differences regarding public pensions, as providing a decent standard of living for the old should (definitely or probably) be the government's responsibility in the eyes of a majority through all age groups in the countries included in the analysis (Canada, Germany, Italy, Japan, Sweden, UK, USA). However, looking at the percentages in detail reveals that this conclusion can hold only for the USA, where the gap in percentages concerning the mentioned attitude is only 3.1% (38.7% for the youngest, 41.8% for the oldest age group in the USA). In all other countries, this gap is considerably bigger, and peaks at 24.3% in Canada.

On the basis of Eurobarometer data, Kohl (2003) also argues that differences in attitudes between age groups concerning the needs for social protection at old age are relatively small, even though he identifies indications of weaker support for the idea of intergenerational solidarity among younger people.

In contrast, Smith (2000, p. 12), analyzing ISSP data, finds systematic differences in support of governmental spending on pensions: "Across age groups the predominant pattern was for support for governmental spending for retirement benefits to rise with age [...]. This occurred in 19 of 25 countries. The generational differences were often quite large". Similar findings are presented in a study by Ponza et al. (1988). Their analysis of General Social Surveys in the USA adds support to the hypothesis that the elderly promote their own interest, as older respondents were least likely to support higher spending for education and least likely to have the view that too much is spent on social security. Furthermore, when asked about their view on increasing expenditure on welfare programs for low-income families, the aged had a larger likelihood than any other age group to view current spending levels as too high and the smallest likelihood to perceive these as too low. To explain these differences, Ponza et al. indeed include some socio-demographic variables in their study, but not the number of children of the respondents.

The only study found that considers this variable in its multivariate analysis of attitudes is that of Logan and Spitze (1995). It compares the levels of support between the age groups 40 to 80+ at 10-year intervals for a series of preferences towards parent–child relations and governmental programs for older people. Programs within the family sector are not taken into account. The data used in this study come from interviews with 1,200 residents of the Albany-Schenectady-Troy metropolitan area, a region in the US state of New York. As a main result, Logan and Spitze conclude from their analysis that older people's attitudes in both mentioned spheres tended to be the least likely to be selfish, i.e. representing the "pro-elderly" position, also if controlled for other variables. Still, the number of children seems to have an effect: "People with more adult children are more likely to adopt attitudes favouring the younger generation".

10.3.5 Conclusions

Are relations between the young generation and the elderly based on self-interested group consciousness of the latter – thereby limiting the scope for future public transfer reforms – or on their altruistic motives? Existing research remains inconclusive concerning this question: some studies claim to identify altruism as the main motivation, whereas other research work, especially in the framework of aging group consciousness, emphasizes the importance of self-interest. To a certain extent, the findings have to be contradictory due to the limitations of the samples or the analytic models.

Compared to, for example, the dataset used by Logan and Spitze, which should further contain the appropriate questions of choice between different transfers as well as necessary information on the differential socialization of the respondents, a study on the basis of data with a larger sample size could add clarification to this area of research.

10.4 Empirical Analysis: Public Intergenerational Transfers in Germany

The following section aims at providing a first step in analyzing the wider research framework developed in Sections 10.2 and 10.3, as well as at contributing to the few existing preference analyses for the German case. In particular, we are interested in whether there is a difference along the age line with regard to transfer preferences. To point out the relevance of Germany as an example, we start with a brief outline of policy-relevant demographic trends and the recent shift in transfer policies which is seemingly putting more emphasis on supporting the younger generation. The empirical analysis will first present descriptive findings from recent survey data, and then introduce a logistic regression model which estimates the age effect on supporting a specific transfer policy measure (significant increase in child benefits).

10.4.1 Policy-relevant Demographic Trends and the Recent Transfer Policy Shift in Germany

As in almost all other European countries, Germany's population has been aging due to persistent low fertility rates and increasing life expectancy, the latter being an international trend persisting at a remarkably steady rate (Oeppen and Vaupel 2002). In 1840, Swedish women had the world's longest life expectancy: under prevailing living conditions, they could expect an average lifespan of about 45 years. Japanese women, today's record holder, can anticipate a lifespan of more than 85. Over the past 160 years, national life expectancy has steadily risen about 2.5 years per decade. Except for the periods of the two World Wars, the trend in Germany has followed the international development with a lag of about 4 to 5 years (see Fig. 10.2).

As a result, the mean age of the German population will increase significantly in the coming decades, from 37.4 years in 2002 to over 44 years in the year 2050 (see Fig. 10.3). The electorate (population aged 18+) is aging as well: its mean age was 43.9 years in 2002 and will go up to the value of almost

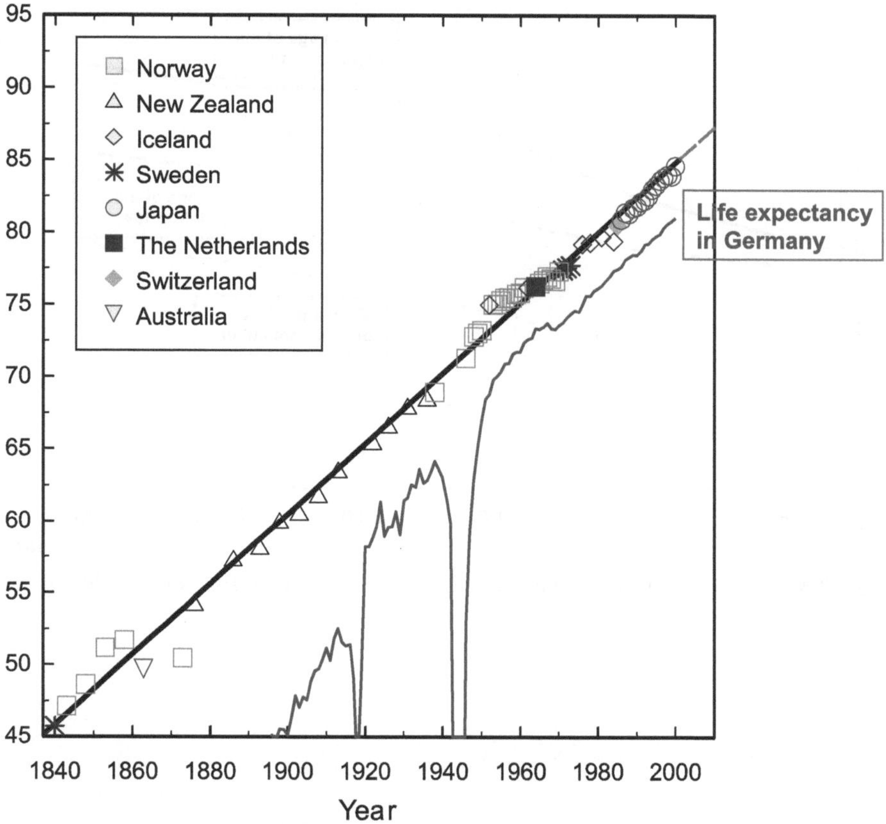

Fig. 10.2 International record life expectancy and trend for Germany (source: Oeppen/Vaupel 2002)

50 years in the next five decades. Examining the age structure of this subpopulation reveals how dramatic the development will be for the relative weight of the younger vs. older generation: the median age of the electorate will rise from 45.8 years in 2002 to almost 56 years, i.e. in 2050 half of the German population will be 56 years or older, and thus close to the current de facto retirement age of 60. With regard to socio-demographic characteristics of the future German population, recent research shows that an increasing percentage of the elderly will be childless and married (Doblhammer et al. 2006). This is due to the relatively high marriage rates in the 1970s and the almost simultaneous increase of couples who remain childless over their whole life course.

More relative political power is given to the elderly not only by a fast-aging electorate but also due to another phenomenon: older people tend to exert their voting rights more often than do the young generation. Figure 10.4 presents the voter turnouts at national elections for the German parliament from 1972 to 2002. While overall turnout rates have been decreasing over time, they increase with age at all elections, peaking in the age range between 60 and 70.

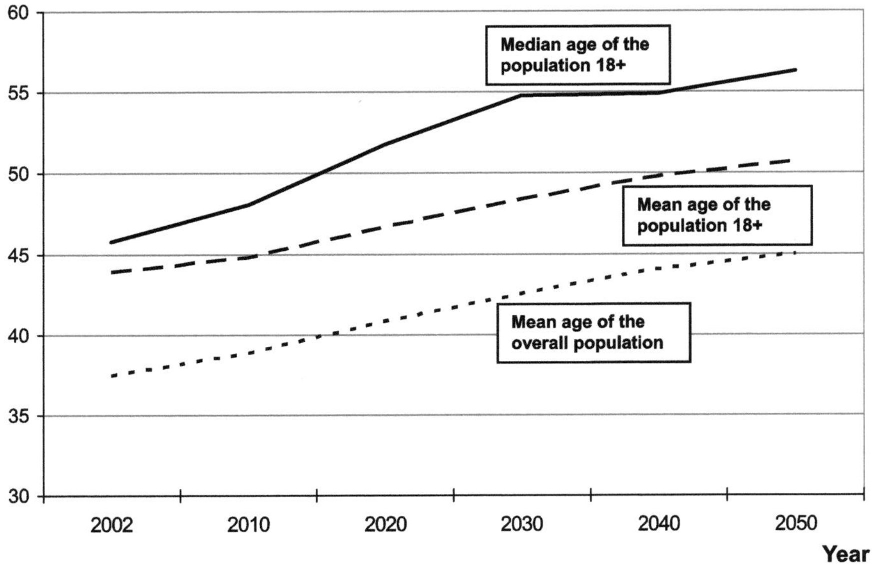

Fig. 10.3 Aging of the German electorate (source: Dickmann (DW Cologne, 2004))

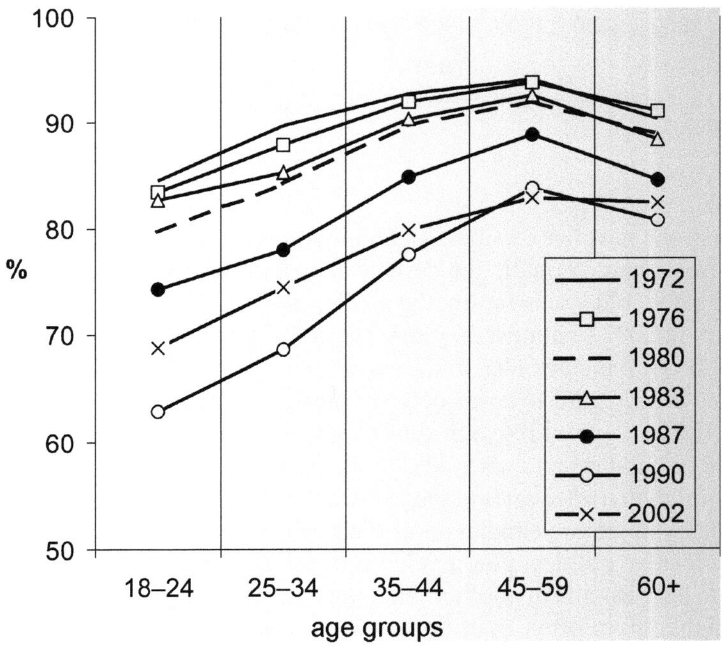

Fig. 10.4 Voter turnouts, Germany national elections 1972–2002 (source: own representation on basis of data from the Federal Statistical Office)

Please note that the highest age group is an open interval, and thus includes also people at advantaged ages at which voter turnouts are declining sharply due to bad health conditions.

Yet Germany is not only experiencing a dramatic change in the age structure of its population, which is of high policy relevance for the question addressed in this chapter. There has also been a remarkable shift in transfer policies over the past years, partly driven by the severe budgetary problems which Germany has been facing, and partly due to demographic considerations. When looking at the public discourse on the consequences of demographic change, the general trend seems to be to advocate reductions in transfers to the elderly and a concurrent increase of transfers for the younger generation. This becomes particularly evident if we look at two policy areas: pensions and family support. Even though pensioners in Germany still enjoy a high-level social security system, there have been major policy changes implemented over the past years resulting in lower transfer levels: decreasing net replacement rates, increasing taxation of pensions (e.g. for health insurance and long-term care) and – very recently decided by the current government's Grand Coalition – a stepwise increase of the official retirement age from 65 to 67. Furthermore, for the first time ever in the history of social security in Germany, the government put through a law in order to secure current pension levels in early 2006.[1] The logic behind this is that in Germany the yearly adjustments of pensions are linked to the per-capita income growth. In the light of high unemployment rates as well as increasing numbers of low-paid jobs, this growth was expected to be negative for the year 2006, which would have resulted in a negative adjustment of current pensions. However, real pensions have already been decreasing since 2003 as their adjustments were frozen to 0%, i.e. they have not been compensating for inflation.

At the same time, the discourse in the area of family policy aims at increasing benefits for the younger generation. On the basis of recommendations by Bert Rürup, a well-known governmental advisor, in 2003 the Federal Ministry for Family Affairs adopted a new paradigm called "Sustainable Family Policy" (Rürup and Gruescu 2003). Its "meta-aim" is to increase fertility rates by providing more transfers for families. This is in line with the general political response to demographic change, as all political parties in Germany prefer strategies to immanently influence population trends by manipulating birth rates, over concepts of adjustments to the demonstrably inevitable population aging (Wilkoszewski 2003).

The first concrete policy reform on the basis of the new political paradigm is the introduction of a rather generous paid parental leave benefit, which came into effect at the beginning of 2007. It includes a monthly payment of 67% of the salary drawn before the parental leave period for up to 12 months. It can

[1] See printed matter 16/794 of the German parliament online at http://dip.bundestag.de/btd/16/007/1600794.pdf. Critics pointed out that a negative adjustment of pensions had not been expected anyhow, qualifying the law as being entirely symbolic.

be prolonged by another 2 months, if the second parent (often the father) also takes a parental leave of at least 2 months. The maximum monthly payment is € 1,800.[2] The additional costs per annum for the national budget are expected to be € 3.9 billion.[3]

10.4.2 Current Preferences Towards Public Transfers: Descriptive Findings from the Population Policy Acceptance Survey 2003

The Population Policy Acceptance Survey is an international survey project which had its first wave in 1992. In 2003, the second wave for Germany was conducted; it contains information on general views about demographic trends as well as intergenerational relations and preferences towards respective policy options. The sample size of 4,110 respondents is sufficiently big for statistical analysis. With an age range of 20 to 65, the 2003 wave also covers the age groups relevant for the research question at hand.

However, the dataset bears two limitations: first of all, it is cross-sectional and, therefore, not suitable for identifying patterns of preference change. The first, 1992 wave could theoretically be used as a reference point in the past; the age range of its respondents, however, is only 20 to 39, which exacerbates conclusions about trends. The second limitation is the design of the questionnaire, which does not urge the respondent to make a choice between transfers for the older or for the younger generation. On the other hand, the dataset does contain all relevant socio-demographic variables, and represents the most recent data collection available for Germany in the area of demography and intergenerational transfers.

The descriptive analysis of the data produces a mixed picture regarding a possible age effect on transfer preferences. When asked for the government's responsibility towards either the younger or the older generation, we find a remarkably uniform pattern of attitudes across all age groups: 35% of the youngest age group (20 to 29) and 48% of the oldest age group (50 to 65) in Germany think that the government's responsibility for the "support of the elderly" is "very high"; 49% (youngest) and 40% (oldest) assess the responsibility as "high". The categories "low" and "very low" find only minor support (see Fig. 10.5a). When asked about the responsibility in the area of family support ("compatibility of work and children"), the patterns are similar: 35% (aged 20–29), 42% (30–39), 43% (40–49) and 35% (50–65) of the respondents see a "very high" responsibility; the corresponding percentages for the category "high" are

---

[2] See the governmental bill online at http://www.bmfsfj.de/RedaktionBMFSFJ/Internetredaktion/Pdf-Anlagen/gesetzentwurf-elterngeld,property=pdf,bereich=,rwb=true.pdf.

[3] http://www.tagesschau.de/aktuell/meldungen/0,1185,OID5621866,00.html.

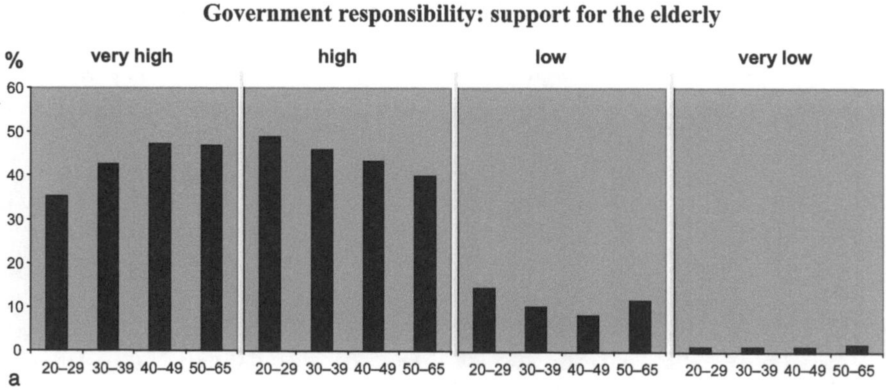

a

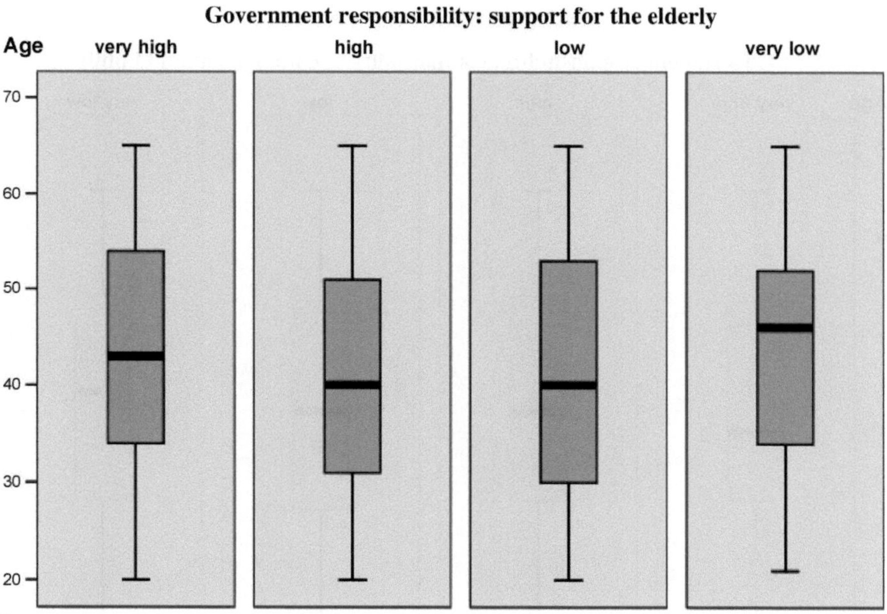

b

Fig. 10.5a,b Population Policy Acceptance Survey 2003: government responsibility: support for the elderly (source: own calculations)

slightly higher: 45, 43, 41 and 45% respectively (Fig. 10.6a). Box plots are another way of displaying the respondent's age distribution in each category by providing 25%-, 50%-, (median, bold line), and 75%-Quartiles. The boxplots in Figs. 10.5b and 10.6b show clearly that there is practically no age effect on the views expressed. These uniform patterns might be due to the political culture in Germany, which is influenced by the legacy of a generous social welfare as well as the politically promoted principle of equalisation of living standards not only in territorial terms but also over the life course.

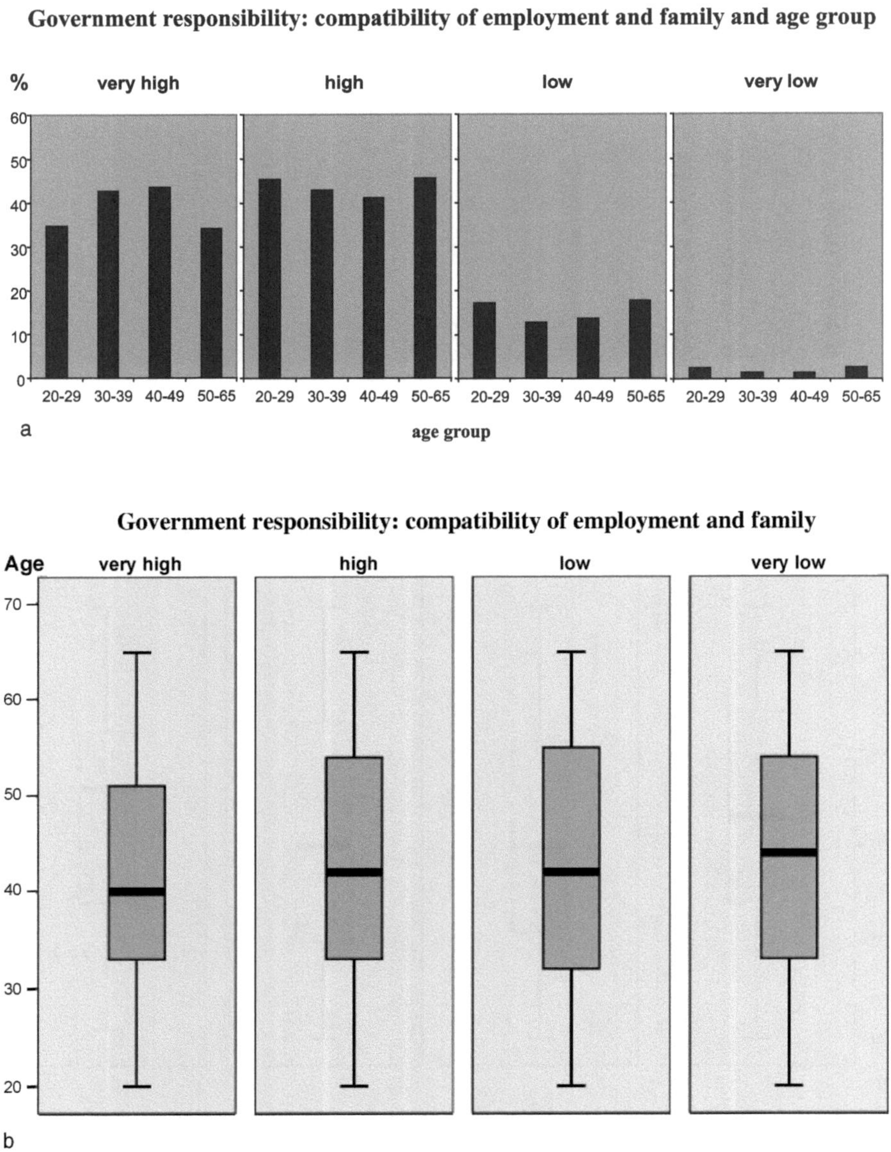

Fig. 10.6a,b Population Policy Acceptance Survey 2003: government responsibility: compatibility of employment and family (source: own calculations)

A mixed picture emerges when the respondents are asked about their views on the general role of the elderly in society: again, a rather uniform distribution across age can be seen with regard to the view "elderly people are not productive anymore" (Fig. 10.7) but, compared to younger people, older people tend to more often reject the view that "elderly people are a stumbling block for (social) change" (Fig. 10.8).

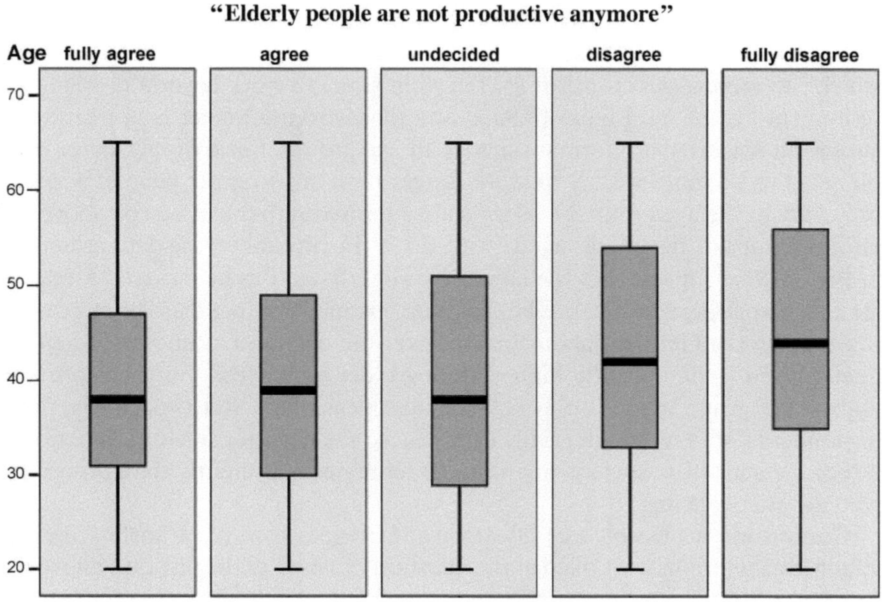

Fig. 10.7 Population Policy Acceptance Survey 2003: elderly people are not productive anymore (source: own calculations)

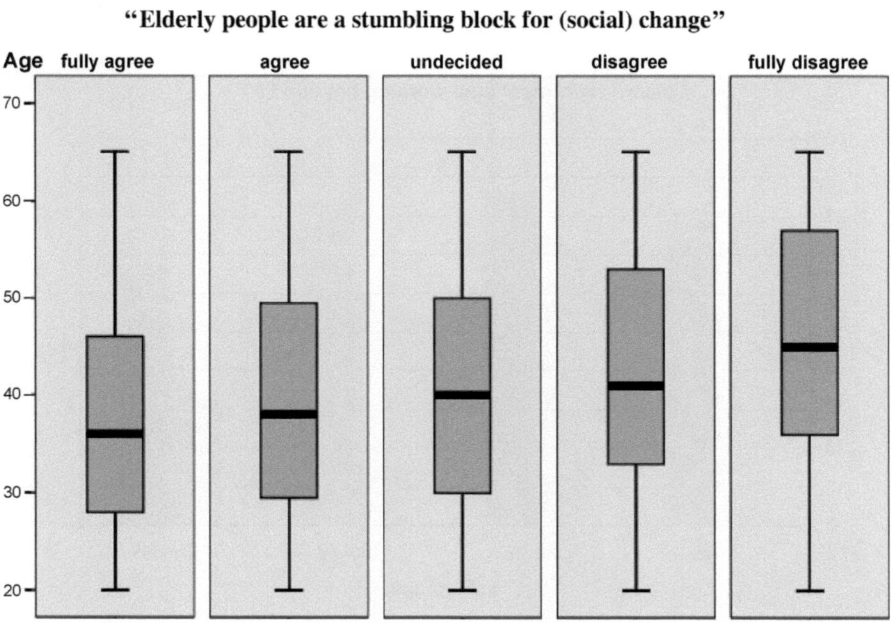

Fig. 10.8 Population Policy Acceptance Survey 2003: elderly people are a stumbling block for (social) change (source: own calculations)

Further indications of age effects can be seen in terms of concrete policy measures: the respondents were asked to give their desired retirement age, which can serve as an indicator for the willingness to work beyond the de facto retirement age of 60. Figure 10.9a shows that working longer is not a preference for a majority of Germans across all age groups. Surprisingly, older people seem to be more willing to work longer than are younger people: whereas only 12% in the age group 30–39 indicate a desired retirement age of above 60, almost a third of the people aged 50–65 do so. Furthermore, the data presented in Fig. 10.9b,c suggest that the latter also slightly tend to be parents. A reason for this surprising result could be that older people have been under increasing pressure on the German labour market over the past years: the risk of getting unemployed is significantly higher among older employees. Furthermore, the highest age group in the survey also includes pensioners. Retrospectively, these respondents, who have potentially experienced the negative side of a functional disengagement from society, might judge retirement differently than do people who are still working.

Concerning a possible age effect on preferences towards transfers for the younger generation, we looked at the question of whether the respondent would support a "significant increase in child benefits", which not only represents a clear-cut policy measure but also indicates that the state would have to spend more money to implement the policy. The boxplot in Fig. 10.10 shows that the median age of respondents who "disagree" or "fully disagree" with this policy option is 4 to 5 years higher than that of people who are in favour of it.

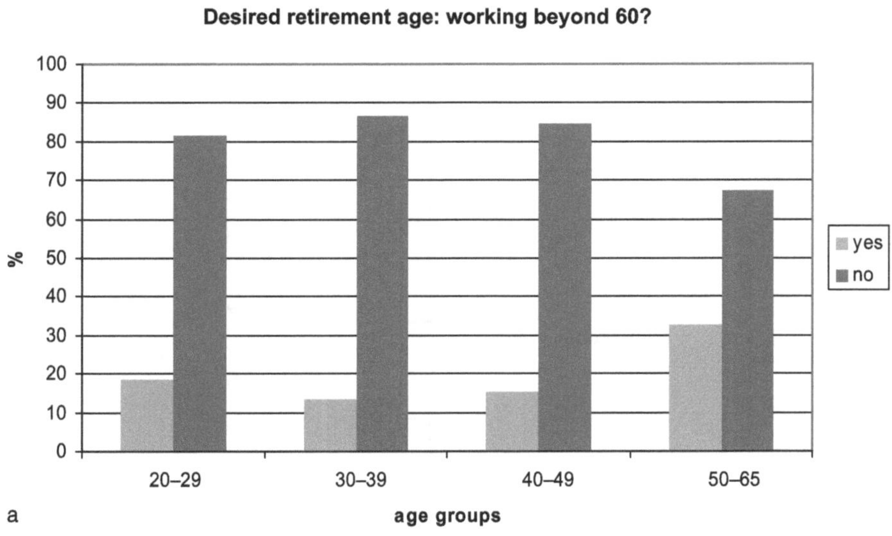

a

Fig. 10.9a,b Population Policy Acceptance Survey 2003: desired retirement age: working beyond 60? Source: own calculations

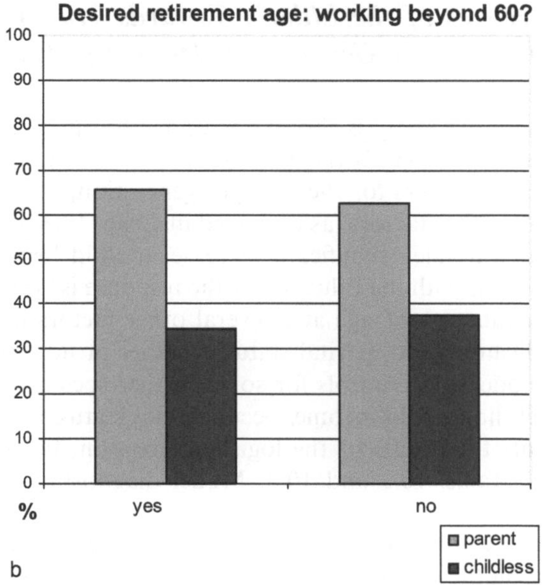

Fig. 10.9a,b *(continued)* Population Policy Acceptance Survey 2003: desired retirement age: working beyond 60? Source: own calculations

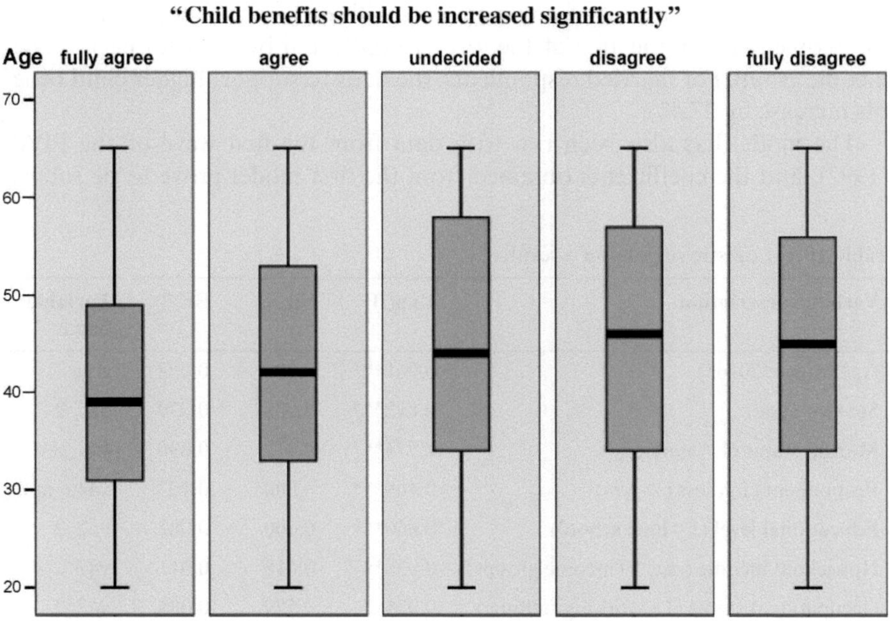

Fig. 10.10 Population Policy Acceptance Survey 2003: child benefits should be increased significantly (source: own calculations)

10.4.3 Preferences of the Elderly Towards Transfers for the Younger Generation: Does Age Matter?

Based on the descriptive analysis above, we decided to run a logistic regression model to analyze how strong is the effect of the observed age pattern in the preference towards transfers for the younger generation, whether it is significant, and what role other factors (as discussed in Chap. 10.3) might play.

The dependent variable "significant increase in child benefits" is recoded into a dummy variable with the value of 1 if the response is "fully agree", which is predicted by a function of age and several other factors including further demographic indicators (sex, marital status, whether or not the respondent is childless). The model also controls for some further socioeconomic variables (educational level, household income, occupational status, area of residence). Table 10.1 presents the results of the logistic regression. For further descriptive statistics, see Tables 10.2 and 10.3. Model diagnostics are presented in Table 10.4.

All coefficients, except for occupational status, are highly significant. We find a clear age effect on the dependent variable: with every year gained in life, the odds to support a significant increase in child benefits decrease by 3.9%, holding all other variables constant. Men are 18.8% less likely to be in favour of the proposed policy measure than are women; the odds for childless respondents to do so are 53.2% lower than for parents. For people with higher education, higher income and those living in Eastern Germany, the odds are smaller as well: they decrease by 34% for respondents with high-school degree, by 37.9% for people living in the area of the former GDR, and by 2.5% for each higher income group. For married respondents, the odds to support higher child benefits increase by 27.4%.

The model has also been run with data from the first wave of the PPAS (1992), and the coefficients obtained from the first model prove to be robust.

Table 10.1 Logistic regression – results

Variable/description	Exp(B)	Sig.	SE	Variable name
Age (range: 20–65)	0.961***	0.000	0.003	Age
Sex (1 = male)	0.812***	0.008	0.079	v37_2
Marital status (1 = married)	1.274***	0.012	0.096	v11_test
Respondent childless (1 = yes)	0.468***	0.000	0.103	v44a_new
Educational level (1 = high school)	0.660***	0.000	0.082	v52_2
Household income (net, 19 income groups)	0.975**	0.018	0.011	v87
Occupational status (1 = working fulltime)	0.975	0.579	0.084	v47_2
Area of residence (1 = West, 0 = East)	0.621***	0.000	0.092	WvsE
n = 3,301	14.718***	0.000	0.206	Constant

Table 10.2 Descriptive statistics of logistic regression model

	n	**Min.**	**Max.**	**Mean**	**SD**
Marital status (1 = married)	4,105	0	1	0.481	0.500
Area of residence (1 = West, 0 = East)	4,110	0	1	0.797	0.402
Sex (1 = male, 0 = female)	4,110	0	1	0.494	0.500
Increase in child benefits (1 = fully agree, 0 = else, missing = undecided)	3,477	0	1	0.494	0.500
Educational level (1 = high school, 0 = else)	4,104	0	1	0.318	0.466
Occupational status (1 = fully employed)	4,103	0	1	0.514	0.500
Age (years)	4,110	20	65	42.269	12.923
Household income (net, 19 income groups)	3,809	1	19	10.605	4.127
Childless (1 = yes)	4,090	0	1	0.364	0.481
Valid *n* (listwise)	3,196				

Table 10.3 Household income, net

Group	**Household income, net (in €)**
1	<150
2	150–300
3	300–500
4	500–700
5	700–900
6	900–1,100
7	1,100–1,250
8	1,250–1,500
9	1,500–1,750
10	1,750–2,000
11	2,000–2,250
12	2,250–2,500
13	2,500–2,750
14	2,750–3,000
15	3,000–3,250
16	3,250–3,500
17	3,500–3,750
18	3,750–4,000
19	>4,000

Table 10.4 Logistic regression – model fit

Omnibus tests of model coefficients				
		Chi-square	df	Sig.
Step 1	Step	254.291	8	0.000
	Block	254.291	8	0.000
	Model	254.291	8	0.000
Model summary				
–2 Log likelihood	Cox & Snell R Square	Nagelkerke R Square		
4,175.997	0.076	0.102		
Hosmer and Lemeshow test				
		Chi-square	df	Sig.
		9.790	8.000	0.280

The age effect is somewhat smaller: for every year gained in life, the odds to fully agree with significantly higher child benefits decrease by 2.9%. However, this smaller effect is not a result of a change in preference structure but rather due to different characteristics of the two survey waves: the data from 1992 cover only an age range of 20–39 years, whereas the PPAS sample from 2003 includes also people aged 40 to 65.

10.5 Summary and Directions for Future Research

This chapter has developed a research framework for analyzing the feasibility of future social policy reforms in the light of demographic trends. Starting from Mannheim's concept of political generations, we demonstrated the importance of preferences when studying public intergenerational transfers and provided a conceptual overview of these.

As a first step of applying the proposed research framework, we used descriptive and analytical statistics on the basis of new survey data for Germany in order to identify possible age effects on transfer-related preferences. Even though the descriptive statistics provided a mixed picture with regard to this issue, our analytical model identified a clear age effect on preferences towards a concrete transfer policy, thus adding evidence to some existing studies. It also gave new insights on the effect of other demographic indicators such as childlessness, sex, and marital status, which do have a significant effect on the attitude examined.

However, these results necessarily have to remain incomplete in terms of answering the question of whether a new political generation of older people with unified transfer preferences is about to emerge in Germany: the data used for the analysis are cross-sectional and do not include all relevant areas of public intergenerational transfer (e.g. education).

Future research within this framework should focus on the analysis of longitudinal survey data in order to identify possible changes in transfer preferences over time. Furthermore, additional qualitative investigations (e.g. focus groups) could help in adding support to the preferences found and in explaining the underlying motivations.

References

Adolph H, Heinemann H (2002) Zur Lebenssituation älterer Menschen in Deutschland. Ausgewählte Daten und Kurzinformationen. Deutsches Zentrum für Altersfragen, Berlin, Diskussionspapier Nr 37

Andreß H-J, Heien T (2001) Four worlds of welfare state attitudes? A comparison of Germany, Norway, and the United States. Eur Sociol Rev 17(4):337–356

Attias-Donfut C, Arber S (2000) Equity and solidarity across the generations. In: Arber S, Attias-Donfut C (eds) The myth of generational conflict. Routledge, Oxford, pp 1–21

Becker GS (1974) A theory of social interactions. J Political Econ 82:1063–1094

Becker GS, Murphy KM (1988) The family and the state. J Law Econ 31(1):1–18

Blekesaune M, Quadagno J (2003) Public attitudes toward welfare state policies. A comparative analysis of 24 nations. Eur Sociol Rev 19(5):415–427

Boeri T, Börsch-Supan A, Tabelloni G (2001) Would you like to shrink the welfare state? The opinions of European citizens. Econ Policy 32:7–50

Bommier A, Lee R, Miller T, Zuber S (2004) The development of public transfers in the US: historical generational accounts for education, social security, and medicare. Paper PAA Annual Meetings 2004, Boston

Börsch-Supan A, Reil-Held A (2001) How much is transfer and how much insurance in a pay-as-you-go system? Scandinavian J Econ 103(3):505–524

Browning EK (1975) Why the social insurance budget is too large in a democracy. Econ Inquiry 13:373–388

Cox D, Soldo BJ (2004) Motivation for money and care that adult children provide for parents. Center for Retirement Research Working Papers 2004. http://escholarship.bc.edu/retirement_papers/11

Cox D, Eser Z, Jimenez E (1998) Motives for private transfers over the life cycle. An analytical framework and evidence for Peru. J Develop Econ 55:57–80

Dallinger U (2002) Das "Problem der Generationen": Theorieentwicklung zu intergenerationalen Beziehungen. In: Dallinger U, Schroeter KR (eds) Theoretische Beiträge zur Alternssoziologie. Leske & Budrich, Opladen, pp 203–234

Doblhammer G, Westphal C, Ziegler U (2006) Pflegende Familienangehörige brauchen mehr Unterstützung – Bedarfsprognosen zeigen einen Anstieg häuslichen Pflegepotenzials in Deutschland bis 2030. In: Demografische Forschung aus erster Hand, Jahrgang 3/Nr 4

Dunham C (1998) Generation units and the life course. A sociological perspective on youth and the anti-war movement. J Political Military Sociol 26(2):137–155

Esping-Andersen G (1990) The three worlds of welfare capitalism. Princeton University Press, Princeton

Esping-Andersen G (1999) Social foundations of postindustrial economies. Oxford University Press, Oxford

European Commission (2004) The future of pension systems. Special Eurobarometer 161/ Wave 56.1. European Opinion Research Group EEIG
Feinerman E, Seiler EJ (2002) Private transfers with incomplete information: a contribution to the "altruism-exchange motivation for transfers" debate. J Popul Econ 15:715–736
Galasso V, Profeta P (2002) The political economy of social security: a survey. Eur J Political Econ 18:1–29
Gehring UW, Wagner M (1999) Wahlbeteiligung im hohen und sehr hohen Alter. Ergebnisse der Berliner Altersstudie. Kölner Zeitsch Soziol Sozialpsychol 4:681–705
Hicks P (2001) Public support for retirement income reform. OECD Occasional Pap no 55
Inglehart R (1977) The silent revolution. Changing values and political styles among western publics. Princeton University Press, Princeton
Kohl J (2003) Principles of distributive justice in pension policies. Cross-national variations in public opinion. Paper Annual Meeting ISA Research Committee 19, August 2003, Toronto
Kohli M (1996) The problem of generations. Family, economy, politics. Collegium Budapest, Public Lectures no 14
Kohli M (1999) Private and public transfers between generations: linking the family and the state. http://www-user.ined.fr/~mad/Rencontres-Sauvy-Paris/Actes/Kohli.pdf
Kohli M (2003a) Intergenerational family transfers in aging societies. Section on Aging & the life course. Distinguished Scholar Lecture, 98th Meet American Sociological Association, 19 August 2003, Atlanta, GA
Kohli M (2003b) Generationen in der Gesellschaft. Forschungsbericht 73, Forschungsgruppe Altern und Lebenslauf (FALL). Freie Universität Berlin, Berlin
Kohli M (2005) Aging and justice. Research Report 74, Research Group on Aging and the Life Course (FALL). Free University of Berlin, Berlin
Kohli M, Künemund H (2001) Intergenerational transfers in the family: what motives for giving. Research Report 71, Research Group on Aging and the Life Course (FALL). Free University of Berlin, Berlin
Lee R (2003) Intergenerational transfers. In: Demeny P, McNicoll G (eds) Encyclopedia of population. MacMillan, New York, pp 542–545
Leisering L (2000) Wohlfahrtsstaatliche Generationen. In: Kohli M, Szydlik M (eds) Generationen in Familie und Gesellschaft. Leske & Budrich, Opladen, pp 59–76
Logan JR, Spitze GD (1995) Self-interest and altruism in intergenerational relations. Demography 32(3):353–364
Lüth E (2001) Private intergenerational transfers and population aging. The German case. Physica, Heidelberg
Mannheim K (1964) Das Problem der Generationen. In: Mannheim K, Wissenssoziologie. Soziologische Texte 28. Luchterhand, Neuwied
Mason A, Lee R, Tung A-C, Lai M-S, Miller T (2006) Population aging and intergenerational transfers: introducing age into national accounts. NBER Work Pap no 12770
McDaniel SA (1997) Intergenerational transfers, social solidarity, and social policy. Unanswered questions and policy challenges. Can J Aging/Can Public Policy suppl 1997:1–21
McGarry K, Schoeni RF (1997) Transfer behaviour within the family. Results from the Asset and Health Dynamics (AHEAD) Study. J Gerontol Psychol Social Sci spec issue 52B:82–92
Niethammer L (2003) Generationen und Geist. Eine Station auf Karl Mannheims Weg zur Wissenssoziologie. In: Schmidt R (ed) Systemumbruch und Generationswechsel. SFB Mitteilungen 580. Universität Jena, Jena
OECD (2004) Education at a glance. OECD Indicators. Organisation for Economic Development and Co-operation (OECD), Paris
Oeppen J, Vaupel JW (2002) Broken limits to life expectancy. Science 296:1029–1031
Opaschowski HW (2004) Der Generationenpakt. Das soziale Netz der Zukunft. Wissenschaftliche Buchgesellschaft, Darmstadt
Parsons DO (1982) Demographic effects on public charity to the aged. J Human Resources 17(1):144–152

Pilcher J (1994) Mannheim's sociology of generations: an undervalued legacy. Br J Sociol 45(3):481–495

Ponza M, Duncan GJ, Corcoran M, Groskind F (1988) The guns of autumn? Age differences in support for income transfers to the young and old. Public Opinion Q 52(4):441–466

Preston SH (1984) Children and the elderly. Divergent paths for America's dependents. Demography 21(4):435–457

Rattinger H (1994) Demografie und Politik in Deutschland. In: Klingemann H-D, Kaase M (eds) Wahlen und Wähler. Analysen aus Anlass der Bundestagswahl 1990. Westdeutscher Verlag, Opladen

Razin A, Sadka E, Swagel P (2002) The aging population and the size of the welfare state. J Political Econ 110(4):900–918

Rosenmayr L (2000) Neue Daten und Thesen zur Generationenfrage. Österreichische und europäische Befunde. SWS Rundsch 40(3):229–248

Rürup B, Gruescu S (2003) Nachhaltige Familienpolitik im Interesse einer aktiven Bevölkerungsentwicklung. Bundesministerium für Familie, Senioren, Frauen und Jugend, Berlin

Schokkaert E (2006) The empirical analysis of transfer motives. In: Kolm S, Ythier JM (eds) Handbook of the economics of giving, altruism and reciprocity, vol I. Elsevier, Oxford, pp 127–181

Sinn H-W, Übelmesser S (2000) Wann kippt Deutschland um? ifo Schnelldienst 28/29:20–26

Smith TW (2000) Public support for governmental benefits for the elderly across countries and time. Report OECD, Paris

Szydlik M (2000) Lebenslange Solidarität? Generationenbeziehungen zwischen erwachsenen Kindern und Eltern. Leske & Budrich, Opladen

Wilkoszewski H (2003) Die verdrängte Generation. Politische Parteien und die alternde Gesellschaft in Deutschland. Tectum, Marburg

Information on the Foundation for the Rights of Future Generations

Who We Are

The Foundation for the Rights of Future Generations (FRFG) is a research institute on the interface of science, politics, and the business world. In 1997, it was founded by a group of students that worried about the future and wanted to promote intergenerational justice in terms of ecology and economy. To FRFG, intergenerational justice means that today's youth and future generations must have at least the same opportunities to meet their own needs as does the generation governing today. Examples for the discrimination of the succeeding generations are the unprecedented ecological destruction, the pension crisis, the disenfranchisement of the young generation, youth unemployment, and national indebtedness. FRFG aims to provoke, challenge, and ultimately, stimulate politicians to recognize the rights of future generations, and to implement measures to protect these. In 1996, FRFG founded the "Institute for a Better Demographic Future" to conduct research on demographic issues such as aging and shrinking of the population, the development of the birth rate as well as domestic migration and immigration policy.

What Are Our Activities?

FRFG takes action whenever the chances of succeeding generations are reduced by measures of the current political establishment.

FRFG organized several congresses, symposia, and meetings. It publishes books that are also understandable for non-scientific readers (for example, the "Handbook of Intergenerational Justice"), and issues policy papers that give precise recommendations or possible future scenarios. The main emphasis of work lays on ecological policies, financial policies, the pension scheme, educa-

DOI 10.1007/978-3-540-77084-8 © Springer 2008

tion policies, labor-market policies, youth policies, and policy of peace. Beside these activities, the FRFG publishes a journal called "Intergenerational Justice Review!", which reaches many thousand of today's and future decision makers (all German members of Parliament, numerous scientific institutions and professors, managers and journalists, as well as 3,000 students from various fields of study).

Through the so-called Generational Justice Price, endowed with € 10,000, young scientists are encouraged to take a close look on issues concerning the future.

Numerous politicians have asked for FRFG's advice in questions concerning Generational Justice, among them the German Minister for Work (reform of the pension scheme) and the Minister for Justice (establishment of generational justice in the German constitution).

Who Supports Us

FRFG is supported by a scientific advisory council that comprises distinguished personalities like Prof. Dr. Mihajlo Mesarovic (Club of Rome), Prof. Dr. Dr. Radermacher (Club of Rome), Prof. Dr. Ernst Ulrich von Weizsäcker (Club of Rome), Lord Ralf Dahrendorf (UK House of Lords), and Kennedy Graham (UN University). Furthermore, an entrepreneurial council with highly reputable members assists the work of FRFG.

Awards

FRFG received the Theodor-Heuss-Medal, and the Medal for Good Citizenship of the town of Oberursel for its engagement. Furthermore, FRFG is associated with the United Nations Department of Public Information (DPI), and the Economic and Social Council (ECOSOC).

We Need You!

We are always looking for people and organizations that want to work with us on reasonable solutions for intergenerational justice. You may become a regular sponsor by joining our association of supporters. On demand, we will be pleased to send you more detailed information on FRFG. Please contact us at kontakt@srzg.de or visit our webpage at http://www.srzg.de.

Join FRFG and make the world with us more generationally just!

Address

Foundation for the Rights of Future Generations
(Stiftung für die Rechte zukünftiger Generationen)
P.O. Box 5115
61422 Oberursel
Germany
Tel.: +49-6171-982367
Fax: +49-6171-952566
e-mail: joerg.tremmel@srzg.de
Web: http://www.intergenerationaljustice.org

Subject Index

Index of Persons

MIX
Papier aus verantwortungsvollen Quellen
Paper from responsible sources
FSC® C105338
FSC
www.fsc.org

If you have any concerns about our products,
you can contact us on
ProductSafety@springernature.com

In case Publisher is established outside the EU,
the EU authorized representative is:
Springer Nature Customer Service Center GmbH
Europaplatz 3, 69115 Heidelberg, Germany

Printed by Libri Plureos GmbH
in Hamburg, Germany